# High Comedy in American Movies

# Genre and Beyond
## A Film Studies Series

**Series Editor: Leonard Leff, Oklahoma State University**

*Genre and Beyond* offers fresh perspectives on conceptions of film as well as cinema's role in a changing world. Books in the series explore often overlooked or unconventional genres as well as more traditional themes. These engaging texts have the rigor that scholars demand and the creativity and accessibility that students and interested readers expect.

### Titles in the Series

*Cinematic Shakespeare*
Michael Anderegg

*High Comedy in American Movies:*
*Class and Humor from the 1920s to the Present*
Steve Vineberg

### Forthcoming in the Series

*African American Film Now*
Mark A. Reid

*Queer Images: Homosexuality in American Film*
Harry M. Benshoff and Sean Griffin

*Killing in Style: Artistic Murder in the Movies*
Steven Schneider

*Film Adaptations*
Christine Geraghty

# High Comedy in American Movies

*Class and Humor from the 1920s to the Present*

Steve Vineberg

ROWMAN & LITTLEFIELD PUBLISHERS, INC.
Lanham • Boulder • New York • Toronto • Oxford

ROWMAN & LITTLEFIELD PUBLISHERS, INC.

Published in the United States of America
by Rowman & Littlefield Publishers, Inc.
A wholly owned subsidiary of The Rowman & Littlefield Publishing Group, Inc.
4501 Forbes Boulevard, Suite 200, Lanham, Maryland 20706
www.rowmanlittlefield.com

PO Box 317
Oxford
OX2 9RU, UK

British Library Cataloguing in Publication Information Available

**Library of Congress Cataloging-in-Publication Data**

Vineberg, Steve.
   High comedy in American movies : class and humor from the 1920s to the present
/ Steve Vineberg.
      p.    cm. — (Genre and beyond)
   Includes bibliographical references and index.
   ISBN 0-7425-2633-X (cloth: alk. paper) — ISBN 0-7425-2634-8 (pbk.: alk. paper)
   1. Comedy films—United States—History and criticism. I. Title. II. Series.
   PN1995.9.C55V56 2005
   791.43'617—dc22

                                                          2004013388

Printed in the United States of America

⊗™ The paper used in this publication meets the minimum requirements of
American National Standard for Information Sciences—Permanence of Paper for
Printed Library Materials, ANSI/NISO Z39.48-1992.

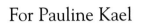

For Pauline Kael

~

# Contents

# Acknowledgments

This book emerged out of a long-time interest in a movie genre that has received sparse attention from film scholars and reviewers. My happy first task was to define it for myself and determine which movies fell within its purview. Over the course of many conversations about movies and theater, my dear friends Polly Frost and Ray Sawhill lent their acute critical intelligence to the problem and helped me, far more than they know, to hone a more complex sense of what high comedy is, and I am very grateful to them. Polly and Joe Mader read the completed manuscript and kindly offered their encouragement—and Joe's eagle eye picked out errors I had missed.

Many of the films and most of the handful of plays discussed here have found their way onto the syllabi for my courses at College of the Holy Cross, which have often served as testing grounds for my ideas. I am indebted, as always, to my students for inspiring me with their own intellectual excitement and the often astonishing quality of their written and oral response to these works. Jonathan Hastings wrote a brilliant senior thesis on twentieth-century comedy that dealt with Philip Barry, John Guare, Preston Sturges, and Robert Altman (among others) in inventive ways that challenged my own perspective. Kerry Skowron's examination of Barry and S. N. Behrman enhanced my understanding of the workings of a distinctly American approach to high comedy. And though they may have long forgotten these contributions, I was shrewd enough to jot down in my lecture notes the insights of two of my American film students, Tim Doherty and Tom McGrath, in a class on Arthur Penn's *Alice's Restaurant*, and have borrowed them for my discussion of the movie.

My former colleague Chris Merrill was generous enough to suggest Rowman & Littlefield as a home for my next book project and introduced me to Dean Birkenkamp, who invited and then accepted my proposal for a book on high comedy. I would also like to extend my thanks to Brenda Hadenfeldt, Erica Fast, and Jenn Nemec for their hard work and editorial assistance.

Portions of this book appeared, in a variety of contexts, in articles and reviews in the *Threepenny Review*, the *Boston Phoenix*, the *Perfect Vision*, the *Chronicle of Higher Education*, *Salon*, the *Christian Century*, the *Journal of Dramatic Theory and Criticism*, and *Millennium Pop*. I am grateful to my editors at those publications and particularly to Wendy Lesser at the *Threepenny Review*, a magazine I feel privileged to have been associated with for the past two decades.

Two song lyrics are reprinted here by special permission.

"Thanks for the Memory" from the Paramount Picture *The Big Broadcast of 1938*. Words and music by Leo Robin and Ralph Rainger. Copyright © 1937 (Renewed 1964) by Paramount Music Corporation. International Copyright Secured. All Rights Reserved.

"All in Fun" by Jerome Kern, Oscar Hammerstein II. Copyright © 1939, 1967 by Universal–Polygram International. Publications, Inc. on behalf of T. B. Harms Co. [ASCAP]. Used by permission. International Copyright Secured. All Rights Reserved.

~

# Introduction

High comedy, also known as comedy of manners, was invented by the British Restoration playwrights in the late seventeenth century. Their brand of comedy, most radiantly exemplified in William Congreve's *The Way of the World*, was distinctly verbal, containing ingeniously sculpted, wittily curlicued language, and it was aimed at educated, aristocratic audiences. Richard Brinsley Sheridan, the most significant writer of comedy of manners in England around the turn of the nineteenth century, considered himself an aristocrat first and a playwright second; reportedly, when asked by a friend why he didn't produce more plays, he replied haughtily, "Sir, I am a gentleman." Conventionally, high comedy is elevated in both style and subject matter: the principal characters are ladies and gentlemen, and class is a felicitously inescapable boundary. In both *She Stoops to Conquer*, by Sheridan's contemporary Oliver Goldsmith, and *The Game of Love and Chance*, by the eighteenth-century French playwright Pierre Marivaux, the hero and heroine, matched up by their fathers, disguise themselves as servants to court each other. They fall in love, naturally, but then they panic under the shared misapprehension that they have found lovers beneath their class. In both plays the happy ending, after the true station of the two lovers is revealed, confirms the wisdom of class barriers: aristocrats are instinctively drawn toward each other as soul mates and life partners.

When most people hear the term "high comedy," they think of *The Importance of Being Earnest* or the plays of Noël Coward. But we Americans have had our own high-comic playwrights, whose period of popularity came

Shakespearish / Greek

between the two world wars, and the best of them are Philip Barry (whose work has endured best), S. N. Behrman, and Samson Raphaelson (who traveled from Broadway to Hollywood and wrote his most distinguished scripts for movies directed by Ernst Lubitsch). As Americans, their approach to class was necessarily—at least superficially—more liberal and modern. In *Holiday* and *The Philadelphia Story*, Philip Barry's most famous plays (and the most beloved examples of Broadway comedy of manners), characters who were not to the manor born *are* permitted to cross the class barrier, and a challenge seems to be thrown down to the morality and lifestyle of the very rich. In *Holiday*, it comes in an appropriately idiosyncratic form: the hero, Johnny Case (a man of humble origins who works his way into the aristocracy), opts for taking a holiday around the world and absorbing life before settling down, rather than dedicating himself to multiplying his small fortune. This impulse seems to his prospective father-in-law—a millionaire who can't imagine anything more exciting than making acres of money—to be a dangerous insurrection on a social scale and a slap in the face on a personal one. In *The Philadelphia Story*, the challenger is a journalist, Macaulay (Mike) Connor, who has written a short story with the epigraph, "With the rich and mighty, always a little patience." When his magazine assigns him to cover a moneyed Philadelphia wedding, he comes prepared to despise his subjects. Significantly, however, Case's rebellion in *Holiday* is the kind that only a man who's just made a bundle on Wall Street can afford, and Connor ends up not only revising his opinion of the Lord family but falling for the bride.

These wonderful plays—which became, as George Cukor movies starring Katharine Hepburn and Cary Grant, the best conventional examples of high comedy in Hollywood—represent a peculiarly American approach to class, a topic that is unmistakably at the heart of this genre. We're Americans, so we're not supposed to believe in the inflexibility of class boundaries. Therefore the heroes of Barry's plays are restless, uncomfortable with their aristocratic status or with the demands it places on their behavior; or else they are nonaristocrats who have somehow infiltrated the club and feel compelled to comment on its strangeness and exclusivity. The problem is that comedy of manners is *about* the manners of aristocrats, and by tradition its tone is complacent and conservative. In Barry's plays and in the Cukor movie versions, both stances—traditional/conservative and American/democratic—end up being compromised (or fudged). And what makes American comedy of manners—which has a much more complex history in the movies than on stage—so fascinating is the ways in which American identity, historically in tension with the distinctly undemocratic substance of the high-comic universe, interacts with that universe to produce a series of variations on the genre. These are unlike the high comedies of England or France or any other European country. American high comedies play with the notion of what constitutes an aristocracy; in the homegrown versions, money is rarely the sole factor in determining who gets to join the club. And, exercising their Yankee right to pull against the class tide, they focus as much on the division between those who belong to the aristocracy and those who don't as on the lifestyle of the aristocrats themselves.

Before addressing some of the ways in which American movies handle high comedy, let me try to define the genre, at least in its modern form. Noël Coward is, after all, a far cry from Richard Brinsley Sheridan, and comedy of manners has taken on a different tone in the disenchanted modern age. High comedy is one of several comic genres known to American audiences; the others are romantic comedy, burlesque, hard-boiled comedy, sentimental comedy, situation comedy, parody, black comedy, satire, and farce. Romantic comedy (sometimes called screwball comedy), the favorite of Americans, begins with a hero and heroine in an adversarial position to each other; in the great screwball comedies of the thirties, one is rich, the other professional or working class. Through a series of adventures that operate like tests of character, they grow to recognize what the audience, with its radar for romantic chemistry, knows from the outset: that they're a match. And they grow to deserve one another. The source of all romantic comedy is Shakespeare's *Much Ado About Nothing*; in American movies, the conventional romantic comedies, which blossomed in 1934, after the introduction of the Hays Code (Hollywood's self-regulating censorship code, which reigned for nearly three decades), include *It Happened One Night*, *Bringing Up Baby*, and *My Man Godfrey*. And there have been hundreds since.

Burlesque is low comedy—Mack Sennett's Keystone Kops, the Marx Brothers in *A Night at the Opera*, the work of the Farrelly brothers. It relies on pratfalls and other kinds of physical comedy, on broad humor; like a nose-thumbing schoolboy, it attacks respectability and thrives on getting away with as much outrageous conduct as it can. Hard-boiled comedy is survivor's comedy, set in a tough, inequitable world where those who succeed are wised-up pros who are skilled at their work and who recognize horseshit when they smell it. Perhaps the most colorful examples are Altman's *M*A*S*H* and the many film versions of the Hecht-MacArthur newspaper play *The Front Page* (the most famous, justly, is *His Girl Friday*). The film musical *Chicago* is the third movie version of another signature American high comedy, the stage play by Maurine Watkins of the same name. There's a significant overlap between hard-boiled and high comedy: in both, the heroes belong to an exclusive club. But it isn't an aristocracy in hard-boiled comedy—it's a band of reporters, or of jailed murderesses, or of army med-ical personnel who share a cynical view of the war and the military. Those without a membership are always suspect and generally the target for wise-cracks and practical jokes. James Harvey in *Romantic Comedy* calls the so-cial landscape of hard-boiled comedy "a community of wiseacres—in a larger society of fakes and fools (as we all at times believe all larger societies to be)."[1]

Sentimental comedy comes in a variety of forms, but in all of them it's a hybrid of comedy and melodrama, and though it seldom represents the best of either, Americans adore it. Chaplin made many of these comedies (like *City Lights*); today they're sometimes called "dramedies" and they're as often found on television, where they tend to work better in a form that is both more economical (forty-four minutes at a stretch) and more extended (in se-ries arcs). In situation comedy, which has also been adopted by TV, it's the dramatic situation, the given of the plot, that dictates much of the humor, for instance, the difficulty of assembling a wedding in *Father of the Bride*; much of the focus tends to be on details of lifestyle or career.

Parody is benign spoof—of soap operas, perhaps (*Soapdish*), or British spy movies of the sixties (like the *Austin Powers* movies, which also contain a large measure of burlesque). Black comedy consigns traditionally dark subjects to laughter, such as a jealous husband's desire to kill his allegedly unfaithful wife (in Preston Sturges's *Unfaithfully Yours*), and it's notoriously unpopular with audiences. Black comedy and satire overlap. Satire, the more savage cousin of parody, is premised on the notion that its target is malignant and de-serves to be exposed: nuclear armament (*Dr. Strangelove*), the American ob-session with staying young (*Death Becomes Her*), anti-Communist hysteria (*The Manchurian Candidate*, a satire presented in the form of a cold war polit-ical thriller), Reagan-era family values (*The Stepfather*, a satire presented in the form of a horror movie).

Finally, farce is the most technical form of comedy, in which the implica-tions of a comic situation, often involving mistaken identity and illicit ro-mantic entanglements, work to reduce characters to mere mechanical figures caught in the cogs of an immense, haywire apparatus. The most memorable sequences in Chaplin's *Modern Times* are farce; Buster Keaton's movies ele-vate farce to the level of great modern art. Sex farce is the mechanism at the heart of some of the most affecting cinematic high comedies, like Renoir's *The Rules of the Game*, Bergman's *Smiles of a Summer Night*, and, in this coun-try, Hal Ashby's *Shampoo*. But then, the boundaries that separate these comic genres are extremely fluid, and often movie comedy thrives on combinations of several different genres; farce in particular is such a common resource for comic filmmakers that it's often more a device than a genre of its own. Romantic comedies often match up heiresses and working stiffs, introducing elements of high comedy into the mix, and sometimes elements of parody, too, depending on how much the film chooses to lampoon the rich. The fatuous mothers of *My Man Godfrey* and *Easy Living*, for example, are cartoon versions of wealthy, spoiled matrons. The appeal of the Farrelly brothers' *There's Something About Mary* is in its application of burlesque to a romantic-comedy premise—the attempt of a persistent goofball to win the woman he's been chasing since high school. The running gag on the HBO series *Sex and the City* was that its main characters, a quartet of glamorous Manhattan women, were high comic in style, low-comic—raunchy—in behavior, and their dialogue reflected both.

In examining the conventions of comedy of manners, it's useful to keep in mind that conventions are made to be twisted, tweaked, even broken; anything is possible so long as the genre continues to *address* these conventions. That's equally true of all American movie genres. For example, the fact that Alvy and Annie don't end up together in *Annie Hall* doesn't mean that the movie isn't a romantic comedy. The way in which Woody Allen disappoints our expectations extends the meaning of the genre to acknowledge that in 1977 America happy endings aren't so easily come by. The disappointment at the heart of some of the most interesting romantic comedies of the nineties—*Notting Hill*, *Runaway Bride*, *Addicted to Love*, and especially *My Best Friend's Wedding*, where the behavior of the Julia Roberts heroine is shrill, selfish, and clearly desperate, and she doesn't wind up with the hero—alters the form of the romantic comedy to make the same point.

Here are the conventions of high comedy. It's worth remembering, when you think about the movies the genre encompasses, that—as with other genres—not every high comedy includes every one of the conventions.

1. High comedy takes place among an aristocracy. Often it is an aristocracy of money; one of the incidental pleasures of this kind of movie is that it gives us a vicarious taste of the way the very rich live. That certainly would have been the case for Depression-era audiences, but on the whole they preferred screwball comedies, where the heiress is taken down a notch by her earthy boyfriend (as Claudette Colbert is by Clark Gable in *It Happened One Night*). But though the air the characters in high comedy breathe is definitely rarefied, the aristocracy may be defined by a shared quality other than money: the protagonists of *Design for Living*, for example, are bohemian artists. Post-Depression comedies of manners are less likely to be about moneyed aristocracies, with some

important exceptions, like the Los Angeles–set movies of Paul Mazursky (*Bob and Carol and Ted and Alice, Blume in Love, Down and Out in Beverly Hills*).

2. Visually the high-comic world is defined by settings and costumes—most conspicuously by the women's gowns and the *objets* that fill the rooms through which the characters travel. In a famous sequence in Ernst Lubitsch's *Trouble in Paradise*, the courtship of the perfume heiress (Kay Francis) and her secretary (Herbert Marshall)—in fact a thief whose original intention in seeking employment in her home was to rob her—is narrated almost entirely through close-up images of a magnificent series of clocks.

3. The exclusive club to which the protagonists belong—as distinctive as the clique to which the heroes of hard-boiled comedy pay their dues—has a definite set of rules (mores) that can't be transgressed with impunity. But these rules vary with the times, and even with the social settings of the individual films, just as they do from one hard-boiled comedy to another.

4. In a 1952 *New York Times* article titled "Query: What Makes Comedy High?" the playwright S. N. Behrman observed, "The immediate concerns of the characters in a high comedy may sometimes be trivial; their point of view must never be. Indeed, one of the endless sources of high comedy is seriousness of temperament and intensity of purpose in contrast with the triviality of the occasion."[2] The presence of a reporter and a photographer from *Spy Magazine* at the wedding of Tracy Lord (Katharine Hepburn) in *The Philadelphia Story*, for instance, is a crisis that has to be handled with a combination of patience, energy, and invention. It is equally true that high-comic characters approach serious matters with great humor. This balance of opposites constitutes in large part the characters' style, which defines them every bit as much as their conduct.

5. In her introduction to *Three Screen Comedies by Samson Raphaelson*, Pauline Kael describes Raphaelson's accomplishment as "the creation of a chimerical world of streamlined elegance. It's a dream of high life, in which lovers are articulate, slim-hipped, and witty. As an adolescent in the thirties I saw his plays performed and, like the plays of S. N. Behrman, they were comedies-of-manners floating in an urban cloudland."[3] In addition to the accoutrements alluded to in number 2 above, the world Kael describes is determined by the factors that Behrman insists are the essence of high comedy: "the articulateness of the characters, the plane on which they talk, the intellectual and

moral climate in which they live."[4] The proof of class—the characters' calling card—is their wit, and their natural environment is language, which they employ with extraordinary skill and delicacy. As Kael remembers, "I listened to the rhythms of the burnished dialogue and knew that only people on the stage talked like that"[5]—or people on the screen, at least in those early high comedies derived from the plays of European and Broadway master craftsmen. They polished their dialogue until (Kael again) "it had the gleam of appliquéd butterfly wings on a Ziegfeld girl's toque."[6]

In act 3 of Coward's *Design for Living*, a minor character overhears the heroine, Gilda, talking to the two heroes, Otto and Leo, both at one time her lovers, when they return to see her in Manhattan two years after she's run out on them to marry a *third* man. "This, really, is the most extraordinary conversation I've ever heard," cries the astonished eavesdropper—and that line could serve as the epigram for the entire genre. Comedy of manners must be the most extraordinary conversation we've ever heard.

6. Behrman's phrase "the intellectual and moral climate in which they live" reflects the qualities of character that distinguish the heroes of high comedy. In his article "*Semi-Tough* or Impossible? Romantic Comedy Today," Brian Henderson lists the virtues of romantic-comedy heroes and heroines, and they represent all the reasons we like their high-comedy counterparts (or sometimes—in the case of Tracy Lord, for one—the qualities that come through when they release their finer selves): spontaneity, wit, intelligence, genuine feeling as opposed to conventional response, adaptable moral response, vitality, and life.[7]  The overlap may explain in part why some high comedies, like the Barry adaptations, are often called romantic comedies, and why performers like Hepburn and Grant are equally at home in both genres. The characters must also display generosity of spirit.

This list portrays the characters as liberal in attitude, even though high comedy itself tends to be conservative (see number 10 below). When Tracy's ex-husband, C. Dexter Haven (Grant), suggests that she's remarrying beneath her, and she retorts that he's a snob, he explains that she's got him wrong: "You could marry Mac, the night  watchman, and I'd cheer for you." Of course, in a twentieth-century American comedy of manners a Philadelphia heiress would no more marry the night watchman than a wealthy young man out of Goldsmith or Marivaux would wind up marrying the maid; liberality of attitude rarely triumphs over the rigorous social code of the aristocracy.

7. There is inevitably an erotic element in a high comedy. In romantic comedy we know the characters are a match if they're capable of having fun together; in the romantic musical comedies of the thirties starring Fred Astaire and Ginger Rogers, the indisputable evidence of their compatibility is how beautifully they dance together. (In fact, as has often been pointed out, their sublime pas de deux are stylized courtship rites—metaphors for sexual union that the movies themselves sometimes kid about.) High comedy supplies three means for ascertaining that the hero and heroine are a matched pair. They must be good sparring partners; they must share a vision of life, which they express eloquently (high-comic heroes generally love to philosophize); and—though this last rule can be bent—they must come from the same world. It doesn't matter that Johnny Case (Grant) in *Holiday* wasn't born rich, like Linda Seton (Hepburn), since she understands the value of the unorthodox future he's mapped out for himself, whereas her sister Julia (Doris Lloyd), his first fiancée, doesn't even try to see his point of view. Of course, the alleged class distance between Case and the Park Avenue Setons isn't very convincing anyway with Cary Grant in the role of Johnny, and in any case Barry has written the role so that, in intelligence, education, and manner of speech, Johnny is the obvious equal of anyone else in the film.

8. Sex is discussed openly; often, in fact, it's the *subject* of high comedy, at least as much as class, though the language in which it's discussed is likely to be more elegant than in, say, hard-boiled comedy. Most of the main male characters in *The Philadelphia Story* make the observation, at one time or another, that Tracy is frigid, but they do so in rather grand, allusive terms, comparing her to a statue of a goddess and so forth. One character is her fiancé, the priggish George Kittredge (John Howard), in response to her asking him if he minds that she's been married before—that is, that she isn't a virgin; but she phrases it with exquisite tact, inquiring if he's bothered by the fact that someone else was once her "lord and master."

9. Alcohol is an essential item in many high comedies. It is often champagne, and in addition to its social importance it has the power to liberate—repressed feelings, romantic ecstasy, forgotten humanity. Of all high-comic writers, Philip Barry offers the most complex treatment of drunkenness, in *Holiday* (where one of the characters is an alcoholic) and in *The Philadephia Story* (where the heroine cannot recover her lost generosity of spirit until she repeats the single drunken night of her life).

10. Comedy of manners may occasionally contain satire, but it's traditionally conservative—that is, pro-aristocracy, pro–status quo. It has usually been written from within: Sheridan was an aristocrat, and when Wilde sent up the high-society Victorians in *The Importance of Being Earnest*, he was talking intimately about the culture in which he'd been brought up. This convention hasn't changed much since high comedy was brought into the twentieth century. Philip Barry came from money; Donald Ogden Stewart, who adapted both *Holiday* and *The Philadelphia Story* to the movies, married into it, and his social circles were literary and gold standard (the Algonquin Round Table, the friends of Hemingway). The characters in Paul Mazursky's Beverly Hills movies, with their hip credentials and glowing skin, were versions of his friends and neighbors. Even the most scathing of contemporary high comedies, John Guare's *Six Degrees of Separation* (filmed by Fred Schepisi), was inspired by an incident that happened to a couple in his Manhattan social set. So the *tone* is hardly ever satirical (though there are some fascinating latter-day exceptions), and though the flaws and follies of the characters are evident, they are presented without moral judgment, as in the works of Chekhov. We may laugh at George the hairdresser's sexual escapades in the bedrooms of the wealthy Angelenos of *Shampoo*, but the filmmakers, Hal Ashby and screenwriter Robert Towne, make sure we feel compassion for him.

11. Hard-boiled comedy is always set in a fallen world, often a seedy one, and its point of view might be described as cheerful survivalism: you can get through if you're smart and resourceful and good at your job. By contrast, high comedy traditionally offers an optimistic vision of the world—the characters have more money than God, so there's no reason to imagine that their story won't end happily. Modern drama has complicated that picture: the rich aren't always heart-whole. And in the most interesting high comedies of the twentieth century, both European and American, the happy endings get compromised; that's the chief way in which they reflect the modern sensibility. (See number 14 below.)

12. High comedy itself is a very delicately crafted thing—a soufflé. In order to work best it must be as light as gossamer and seem easy and slight and entirely superficial; that's how writers and directors produce what, in Kael's view, Raphaelson and Lubitsch produced: "almost perfectly preserved iridescent, make-believe worlds."[8] What the finest high comedies accomplish is to seem superficial while actually being

profound. But if you play a high comedy too seriously—if you give in to the sadness that often lies at its heart—then you wreck it.

13. Vitally important to the success of the high comedy project detailed in number 12 is the style and technique of the performers. Delineating the difference between the era that produced the first plays of Barry, Behrman, and Raphaelson and the contemporary one in which she was writing, Kael explains,

> Actors now don't really know how to move and speak and wear their affectations in the way that the performers of forty or fifty years ago did; they're not trained to be radiant. . . . The plays are entertaining in revivals . . . but they don't have the glitter and dash they once had, when, just at the right, carefully prepared moment, capricious actresses such as Ina Claire and Gertrude Lawrence made their entrances and stood stock still, with a faint, amused air of surprise, as the audience burst into applause.[9]

(As Margo Channing in *All About Eve*, Bette Davis does precisely that when she takes her solo curtain call in her hit show, *Aged in Wood*.) The actors who starred in Hollywood high comedies in the thirties didn't have audiences to play off with that delightful air of self-consciousness Kael pinpoints, but in her few movies Claire brought something of the filigreed splendor of Broadway comedy of manners to the screen. And there were others whose styles contained a pleasurable layer of artifice (even under the glare of the camera, which demands a greater degree of realism from actors)—Hepburn and Grant, of course, John Barrymore and Fredric March (both, like  Hepburn, stage trained), Margaret Sullavan, Miriam Hopkins, and Claudette Colbert. Though *It Happened One Night* is a romantic comedy from start to finish, Colbert gives the impression of having stepped out of high comedy; she always does. Her presence and Barrymore's, as well as the Paris settings, give *Midnight* (another romantic comedy) the shimmer of high comedy.

Yes, those styles have vanished forever from our screens, but we still have actors who can perform miracles of style with the right material—the women on *The West Wing* accomplish them week after week. Judy Davis has created a contemporary high-comedy style from the neurosis of the characters she plays in movies like Woody Allen's *Husbands and Wives* and Michael Tolkin's *The New Age*. Imagine a revival of Noël Coward's *Design for Living* with Kevin Kline, David Hyde-Pierce, and Christine Baranski.

14. Comedy of manners has a distinctive style—highly polished, very brittle, tremendously elegant, and graceful. Modern comedy of manners has a distinctive tone—comic, somewhat sardonic, somewhat satiric, with an aftertaste of melancholy. It's the tone of characters who pretend to be gay and carefree and free-spirited but in truth care passionately and mourn their losses with heavy hearts. In the midst of a commitment to the fleeting, the ephemeral, is the acknowledgment of the bitter taste of death. William Bolitho, trying to get at the quality of Noël Coward's play *Bitter Sweet*, suggested, "You find it faintly when you look over old letters the rats have nibbled at, one evening you don't go out; there is a little of it, impure and odorous, in the very sound of barrel organs, in quiet squares in the evenings, puffing out in gusts that intoxicate your heart. It is all right for beasts to have no memories; but we poor humans have to be compensated."[10]

There is, of course, a serious kernel enclosed deep inside most comedies. Behrman writes, "The essence of the comic sense is awareness: awareness of the tragedy as well as of the fun of life, of the pity, the futility, the lost hopes, the striving for immortality, for permanence, for security, for love."[11] But the great high comedies of the twentieth century are perhaps the saddest of funny plays and movies; they comprehend at how deep a level laughter is linked to sorrow. That's why, in *Smiles of a Summer Night*, when the callow virgin Henrik (Björn Bjelvenstam), with all the strained self-seriousness of youth, explodes in the middle of a dinner party at "the lies, the compromises," his hostess, the magnificent middle-aged actress Desirée (Eva Dahlbeck), encourages him sympathetically to try laughing at them. He can't—he says it hurts too much to laugh; he isn't wise enough to see that that's precisely why we do. In his introduction to the published version of *Design for Living*, Noël Coward mentions that the ending—the curtain falls on the three protagonists laughing—has been widely interpreted and wondered at, the play's critics finding the laughter (which they took to be at the expense of one of the other characters) rather offensive. But Coward insists that the heroes are laughing at themselves. Laughter is the only salvation of poor, pathetic mortals.[12]

In Coward's *Private Lives*, Amanda and Elyot, divorced from each other and on their second honeymoons with other spouses, run into each other on the Riviera—damnable luck! Their honeymoon suites are at the same hotel, right next door to each other. And then, as they stand on their adjacent balconies, befuddled by the fate that's brought them together at this most inopportune of moments, the orchestra strikes up their song, a tender romantic ballad. They're furious because, quick-witted as they are, they have absolutely no control over their still-vibrant, though long-buried, feelings for each other, and now this goddamn song has them at its mercy. "Extraordinary how potent cheap music is," Amanda quips. Comedy of manners can be explained, on one level, as the remarkably sophisticated, gold-leafed, buoyant, and hilarious high style erected to mask, then reveal, then mask again, the potent cheap music that makes a holy mess out of our lives.

Among American lyricists, Cole Porter wrote the best examples of high-comic style, and Lorenz Hart the second best. But one of my favorites is a lyric by Oscar Hammerstein II, set to a Jerome Kern tune and called "All in Fun":

We are seen around New York
El Morocco and the Stork
And the other stay-up-late cafés
I am on the town with you these days
That's the way it stands.

Just a fellow and a girl
We have had a little whirl
And our feet have left the ground a bit
We've played around a bit
That's the way it stands.

For we are strictly goodtime Charlies
Who like to drink and dance around
And maybe kick romance around
And that's the way it stands.

All in fun
This thing is all in fun
When all is said and done
How far can it go?

Some cocktails, some orchids, a show or two
A line in a column that links me with you.

Just for laughs
You're with me night and day
And so the dopes all say
That I'm "that way" 'bout you.

Here's the laugh
And when I tell you
This'll kill you
What they say is true.

# Notes

1. James Harvey, *Romantic Comedy in Hollywood, from Lubitsch to Sturges* (New York: Alfred A. Knopf, 1987), 90.

2. S. N. Behrman, "Query: What Makes Comedy High?" *New York Times*, May 30, 1952, XI, 1.

3. Pauline Kael, introduction to *Samson Raphaelson: Three Screen Comedies* (Madison: University of Wisconsin Press, 1983), 13–14.

4. Behrman, "Query," XI, 1.

5. Kael, introduction to *Samson Raphaelson*, 14.

6. Kael, introduction to *Samson Raphaelson*, 15.

7. Brian Henderson, "*Semi-Tough* or Impossible?: Romantic Comedy Today," *Film Quarterly* 31, no. 4 (1978): 13.

8. Kael, introduction to *Samson Raphaelson*, 14.

9. Kael, introduction to *Samson Raphaelson*, 14.

10. William Bolitho, "The Egg," *New York World*, February 7, 1929. Quoted in Noël Coward, *Play Parade* (New York: Doubleday, Doran, 1934), xii.

11. Behrman, "Query," 1.

12. Coward, *Play Parade*, xvii.

# CHAPTER ONE

~

# Europe in Hollywood

One of the most intriguing impulses in American movies in the thirties was an attempt to use Hollywood resources to create a vision of Europe on the screen. The source material for these movies was often European novels  and plays, though the actors were usually American (with some notable exceptions, like Garbo and Dietrich), and the results were curious hybrids—unmistakably Hollywood, yet not quite like other Hollywood movies produced in this decade. The Paris, Vienna, and Budapest settings became metaphors for elegance, exoticism, magic; films like Frank Borzage's *Liliom* (1930), Rowland V. Lee's *Zoo in Budapest* (1933), and William Wyler's *The Good Fairy* (1935), whatever other genres they might lay claim to, were modern fairy tales.

This Hollywood fascination with Europe can be traced to a number of sources. European theater had a strong hold on Broadway in the experimental years of the twenties and thirties, especially through the efforts of the powerful Theatre Guild to bring the best of England and the continent to New York audiences. And when sound came in at the end of the twenties, Hollywood relied on the stage more than ever to supply scenarios. At their  worst, the early talkies were uneasily transported theatrical experiences, with the camera more or less rooted in the fifth row orchestra center, and the imprimatur of the Broadway house imparting class, however secondhand, to the proceedings. In addition, though, American filmmakers were often excited by the movies they saw from Europe, especially Germany, where the most visually imaginative films in the world were being made in the twenties and early thirties. You can spot the influence of the German romanticists on Borzage movies like *Little Man, What Now?* (1934) and *Three Comrades* (1938) (both adaptations of German novels), and even on his captivating Depression romance *A Man's Castle* (1933), where he turns a Hooverville into an echt-European village. Similarly, the quicksilver touch of the French director René Clair, who made some of the first authentic movie musicals, is evident in Lewis Milestone's 1933 *Hallelujah, I'm a Bum!* despite its Rodgers and Hart tunes and its Manhattan setting and the ineffable presence of Al Jolson. Finally, there were émigré Europeans on the scene in Hollywood as early as the late silent period, and their sensibilities and styles became part of the mix. Most of them wanted to work on American subjects, even though in Fritz Lang's hands a gangster picture like *You Only Live Once* (1937) or a social-problem picture like *Fury* (1936) had a distinctly foreign flavor. But there were exceptions—one in particular. The Berlin-born high-comedy master Ernst Lubitsch, who began to direct movies in the middle teens and came to America at the behest of Mary Pickford in the early twenties (he was the first of the German transplants, anticipating F. W. Murnau's arrival by half a decade), was continually attracted to material set in the Europe he'd left behind.

From the outset the European flavor of the early sound comedies of manners was bizarrely at odds with the natural inclination in American talkies for tough talk, pragmatic heroes, and contemporary situations. The movies now known as "pre-Code"—that is, produced before the self-censoring Production Code (popularly known as the Hays Code) went into effect in 1934—featured raucous, wisecracking characters, many from the working class. The best of these pictures displayed a cheerful amorality. Against these crackling comedies and gangster melodramas are pitted the highly self-conscious style and conversation of the figures of high comedy, whose conduct is measured by the standards of an elevated social enclave with its origins in another time and place. Anthony Lane has written of Max Ophüls, the German-Jewish filmmaker whose career took him around the world as he raced to keep one step ahead of the Nazis, that all of his movies, wherever they're set, "seem to be rooted in some Vienna of the imagination, at the unchanging turn of the last century: a place where the bindings of good conduct can shape you as gracefully as the bodice of a new dress, even if the pressure means that, as the day wears on, you find it impossible to breathe."[1] This sensibility, which made Ophüls the ideal interpreter of Schnitzler's plays, also made him an uncomfortable fit for Hollywood (though he made a couple of his best pictures there, in the late forties). Yet the pioneering, pre-Code high comedies were conceived in a style that Ophüls would have recognized and felt at home in.

The other tension between the high-comic attitude and the culture of the early thirties emerged out of social and political realities. One of the most interesting artifacts of this period is the 1932 Paramount comedy *If I Had a Million,* an anthology picture representing the work of sixteen writers and seven directors. In it, an ornery millionaire (Richard Bennett), believed to be on his last legs, elects to dole out his money, one million at a time, to men and women picked at random from the Manhattan telephone directory. (The popular fifties TV program *The Millionaire* was derived from *If I Had a Million.*) The film's purpose as a Depression-era wish-fulfillment fantasy is underscored by the fact that every single beneficiary of Bennett's fortune turns out to be a little guy who's up against it—a nervous salesman in a china shop who's forever paying for the breakage he causes; a prostitute who longs for one night alone; a sympathetic youth on Death Row; a silent, woebegone clerk whose response to receiving his check is to march up to the office of the big boss and give him the raspberry. (Lubitsch directed this last episode, which has a René Clair–like vaudevillian springiness.) How can high comedy, with its tacit dedication to the status quo and its heroes enslaved to outmoded codes of behavior, survive in the atmosphere reflected by a movie like *If I Had a Million?* It would eventually have to undergo a strange metamorphosis—or bond with other elements of Depression comedy to create new variants.

The studio most likely to reproduce the highly respected European stage comedies of the day was M-G-M, whose movies had a glossy patina and a genteel tone. One of the classiest directors on the M-G-M roster, Sidney Franklin, was entrusted with the task of bringing both *The Guardsman* and *Private Lives* to the screen in 1931. *The Guardsman,* translated from a play by the Hungarian Fernc Molnár, had been a 1924 success for the Theatre Guild and a triumph for its stars, Alfred Lunt and Lynn Fontanne, who came to Hollywood to put it on film. The aristocracy to which the Lunt and Fontanne characters in *The Guardsman* belong is the aristocracy of the theater: they are Austrian stage stars, known only as the Actor and the Actress, who, after many shared kudos, have finally married each other (just as Lunt and Fontanne did)—a union as unsurprising as the intermarriage of European royalty. The only other character in the movie, besides a pair of servants (ZaSu Pitts and Maude Eburne) and a creditor with two brief scenes (Herman Bing), is the Critic (Roland Young), who dances attendance on the stars and who, like George Sanders's Addison De Witt in the much later *All About Eve* (1950), is an essential member of their club. The plot is a trifle with the sex-farce underpinnings of many high comedies. Prompted by sexual insecurity to test his wife's fidelity, the Actor invents a Muscovite guardsman to woo her, playing the role himself under heavy disguise. Just as he congratulates himself that she has resisted the advances of his alter ego, the Actress succumbs. When he reveals his true identity to her the next day, she laughs in his face, claiming she knew him all along. The comedy ends on an intended note of mystery: Did she or didn't she?

It's not much of a script, though you can see the variation Molnár plays on the masquerading ruses of the characters in prototypical high comedies like *She Stoops to Conquer* and *The Game of Love and Chance*, and the idea that the Actor's jealousy drives him to create the very rival he feared is clever. The play, with its nonstop affected banter, is all about acting style; the joke it's built around has to do with who's acting when, and how effectively. Accordingly, *The Guardsman* exists as a vehicle for show-off stage technique (I once saw Maggie Smith and Brian Bedford perform it at Canada's Stratford Shakespeare Festival), and, for theater-historical reasons, the movie's preservation of the Lunts' performing styles is invaluable, especially since it was the only film they ever made. And you can see why: they weren't ideal for the camera. Fontanne's face is both too angular and oddly mandarin from some angles; when she's shot in profile, her pointed nose and chin and knobby cheeks are accentuated by the pulled length of her face and the glittering earrings dripping from her lobes. And her stage voice comes out a little mushy. Lunt translates better, especially when he's posing as the Russian, shellacked like a toy soldier, pressing his eyes shut so they look Asian or making them unnaturally wide, his ears almost Vulcan under an absurd wig and set off by eyebrows like squiggles. But these two weren't movie stars. James Harvey pinpoints the reason: "The Lunts have no moral presence. They give the effect of standing for nothing but themselves more or less as they appear before us—of embodying their own theatrical life rather purely. As a result, they are fascinating—but, in some crucial way, not interesting."[2] The movie has its pleasures, but they're supplied mostly by the tiny supporting cast, who are somehow more present than the stars.

The movie does make one concession for American audiences. The play we see the Actor and the Actress perform the end of, in the opening scene, isn't some European classic, but Maxwell Anderson's *Elizabeth the Queen*. Of course, Anderson was, of all playwrights in the first half of the twentieth century, the one most fervently dedicated to trying to extend old-world theatrical values to the American theater—he wrote blank-verse tragedies. (His work hasn't worn well; almost no one revives it.) And *Elizabeth the Queen* was one of his few plays on a non-American theme. So M-G-M's *The Guardsman* is about as close to an import as a movie without foreign actors could be.

*Private Lives* is considerably better. Coward wrote the play for himself and his favorite leading lady, Gertrude Lawrence, in the late twenties, and they performed it both in London's West End and on Broadway, where a very young Laurence Olivier played Victor, Amanda's ill-chosen second spouse. Reportedly M-G-M had the Broadway production filmed to show Franklin and the cast. The thought is enough to make theater mavens salivate, but evidently the studio destroyed the copy immediately afterward. A recording was made independently, however, of an excerpt from one of Coward and Lawrence's scenes, and it conveys the rarefied atmosphere of the piece and the tightrope act in both the writing and the acting, which achieve a sublime self-consciousness without ever becoming arch; these two were peerless exemplars of high style. The movie's stars, Robert Montgomery and the studio's favorite grand lady, Norma Shearer, aren't quite in that category. But Shearer is more than adequate: she shows surprising skill with the language, and only occasionally does she slip into the high-toned playacting mode of her melodrama roles. And though Montgomery's Americanness takes some getting used to, especially if you've seen the role of Elyot played on stage by a deft Brit like Brian Bedford or Alan Rickman, he's handsome and likable and highly accomplished. Franklin must have taken the lesson of the Broadway version—his camerawork, especially in the famous opening scene, grooves with the rhythms of the play. The film is much speedier than *The Guardsman*: Franklin covers the whole play in ninety minutes—half an hour per act.

Officially the characters are English, and the settings are continental (a hotel on the Riviera and—after Amanda and Elyot slip away from their respective second honeymoons to recapture, illicitly, their broken relationship—a Swiss chalet), but the two stars don't bother with accents. It turns out to be a wise choice—that's one obstacle they don't have to climb over. Reginald Denny, who plays Victor, happens to be British, but Una Merkel, as Sybil, Elyot's fatuous second wife, uses a southern accent that gives her a spoiled-plantation-belle quality. (She's fluttery, and her lines sometimes come out sibilant—the vocal equivalent of frilly doilies.) The movie is skillful enough to allow us to relax into the pleasures of the play, one of the great comedies of the twentieth century. Amanda and Elyot have been so damaged by their break-up that they've fled into horrendous rebound second marriages, but Coward makes it obvious why. She's drawn to a second husband who treats her gently and respectfully and wants to take good care of her; he's drawn to a second wife who's the portrait of traditional femininity and has a childlike charm. That both of these choices lack depth and judgment is obvious the moment the protagonists meet again and see their second spouses juxtaposed with their first. The attraction suddenly runs thin; Elyot and Amanda realize that they've never stopped loving each other. Part of what makes *Private Lives* a high comedy rather than a romantic one is its attitude toward love and sex. When Elyot grows pouty over Amanda's refusal to make love to him because it's too soon after dinner (she explains vaguely that their "thingummies" aren't in sync), Coward's acknowledgment that they're at the mercy of their biological makeup is an explanation you certainly won't find in a romantic comedy. High comedy may be optimistic by nature, but that optimism is tempered by the awareness of limitations (mainly the big one—that we're not long for this world). The characters live for the moments when they're deep in their passion, but even then they can't forget how fleeting those moments are. "What's so awful is that one can't stay happy," Amanda muses. When, weary of Elyot's jealousy, she interjects an ironic comment about making herself fascinating for him, he snaps back, "That reply has broken my heart." It takes so little to break their hearts.

The heroes of *Private Lives* are representatives of a new sort of aristocracy: they flout convention by walking out on their new spouses to live together, yet, like their precursors, they remain true to a code that outsiders cannot comprehend. Amanda and Elyot are a world unto themselves. That sounds like it should be a rule of *romantic* comedy, but in fact in romantic comedy most of the supporting characters are accessories to the romance. (Think of the bus riders in *It Happened One Night* [1934], the shop clerks who work alongside Jimmy Stewart and Margaret Sullavan in *The Shop Around the Corner* [1940], or Garbo's Russian comrades in *Ninotchka* [1939].) It's both ingenious and radical of Coward to create an exclusive club with only two members. What ensures that his version doesn't alter the essential high-comic form is that Amanda and Elyot's standards hold for the comedy: We see Victor and Sybil through their eyes and find them pitifully wanting. Maybe Amanda and Elyot make each other miserable half the time, but to settle for Victor and Sybil they'd have to cut themselves down to ordinary size—to lose the independence of spirit and the discriminating intelligence that make them, in high-comic terms, heroic.

In *Design for Living,* Coward's other masterpiece, written for himself and the Lunts, the club has *three* members: Gilda and her two swains, Otto and Leo, between whose beds she travels, like Catherine in *Jules and Jim* (1962) (which is also a comedy of manners about an experiment in living), until the three of them reach the inevitable conclusion that they were meant to be an inseparable trio. They're an aristocracy of bohemians, artists, and, like Amanda and Elyot, they're faithful to their own code and spirit when they refuse to compromise for the petty bourgeois standards they abhor. The dead respectable society they stand against is embodied in Ernest the art dealer, whom Gilda marries for a while for safety and security before she realizes that, as Leo explains to him just before they take her away, "Gilda could be married to you fifty times and still not be your wife." Ernest, who's written with as much malicious wit as Victor and Sybil are, is also a brilliant device—the figure the protagonists need to define themselves against. When Gilda tries to explain their point of view to him and he answers, "I see," she asks, "Do you? Do you really? I doubt it. I don't see how anybody outside could."

The 1932 Paramount film version is billed as "an Ernst Lubitsch production of Noël Coward's *Design for Living*," but that's misleading, since the screenwriter, Ben Hecht, threw out Coward's dialogue and thought up his own. (He took pride in having retained only one line of the original.) His script is sharp witted and slightly lunatic—a true Paramount rendition of high comedy; the lines contain extravagant flourishes and a special, sprung rhythm. "It's clear that you've been behaving like a rather ordinary rat," the playwright Tom (formerly Leo and played by Fredric March) complains to the painter George (formerly Otto and played by Gary Cooper) when he learns that George and Gilda (Miriam Hopkins) have violated the no-sex "gentleman's agreement" all three entered into when they decided to move into a Paris flat together. (The arrangement, in the Hecht version, was meant to be a sort of miniature artists' colony, with tough-eyed Gilda nurturing—and criticizing—both men's work.) Dictating a letter to his friends from London, where his first play is being produced, Tom writes affectedly, "My heart is in the highlands of Montmartre, and the night finds me pale and thoughtful." When Gilda explains to the men why she can't choose between them, she compares George to a slightly misshapen straw hat and Tom to a piquant fedora worn over one eye that you have to watch carefully on windy days.

Hecht must have written that last line to suit the actors: The stylish, insouciant March and the corn-fed Cooper are a study in contrasts. Cooper isn't ideally suited for this kind of comedy, but he's an astonishing camera subject and terribly amiable, and he's a lot better than you might expect. The difference is that he has to work at it, whereas March barely breaks a sweat, even on tonal shifts that make you gasp—like the one where, receiving the news at his London hotel that Gilda and George have once again become lovers in Paris, he throws away the elaborately mocking letter he was in the midst of writing them and tosses off congratulations instead, muting his own deep disappointment. March is brilliant, while the madcap Miriam Hopkins turns her wondrous technique on the role of Gilda, and the indispensable Edward Everett Horton plays Max (formerly Ernest).

Hecht is sufficiently faithful to the *plot* to make it scandalous enough. Paramount got the movie in under the wire in 1933, before the Hays Code kicked in. (Hollywood officially adopted the Production Code in 1930 but didn't create an administration to police it until 1934.) It would be nearly another four decades before anyone could film material that presented this kind of sexual behavior nonjudgmentally. But the changes Hecht makes to Coward's original alter its philosophical underpinnings—its moral ethic—so that the more you think about the movie, the less you recognize the play in it. Max runs the ad agency where Gilda works (as a commercial artist, designing underwear ads featuring Napoleon); Hecht reconfigures the philosophical conflict so that the forces aligned against each other aren't convention and bohemianism but business and art. When Gilda leaves Max at the end, she persuades him that she's doing him a favor, because her departure will be good for his business.

The best scene in the film is George and Gilda's homecoming after they've seen Tom off on the train to London. Lubitsch shoots it from outside the window of their Left Bank flat, so that they seem foreshortened as they walk in the door. George is blue because his pal is gone, and because he hasn't been able to get his paintings shown, and though he won't state it outright he's envious of Tom's success. Lubitsch gets the mood expertly, and all the complicated reasons for it, none of which the script has to lay out for us. George tries to get Gilda to go to the movies because he feels he's lousy company, and she talks about moving to a hotel while Tom is away. But he doesn't throw her out and she doesn't leave, and after they pace the room for a while they wind up in each other's arms. "We're unreal, the three of us, trying to play jokes on nature," says George.

This scene is a fair example of how Lubitsch works. He loves to get at the feelings of his women and men by indirection, which makes him the ideal director for high comedy, where what the prodigiously articulate characters don't or can't say is at least as important as the bons mots that float effortlessly out of their mouths. It seems strange to think of high comedy as predating the advent of sound, but among Lubitsch's first movies in America were two theatrical adaptations, Lothar Schmidt's *The Marriage Circle* (1924) and Oscar Wilde's *Lady Windermere's Fan* (1925). In structure both are amorous roundelays and farces; in genre they combine comedy of manners with melodrama. Wilde loved that mix: except for *The Importance of Being Earnest*, all his so-called comedies shift tones in midstream. I've never cared much for them on stage (and the 1999 film of *An Ideal Husband* didn't convert me), but Lubitsch's exquisitely nuanced version of *Lady Windermere's Fan*, updated from the Victorian age to the twenties, is close to sublime; he may be the only director who's ever understood what Wilde was after. May McAvoy plays the title character, a married woman who's fallen in love with the rakish Lord Darlington (Ronald Colman, amazingly suave in a moist little mustache and oiled hair). But she's distracted by the sudden appearance of Mrs. Erlynne (the gorgeous, tragic-faced Irene Rich), an older woman with a scandalous reputation who seems to be advancing on Lady Windermere's husband (Bert Lytell). In truth, Mrs. Erlynne is her mother, at first determined to squeeze money out of Lord Windermere in return for keeping silent about the illegitimacy of his wife's birth but in the end dedicated to saving her daughter from making the same mistake she did and ruining her life. Lubitsch directs the sumptuously clothed actors with remarkable skill, and the movie has the same lightness of touch and fluidity associated with his work on the effervescent comedies he made once sound came in. Of course, it isn't really a comedy at all. He goes right for the regret at the heart of the play. And he revels in its theatricality, framing the actors in long shots that point up the eloquence of the staging.

One of Lubitsch's German silents, *The Oyster Princess* (1919), contains a choreographed scene in which a crew of men, back from a night of carousing, tramp wearily through a snowy park, falling off one by one to sink onto discrete park benches. *The Oyster Princess* isn't a musical, obviously, but this sequence suggests what an operetta by Oskar Straus or Victor Herbert around the turn of the century might have looked like (under the hand of a gifted director, that is). When Hollywood was overtaken by the talkies, Lubitsch made real operettas—*The Love Parade* (1929), *Monte Carlo* (1930), *The Smiling Lieutenant* (based on the Straus operetta *A Waltz Dream*; 1931), *One Hour with You* (a musical version of *The Marriage Circle*; 1932), and *The Merry Widow* (a film of the most beloved of all operettas, with the Franz Léhar music; 1934). Maurice Chevalier and Jeanette MacDonald were paired in most of them—he isn't in *Monte Carlo*, she doesn't show up in *The Smiling Lieutenant*. Except for *The Merry Widow*, which is both sumptuous and light fingered, they're far from the best movies Lubitsch ever made, but you can see why he made them. They're high comedies set to music, frivolous and farcical and bejeweled, with glittering pockets of melancholy, like the moment in *The Smiling Lieutenant* where Claudette Colbert, as the musician who loses Chevalier's amorous Viennese soldier to a princess (Miriam Hopkins), leaves him a farewell note with her garter pinned to it. *The Merry Widow* is, of all these pictures, the least encumbered with the whipped-cream silliness that seems to be part and parcel of the operetta style; Lubitsch, working with Samson Raphaelson (as coscreenwriter with Ernest Vajda) and Rodgers and Hart (who adapted the songs), even parodies the expensive form he's working in. The title character, Sonia (MacDonald), the richest woman in the kingdom of Marshovia, circa 1885, has a huge wardrobe, but all her clothes are black, including her corsets, and one of her maids brings her a little black dog; Lubitsch turns her mourning into a fashion statement. But though the plot doesn't take her widowhood any more seriously than, say, *Twelfth Night* takes Olivia's mourning over her dead brother, Sonia's experience deepens her in ways that both MacDonald's performance and Lubitsch's direction touch on subtly. When she tells Danilo (Chevalier) that he doesn't know what love is, we understand that Sonia, who loved a man she lost, does, and a few bars of the score's plaintive ballad, "Vilia" (which she sang earlier, in one of the film's most enchanting sequences), sneak in.

The *Merry Widow* appeared after Lubitsch had mostly stopped making his operettas; it was in the nature of a reunion with MacDonald and Chevalier, and it occurred at M-G-M rather than Paramount, which had released the previous ones. By then Lubitsch had already directed Samson Raphaelson's screenplay of *Trouble in Paradise* (1932), based on a Hungarian play by Aladar Laszlo and one of the high points of thirties comedy. It's a deliciously inconsequential movie—pure, sparkling surface, with Lubitsch's camera swirling around Raphaelson's delirious dialogue. Coming off his operetta series, Lubitsch employs music in a lightly parodic way, as a transition between sequences. There are a ridiculous ad for perfume, sung by a mustachioed crooner, and a few bars of mock opera that briefly recall Clair's *Le Million* (1930), quietly deflating the pomposity of the setting and the opera-house audience while moving us toward the moment when the master thief, Gaston Monescu (Herbert Marshall), makes his appearance in the life of his next mark, Mariette Colet (Kay Francis).

The movie has the feel of a musical, just as Lubitsch's operettas feel like high comedies, and in fact Lubitsch makes a joke out of genre in the opening scene. Behind the credits a tenor croons the title song and we see a regal bed suspended in the air, hinting at erotic paradise and a fairy tale. But as the image fades into mist, we see its reverse—a Venetian garbageman loading up his gondola. Then a thief leaps off a hotel balcony, leaving behind a body stretched out inside one of the suites. Are we watching a thriller? The victim (Edward Everett Horton) isn't dead, just stunned, and when he tries to rise he buckles again. Lubitsch's camera glides across Venice to a restaurant where "the Baron" (really Gaston) smokes, his mood contemplative and perhaps a trifle sad. He's awaiting a lady, and the waiter is inquiring about the wine he wants to anticipate the meal. "That's not so easy. Beginnings are always difficult," the Baron replies—though not, apparently, for Lubitsch. The Baron tries to set the romantic scene he imagines for the waiter: "If Casanova suddenly turned out to be Romeo, having supper with Juliet, who might become Cleopatra"—and this frivolous little line shifts the tone from comedy of manners to romantic comedy and back again (Casanova and Cleopatra are too mature, too worldly for romantic comedy, Juliet too young and untried for comedy of manners). When the Baron orders a "marvelous" supper—"We may not eat it, but it must be marvelous"—and insists that they be able to see the moon in the champagne, Lubitsch and Raphaelson are deliberately straddling the line between these two kinds of comedy: the setting invites romance, but the calculation and self-consciousness eliminate the possibility of innocence. Enter "the Countess" (Miriam Hopkins), on a gondola, in a stunning lamé gown with a slung décolleté that cradles her breasts like nest eggs, fur encircling her elbows like ribbon around a gift. Hopkins's version of high style is loonier than Marshall's more brittle English approach. "One gets so tired of one's own class," she complains, "princes and queens and dukes and kings." And while, in an opera buffa–style scene, Horton's brained hotel guest, François Filiba, explains to the police, through an interpreter, how he was robbed by a man who claimed to be a doctor examining his tonsils, "the Baron" and "the Countess" play a romantic interlude that is just as artificial. Across their dinner plates, she tells him that she knows he's the crook who robbed Filiba, and he replies that he knows she's a thief who stole his wallet (she tickled him when she lifted it). He gets up and locks the door, then takes her by the shoulders and shakes loose the wallet secreted beneath her clothes. In this hilarious variation on a seduction scene, they keep revealing the items they've stolen from each other. The one he won't return is her garter, and this erotic theft seals the deal, along with his confession that he's the notorious Gaston Monescu. "Gaston!" she cries in delight, while he calls her "my sweet little pickpocket." They're made for each other.

The aristocracy in this movie is the faux royalty of thieves ("the Countess" is actually Lily), which interacts with the real aristocracy of the very rich—Mariette Colet's social set in Paris, where most of the action takes place. This link is particularly funny and feels particularly right in a comedy from the Depression, where the moneyed classes are so distant they might as well be the figment of a screenwriter's imagination, and where there's no appreciable difference between the paradise old money creates and the paradise that mock aristocrats build in the air with stolen loot. Once or twice Raphaelson reminds us of the economic realities that his and Lubitsch's sublime artifice masks: when, in the midst of a dry spell (before they fasten onto Madame Colet), Gaston assures Lily, quoting Coolidge, that prosperity is just around the corner, and again in his first encounter with Mariette. He
steals her jeweled handbag, then returns it for the reward (a practical decision, since she's offering more than he'd get from a fence), pretending to be a gentleman in temporary decline, a member of the "nouveau poor" (the

stock-market poor). The filmmakers introduce the reality so well known to their audience in a way that acknowledges the distance between them and the fantasy world on the screen, the comedy-of-manners world where there's money everywhere, parties and bank accounts and magnificent haute couture. (There's also a quintessential thirties bit with Leonid Kinsky as a Russian with overgrown hair who disapproves on political principle of Mariette's offering so extravagant a reward for a lost bag.) The movie's ironic self-awareness is one of its distinctions. James Harvey writes, "The glamour is always lightly undercut . . . by the comic exaggerations of glamour. So that the special quality of the film is both excited and dry."[3]

The two female stars are opposite numbers. Hopkins, with her marcelled hair and speed-of-light line delivery, is the modern Yankee equivalent of a Restoration heroine, a peerless chatterer, while the languorous Kay Francis exists for the camera—she's an objet d'art—and her slight speech defect (she blurs her r's) is terribly sexy. What they have in common is that they're both superb clotheshorses, and it's hard to think of half a dozen movies that contain gowns as stunning as the ones Travis Banton designed for these two actresses. Herbert Marshall partners both women with distinctly British flair, as if Noël Coward had written the script. He shares a seduction scene with each—the scenes are mirror images of each other—in which the verbal playfulness and the shimmering self-consciousness of the dialogue are as much aphrodisiacs as the pull of the exotic and the dangerous that Gaston's and Lily's profession represents. At the same time, the twin running gags of the movie are the ones introduced in the opening sequence, with Lubitsch gliding from the robbery to the love scene: the tension between the aristocratic style (and splendiferous settings) and the underworld reality of the protagonists, and the line between romance and pragmatism, which is continually vanishing. "So far as I'm concerned, her whole sex appeal is in her safe," Gaston, now employed as Mariette's secretary (a ploy so he can be in a position to rob her), tells Lily, now ensconced in Mariette's house as *his* secretary, but beginning to suspect that her lover has more than a professional interest in their employer. And she's right to be suspicious—whatever he says, Gaston has fallen in love with Madame Colet. So Lily robs the safe herself, claiming, "I wouldn't fall for another man if he were the biggest crook on earth" (one of Raphaelson's best lines), and then she insists, "That's what I want—this is real. Money—*cash*." Romance is an illusion—the moon in the champagne. Or is it? Gaston comes back to Lily in the end; they're members of the same club. But he doesn't leave Mariette precisely unsatisfied—he exposes a bigger thief (her business manager, played by C. Aubrey Smith, who's been robbing her for years), and though he takes away the bracelet Lily coveted, he leaves Mariette with a memory of a romance that, once he's confessed his feelings for her, his baser motives somehow haven't tainted.

Lubitsch's treatment of the *objets* in the movie, like the clocks and the cunning art deco telephone in Mariette's Paris home, conveys not only the style and genre of *Trouble in Paradise* but his attitude toward both. James Harvey's reading is that in every way the movie inclines toward abstraction because it's about modernity:

> The film . . . has the lean, sleek 'lines' of that hallway clock—aspires to the emotional equivalents of the art deco style it is always showing us in the wonderful Hans Dreier sets. There's hardly a frame of the film that doesn't emphasize the clean gleaming outline of an object, a stairway, a gown. Those clocks . . . are just the sort of thing Lubitsch wants us to look at in this film: images of the *moderne*, the streamlined.[4]

I'd say that the clocks, the telephone, the jewels, with their modern splendor, are metaphors for the style or, perhaps, clues to it, displacing the concealed emotion with something for us to look at and admire. Farce operates the same way in many modern comedies of manners (including this one). The movie is full of images of doors and mirrors: the mirrors, as is often the case in movies, are about image and what lies beneath it, and the doors suggest the farce corollary—that the intimate truth is hidden behind them. When Mariette returns from a party given by one of her two unsuccessful swains, the Major (Charlie Ruggles)—Filiba is the other—she enters Gaston's room, where the safe is, takes off her jewels, and inquires, "When a lady takes her jewels off in a gentleman's bedroom, where does she put them?" His reply acknowledges the pass: "On the night table." This moment answers an earlier one, a highly conscious visual that I particularly love, where these two kiss for the first time. We see the kiss in their reflection in the mirror, then in silhouettes cast on her bed, before we see the actual embrace—first the image, then the possibility, then the reality. *Trouble in Paradise* is a silvery crescent moon of a movie.

In *Desire*, directed by Frank Borzage four years later (and, significantly, produced by Lubitsch), the thieves who impersonate royalty are the only aristocrats. This ingenious comedy, also based on a European source (a play by Hans Szekely and R. A. Stemmle) and featuring dazzling Travis Banton gowns, is a blend of high and romantic comedy in that it concerns crossing class boundaries—but not the ones the hero, a vacationing car salesman named Tom Bradley (Gary Cooper), expects. When he falls for Madeleine (Marlene Dietrich), "the Countess de Beaupré," and winds up as a guest of her and her supposed uncle, the "Prince Margoli" (John Halliday), he says he

*Sublime artifice, verbal playfulness, shimmering self-consciousness: Miriam Hopkins and Herbert Marshall in Ernst Lubitsch's* Trouble in Paradise *(1932). Credit: Paramount/The Kobal Collection*

feels like a stevedore sitting down to a banquet. He admits to her privately that he's been exaggerating his job and his salary to impress her, and she reminds him gently that they come from different worlds—that a match between them is impossible. He assumes he's getting the brush-off because he's a mere commoner who can't buy her pearl necklaces. He's both right and wrong: it *is* a pearl necklace that separates them, but not the way he thinks. She's just stolen some pearls from a Paris jeweler (in an extended scam that is one of the film's delights), and she slipped them into his pocket at the Spanish border to avoid detection; she and Carlos (the "prince"), her partner in crime, are entertaining Bradley just long enough to get them back. By this time, Madeleine has fallen for Tom, too, but he's a civilian and she's a crook—different worlds indeed. So she tells him the truth, she says, so he won't think that she's even worse than she is, that is, a snob who can't value love rather than a thief who can only dream of it.

Until her confession, Madeleine and Carlos play brilliantly at the masquerade of being high class. Her original treatment of Tom seesaws between friendliness and hauteur, depending on when she needs his help on her travels, and she even steals his car out from under him. So the thieves have to stage a scene where the "prince" apologizes to the American for the conduct of the "countess" to him, which he calls "a black spot on the escutcheon of the de Beauprés that will have to be wiped away." He tells Tom, in a confidential tone, that the aristocracy is being educated badly these days: "No respect for other people. Treating everyone like subjects." He even threatens to disown his niece, which allows Dietrich to imitate an air of contrition, drawing on her weird talent for candied pathos. This movie isn't as self-conscious as *Trouble in Paradise* (it has moments of melodrama), but you cherish the moments when it addresses its own style—as when Carlos meets Madeleine at her hotel with flowers and compliments for her appearance, and she quips, "Thank you for your words and your flowers. It's difficult to tell them apart."

You can see why Cooper feels like such a galoot around Dietrich, with her half-moon eyebrows and her burry, delicately ironic line readings. The movie makes a wonderful joke out of the contrast between her continental style and his drawling, earthbound Americanness, and they're marvelously odd together, as they were half a dozen years earlier in *Morocco*. (Early as it is in Cooper's career, this is his last good comic performance—the last time he was permitted to be light and free.) The script (by Edwin Justus Mayer, Waldemar Young, and Samuel Hoffenstein) fudges the obstacles in the romance—and incidentally betrays the elegant amorality of the opening sequence (the theft of the pearls)—by providing an explanation for Madeleine's behavior: Carlos helped her when she was needy, so she's stolen the necklace to return the favor. Thus it's up to Tom to figure out a way to get her out of it, and he does by pitting his American brawn against Carlos's sneaky European manners. This is probably a bad idea, and the resolution loses *Desire* its highcomic credentials. But the scene where the two men stage a quarrel over her but present it like a political debate, referring to each other as "America" and "Europe," is amusing nonetheless. "You can't underestimate America," Carlos sneers. "It's a big country." "Six foot three" is Tom's laconic reply.

You wouldn't expect a truly amoral comedy after the institution of the Hays Code, anyway. Borzage and the stars do what they can: Bradley can't sleep with Madeleine, of course, but the shot of her in bed the morning after their romantic interlude has a languid, postcoital mood, and the dialogue insinuates that she and Carlos have been lovers when she tells him she's removing the royal crest from her stationery, her lingerie, and her life. This is a little confusing, since Halliday comes across as gay, but since Edward Everett Horton does too in *Trouble in Paradise* (and every other movie he made), it's probably not worth worrying about. The Hays Code is one of the main reasons why romantic comedy was far more common than high comedy from 1934 on—the obstacles the screwball premise throws in the way of sex (the fact that it takes the hero and heroine, who begin as adversaries, the entire movie to realize they belong together) provided writers and directors with ingenious ways of handling the new restrictions imposed on them while still making their comedies sexy. The Hays Code compromises modern high comedy, where sex isn't an issue but an element. So high-comedy filmmakers usually have to invent a romantic-comedy excuse for eliminating it.

There's an implicit social comment in the idea of thieves as aristocrats: in the modern world, the real aristocracy is fading. The protagonist of Jack Conway's 1932 *Arsène Lupin,* played by John Barrymore, is a French duke who becomes a thief (of jewels and art) because his legacy is bankrupt. The young woman he falls for (Karen Morley) turns out to be an ex-con promised parole if she'll help the chief of police (Lionel Barrymore) trap Lupin. The lifestyle the duke clings to provides the trappings of high comedy. The corruption of the idle classes is an occasional theme in caper movies; it's partly the reason Norman Jewison's *The Thomas Crown Affair,* three and a half decades later, is a kind of high comedy. (Crown, played by Steve McQueen, is a wealthy man who becomes a master thief out of ennui.) And of course Barrymore plays the same kind of role straight, the same year as *Arsène Lupin,* in Edmund Goulding's *Grand Hotel,* where he's a baron forced by financial embarrassment to try to steal the jewels of a famous ballerina (Greta Garbo).

*Grand Hotel* isn't a comedy, but it needs a high-comic structure for its ironic point about fate and fortune to bounce off. All the aristocrats in the movie are in deep trouble—the Baron because he has no money, the industrialist Preysing (Wallace Beery) because he's about to lose his business, the ballerina Grusinskaya because she's lost the will to dance and almost the will to live. She and the Baron fall in love and it's the real thing, but they find each other too late to give each other salvation; the dice have already been rolled and come up against them. Otto Kringelein (Lionel Barrymore), who works as a clerk in Preysing's company, is also unlucky—he's been diagnosed with a fatal illness—but since he has no possibility of salvation, he gets everything he's ever wanted in his final days: friends and gaiety and the license to live like an aristocrat with the money he's saved. The friendship between Kringelein and the Baron, who becomes a kind of counselor to him, is the sweetest subplot in the picture.

*Grand Hotel,* which won the Academy Award for 1931–1932, presents a peculiarly Hollywood version of Europe, with one genuine European (Garbo), two American stage stars representing a kind of American royalty (the Barry-

more brothers), and some of the most sheerly American types you can imagine, like Beery, Lewis Stone as the doctor with the burned face, and Joan
Crawford (still in firm possession of her flapper charm) as the vibrant stenog-
rapher Flaemmchen. It's one of those fascinating melodramas that shuffles the
elements of comedy of manners but alters its tone; *Camille* (1936), beautifully
directed by George Cukor and based closely on the mid-nineteenth-century
play by Alexandre Dumas *fils* (which also inspired *La Traviata*), is another. In
*Camille* the line is drawn between the respectable upper-middle-class Duvals
and the demimonde, and it can't be crossed, even though the demimondaine,
Marguerite Gautier (Garbo, in possibly her most extraordinary performance),
can be kept by a baron (Henry Daniell). Armand Duval (Robert Taylor) falls
in love with Marguerite, and the sincerity of his feelings purifies her; she re-
grets her past and, reluctantly at first—because she feels she isn't good enough
for Armand—she allows him to take her out of her phony Parisian life. She
claims that Armand is her first encounter with sincerity since she left the farm
where she grew up to become educated in the ways of the city (like Lady Tea-
zle in *The School for Scandal*), but it must be said that, as Garbo plays her, Marguerite herself is never anything *but* sincere. Armand whisks her away to the
country, which is good for both her moral and her physical health (she's consumptive). But one day his father (Lionel Barrymore) comes to see her privately, and tells her that her union with his son will create enough of a scandal to ruin his family. So she sacrifices the relationship for Armand's sake,
pretending to be tired of him and returning to the supercilious—and far
wealthier—baron. Armand is callow enough and hurt enough by her actions
that he can't see through them; he thinks she's superficial. It isn't until she becomes mortally ill that he learns the truth—that the farm girl is an aristocrat
of the spirit, and it's he who is just barely worthy of her.

    *La dame aux camélias,* as the play is more properly called (Marguerite's
trademark flower is a camellia), was written at the intersection of romanticism and realism, but the story resides in the romantic camp, and it lacks the
irony, perhaps, that would swing it over the edge from melodrama into high
comedy. (A good contrast would be Max Ophüls's 1953 film *The Earrings of
Madame de . . . ,* where the setting is also the aristocracy and the outcome is
also tragic, but the plot is informed with irony at every turn.) But *Camille* explores the flip side of high comedy—class and manners are its stock in trade.

    Other movies take different approaches to treating the waning aristocracy.
The house of assignation Dietrich visits in Paris in Lubitsch's *Angel* (1937) is
run by a Russian countess (Laura Hope Crews), whose status and tone of elegant discretion lend the illicit goings-on a soigné air. Emigré white Russians show up in Paris in both *Tovarich* (1937) and *Ninotchka,* though the

two comedies have contrasting points of view toward them. Charles Boyer and Claudette Colbert play the protagonists in *Tovarich* (based on Robert E. Sherwood's Broadway version of a Jacques Deval play), Mikhail and Tatiana, who hire themselves out as servants to a pair of nouveaux riches. It's a little odd to see Colbert, with her French background and her vaguely mid-Atlantic accent, and Boyer, the most famous Frenchmen in Hollywood, playing Russians, but they're certainly convincing as aristocrats (and they give charming performances—especially Boyer, who is buoyant and nutty). Anatole Litvak's direction is a little arch, especially in the early scenes—he was more at home directing Boyer in the French romantic melodrama *Mayerling* the year before—but the movie is playful. It begins with the couple walking through Paris on *quatorze Juillet*, intrigued by the dancing in the streets but unable to learn at first exactly what the holiday is about; when they find out it's a celebration of a revolution, they want nothing to do with it. This is a good joke, and it establishes the high comedy. Mikhail and Tatiana distance themselves from the dancing plebs; they hold onto their identity as royals. That's what makes their decision to apply as domestics comic. They tell their new employers, a banker (Melville Cooper) and his pixilated wife (Isabel Jeans, in a role played much better in other comedies of this period by Billie Burke and Alice Brady), that they used to be in the service of a Russian prince and duchess. And they tell themselves they can carry it off because it won't be much of a stretch from their former roles as chamberlain and lady-in-waiting to the czar's family. The gimmick is essentially the same as the one in plays like *She Stoops to Conquer* and *The Game of Love and Chance*, but the motivation for the masquerade is different. And of course Tatiana and Mikhail turn out to be tremendously skillful at these new jobs; they win over not only the banker and his wife, but also their college-age daughter and son. The family scenes aren't so much comedy of manners as the kind of over-the-top daffiness (part screwball comedy, part situation comedy) you find in *My Man Godfrey* and *You Can't Take It with You* (where a Russian grand duchess who works at a restaurant makes blintzes for everybody). But the whole idea of the movie is a high-comedy one that, structurally, hits its high point in the scene where Cooper and Jeans discover their servants are really their betters and don't know precisely what to do about it. (There's a funny bit where one of their dinner guests recognizes Tatiana as she's serving hors d'oeuvres and instinctually stands up out of respect.)

The villain, insofar as there is one in this picture, is the Soviet commissar (Basil Rathbone) who speaks philosophically about the "necessary night-mare" of the revolution, with its rivers of blood. (Rathbone isn't very plausible as a Soviet; he sounds more like an aristocrat.) The political shoe is on the other foot in Lubitsch's *Ninotchka,* written by Billy Wilder, Charles Brackett, and Walter Reisch. Garbo plays a Soviet agent sent to Paris to negotiate the return of jewels that once belonged to the czar's family and falls in love with a debonair Frenchman named Leon (Melvyn Douglas). It's a romantic comedy, but the presence of Ina Claire as the Grand Duchess Swana, who used to own the jewels and wants them back—and who is, incidentally, keeping Leon (though the Hays Code–approved screenplay doesn't exactly say as much)—adds a high-comic element. Claire was one of the glories of the Broadway stage in the twenties and thirties, celebrated for her technique, especially in high comedies like S. N. Behrman's *Biography*. She made only a handful of movies, including the first (now lost) version of *The Awful Truth* (1929), George Cukor's adaptation of the George Kaufman–Edna Ferber play *The Royal Family* (called *The Royal Family of Broadway* on screen; 1930) in the role inspired by Ethel Barrymore, an adaptation of the Donald Ogden Stewart play *Rebound* (1931), and an extremely entertaining picture called *The Greeks Had a Word for Them* (a.k.a. *Three Broadway Girls*; 1932). This last is a hard-boiled comedy, and Claire, playing a scheming narcissist, gives it a varnished toughness. She does all sorts of clever things with her eyes and her arms and her hips, and there's an image of her in a satin gown, stretched out half-asleep on a couch at a late-night party, one arm extended behind her, that's like a marvelous line drawing. *Ninotchka* gives a better impression, though, of the kind of work Claire must have done on stage in classier parts. Wearing her Adrian gowns with the easy elegance of a woman who has worn only the finest clothes all her life, she strides through the performance with a combination of quick-wittedness and regal entitlement. As brilliant a technician as she is, she knows how to make a gesture count: when she tells Leon, quoting her lawyer, that France has recognized Soviet Russia and isn't prepared to fight a war for the sake of "my poor jewels," she sweeps her hand up the back of her hair as if she could still feel a tiara there. It's one of those theatrical effects that's meant to seem like an unconscious move on the character's part, and it's so precise and expertly timed that, emblematic though it may be, it works. A Stanislavskian actor would roughen it at the edges to make it look unplanned, but Claire is the master purveyor of the gesture that is as clean of line as a ballet step.

Unlike Mikhail and Tatiana in *Tovarich*, Swana is the villain of the piece—she has a loyal countryman, who works at the hotel where Ninotchka is staying, steal the jewels back and then blackmails her into returning to the Soviet Union so Swana can get Leon back. (It works for the moment, but not, of course, in the long run.) And the script, so clever and satisfying in most ways, loses its panache in the first exchange between Swana and

Ninotchka, where Swana encounters her with Leon in a nightclub. They exchange cracks about the Cossacks with their whips that seem programmed to make us see the grand duchess as the embodiment of the careless cruelty of the Russian royals. Luckily, you don't concentrate on the lines as much as you do on the contrast in acting styles, here and in the later scene between the two women, where Swana makes her deal for Leon. Garbo, the Eleonora Duse of the screen, is all smoldering emotion, and her mastery of the camera is so comprehensive that it feels like an extension of her body. Claire, as always, represents the more old-fashioned virtues of theatrical performance. Pauline Kael characterizes the scene as an acting contest of sorts,[5] and unquestionably it is, enhancing the competition between the two Russians, though the two actresses play to a draw. In the nightclub scene, Claire's Swana glides over to Leon and Ninotchka's table, deliberately excluding her rival by wrapping Leon up in private chatter about their circle; then, with smiling condescension, she turns back to Ninotchka to decode the references for her benefit. But Ninotchka assures her, matter-of-factly, that everything she just said was perfectly understandable, piercing her bubble of exclusive self-importance. "Oh, dear me," Swana replies, "I must be losing my finesse. If I'm not careful I'll be understood by everybody"—and the skill in Claire's line reading lies in her concealing the sting in a velvet cushion of pretend affability. She wins both match and set (as we see in the later *scène à deux*) by remaining utterly unruffled, whereas Garbo's Ninotchka, who lacks the aristocratic training to bury her feelings, always shows her wounds. Even when Swana touches on an issue that she feels deeply—in their return encounter, she talks about all the things the Soviets stole from her—Claire sees to it that the emotion takes the dignified shape of a statement of fact, tinged ever so lightly with sorrow and anger, as if these were merely reflected colors. *That's* high-comic style.

*Reunion in Vienna*, Sidney Franklin's 1933 version of the Robert E. Sherwood comedy the Lunts made famous in New York, stars John Barrymore as a refugee from another ousted royalty, Archduke Rudolf of the Austrian Hapsburgs, now working as a taxi driver in Paris. In this barely transplanted stage play, a group of friends who, in sunnier days, frequented the Schönbrunn, the emperor's summer palace, returns to Vienna for a reunion, and Rudolf braves the police to return illegally to his home. Barrymore gives the sort of outrageous performance he was famous for on the screen, but the focus of the film isn't Rudolf but Elena (Diana Wynyard), Rudolf's former mistress, now happily married to a psychiatrist (Frank Morgan) whose lectures exhort his listeners to expel the delusions in their subconscious just as Austria expelled the Hapsburgs. Dr. Anton Krug represents the modern world: he and Elena live in an art deco manse where the latest in electronic equipment (all deco, too, of course) substitutes for the antiques another man of his income might collect. As for Elena, she has decidedly mixed feelings about her past: she takes a tour of the Schönbrunn, lingering behind the other oglers to return to the bedchamber—accessible by a secret panel the guide assured the tourists no one has ever located—where her portrait still hangs over the mantel and where she made love to the archduke. She claims she has put her aristocratic youth behind her, and when her old friends visit and urge her to attend the reunion, she turns them down—though perhaps it's the thought of seeing Rudolf, rumored to be in Vienna, that she balks at. Anton persuades her to go: he thinks it would be healthy for her to confront the reality that her memories have romanticized. This is Krug's therapy for patients who cling stubbornly to their illusions. And we know it isn't going to work, any more than it works when the doctor attending the title character in Pirandello's play *Henry IV* attempts it to cure his patient, a man who believes he is a long-dead Italian monarch. *Henry IV* is a high comedy that catapults unexpectedly into tragedy when the doctor's experiment backfires. *Reunion in Vienna* is a kind of ersatz-Shavian comedy of manners—Shaw as only a straining American playwright would render him—where both the sanctimonious shrink and the entitled ex-royal (who has as little regard for Elena's married state as he does for the fact of his exile) wind up having their expectations reversed. Elena neither sleeps with Rudolf nor rejects her past (though she stays with her husband), and Anton behaves with nobility when he uses his contact with the prefect of police to secure safe passage back to France for Rudolf. (The prefect's wife is a patient of Anton's, psychoanalysis being a necessary accoutrement for the neoaristocracy that has replaced the old one presided over by the Hapsburgs.)

   *Reunion in Vienna* isn't a very good movie, but it's an interesting remnant of a self-serious style of high-comic writing that's long vanished from the American stage. (Sherwood's plays, which come equipped with morals—*The Petrified Forest* and *Idiot's Delight* are the most famous—haven't aged much better than Maxwell Anderson's.) And it's perhaps the best example of Diana Wynyard's stage-trained technique. Wynyard played the all-enduring British matriarch in the suffocating film of Noël Coward's *Cavalcade* (the same year as *Reunion in Vienna*), and seven years later she was the Victorian woman whose husband (Anton Walbrook) tries to drive her mad in *Gaslight*, the British movie of the Patrick Hamilton warhorse *Angel Street*—the role Ingrid Bergman made famous in Hollywood. In both *Cavalcade* and *Gaslight* the camera picks up too much of Wynyard's theatrical preparation—everything feels laid out. But in the scene in *Gaslight* where she looks at herself in the mirror and tells her housekeeper that she's losing her mind and is beyond help, you can see what she must have been able to achieve on stage, and in *Reunion in Vienna*, playing off that exuberant hambone Barrymore and parrying his often deliciously witty line readings, she reins herself in and attains a subtlety those other, better-known performances don't rise to.

Barrymore shows up in another movie with a European setting and a plot involving royalty, Mitchell Leisen's 1939 *Midnight*, which, like *Ninotchka*, has a script by Wilder and Brackett. Like *Ninotchka*, too, it's a romantic comedy enhanced by some high-comic elements. You can tell the former is leading the latter in the opening scene where a train pulls into Paris in the early-morning rain and the conductor finds Claudette Colbert, in a hooded lamé gown, sleeping on a seat in one of the compartments: she peeks out and quips, "So this is Paris, huh? . . . Well, from here it looks like a rainy night in Kokomo, Indiana." Here the royalty is phony. Down on her luck, Colbert's Eve Peabody crashes a ritzy party, pretending to be someone called "the Baroness Czerny." It's a made-up identity; the name belongs to a definitely non-regal Paris cabbie (Don Ameche), a Hungarian immigrant who was kind to her earlier. (The party features an authentic member of royalty, a white Russian prince with wild, thick hair arranged like a nest around his bald spot, who gets up to play a Chopin étude. In Wilder and Brackett's Paris, Russian émigrés are all the rage in the best social circles.) Barrymore plays George Flammarion, who spots Eve as a *poseuse* straight off but is taken with her nerve. He bankrolls her charade on the condition that she seduce the worthless gigolo lover (Francis Lederer) of his wife (Mary Astor) away from her. Hélène Flammarion isn't dumb enough to fall for Eve's act, but just as she's about to expose her, Czerny (who is in love with Eve) appears, pretending to be a baron. In *Midnight*, royalty is just a ruse—and a plot device—and finally the movie doesn't have much time for the official aristocracy. Flammarion is immensely likable, but largely because he isn't like his wife and her superficial companions: all he wants is to save his marriage. And he and Eve are in some way kindred spirits—survivors with resources. Eve is a gold digger who's learned that "you don't just land in a tub of butter, you jump for it." That these two are simpatico is underlined by the skillful interplay between Barrymore, who may never have seemed more effortlessly relaxed on camera, and Colbert. The last act of *Midnight* would be more satisfying if they wound up together, but—after a rather frantic interlude in a courtroom—Eve ends up with Tibor Czerny, while Hélène (with a gentle resignation that surprises us) returns to George.

The presence of performers like Barrymore and Ina Claire almost guarantees a degree of high comedy. Charles Boyer is another example. In *History Is*

*Made at Night* (Frank Borzage, 1937), he's Paul, a gifted French headwaiter working in London, where he's in partnership with a chef named Cesare, played by Leo Carrillo. But Boyer makes Paul the most distingué headwaiter imaginable, and in fact for the entire first section of the movie we have no idea he isn't an aristocrat. Nor does Irene Vail (Jean Arthur), whose half-mad shipbuilder husband (*Frankenstein's* Colin Clive, doing his specialty, tic-ridden obsession) is trying, through various underhanded means, to keep her from divorcing him. Vail is so convinced that she's left him for another man that he agrees to the divorce only if she can remain celibate for six months, and then when his suspicions fail to bear fruit, he sends his own chauffeur (Ivan Lebedeff) to her apartment to compromise her for a detective's camera. But Paul, who's in the next suite—putting a drunken customer to bed, we learn later—steps in to rescue Irene, posing as a jewel thief and staging a kidnapping to throw off Vail and the detective. The set-up is high comedy, and the combination of Boyer's continental style and Arthur's astonishingly delicate line readings confirm the genre. She's simultaneously brittle and cottony, balanced between romantic comedy and plaintive longing—vulnerability, a history of sadness. Paul takes Irene to Cesare's for his signature dish, though it's closing time; he presses the musicians into service, paying them off in champagne. And he tries to get Irene to talk about what's happened between her and her husband, but she keeps it at bay, burying it under the lovely veneer of this romantic interlude.

*History Is Made at Night* turns out to be a bizarre mix of high comedy, romantic comedy, and melodrama. Technically Paul is an outsider, not an aristocrat, but his conduct and manner suggest the opposite. And it isn't because Irene has married into the aristocracy that her life is miserable—it's because she had the misfortune to get stuck with a jealous bastard. So this is a strange case for high comedy, and it gets stranger as the plot unwinds. Bruce Vail kills his chauffeur and frames Paul for the murder; to save him (she doesn't know he's innocent), Irene returns to her husband and sails for New York. Paul and Cesare follow, opening a new restaurant that becomes, of course, the toast of Manhattan, just as the old one was the toast of Paris. While Paul waits for the inevitable night when Irene will walk in and take the table he keeps reserved for her, she runs out on Vail, taking a job as a model in a dress shop. (The Irene–Paul relationship is almost a blueprint for the marriage between Barbara Bel Geddes and the Howard Hughes–inspired millionaire played by Robert Ryan in Max Ophüls's *Caught*, which came out a decade and a half later.) At this point the plot becomes too complicated to be summarized here. It shifts permanently to melodrama when Vail, who owns the ship on which Paul and Irene are sailing back to Paris, orders the captain to set a new speed record, fog and ice notwithstanding, so he can kill the lovers in a smash-up, and the ship dutifully hits an iceberg. The movie's such a mish-mash of genres and intentions that you wonder if the four writers (Gene Towne, Graham Baker, David Hertz, and Vincent Lawrence, who wrote high comedies for the stage) each submitted a different script and Borzage tried shooting different parts of each one.

Borzage is one director whose imitation-European approach often mined the resources of high comedy, even if the material leaned in other directions. He liked to work with Margaret Sullavan, whose silvery fragility automatically conferred a high-comic aura on the movies she starred in, like William Wyler's *The Good Fairy* (a Molnár adaptation) and H. C. Potter's remake of the Nancy Carroll early talkie *The Shopworn Angel* (1938), one of three movies that starred her opposite Jimmy Stewart. (They were the great forgotten duo of thirties movies, as marvelous together as Hepburn and Grant, Astaire and Rogers, William Powell and Myrna Loy.) Sullavan would have made as great a Camille as Garbo; you can see it in *The Shopworn Angel*, where, as a cynical showgirl melted to a core of genuine feeling by the adoration of Stewart's hick soldier, her head covered in curls like filigree, she blankets herself in a feathered cape as if it could afford protection against the damage of the world. Borzage used her for her *Sea Gull* waif quality in *Little Man, What Now?* where she and Douglass Montgomery (Laurie to Katharine Hepburn's Jo in the Cukor *Little Women* [1933]) struggle to get through the German Depression, and where she has an indelible moment, childlike and sorrowful, on a merry-go-round. And he used her again as the tubercular heroine—a former aristocrat fallen on hard times—of *Three Comrades*, which F. Scott Fitzgerald and Edward A. Paramore culled from an Erich Maria Remarque novel set in post–World War I Germany. It's a very bad movie, but Sullavan has some great scenes in it, and sometimes she's supported by the dialogue, especially when you can hear Fitzgerald's voice in it. The best example is the scene where her boyfriend (Robert Taylor) comes home drunk and, smelling his breath, she murmurs, "Rum, cognac, whiskey—League of Nations, darling." Only one man could have written that line, and no one else could read it with Sullavan's gallantry (Pauline Kael's word for her[6])—that blend of tolerance and reckless emotional commitment. The movie is high-toned romantic melodrama, but that line and that reading, in a certain way, define high comedy.

Sullavan gave her greatest performance—opposite Stewart—in the only movie either of them did for Lubitsch, *The Shop Around the Corner*, which came, like Cukor's *The Philadelphia Story* and Hawks's *His Girl Friday*, in 1940, before the war changed the atmosphere in Hollywood. These three movies represent, in their distinct ways, the apotheosis of the various comic strains peculiar to thirties comedy—*The Philadelphia Story* is a bona fide example of American-bred comedy of manners, *His Girl Friday* is a hard-boiled comedy (Hecht and MacArthur's *The Front Page*) converted miraculously into romantic comedy, and *The Shop Around the Corner*, adapted by Samson Raphaelson from a Hungarian play by Nikolaus Laszlo, is a romantic comedy with high-comic elements. It's also perhaps Lubitsch's finest achievement. The two movies he turned out between the early and late thirties—that is, between *The Merry Widow* and *Ninotchka*—are failed high comedies. *Angel* has a Raphaelson script and Marlene Dietrich; *Bluebeard's Eighth Wife* (1938) stars Claudette Colbert and Gary Cooper and was written by Wilder and Brackett. (The source is a French play by Alfred Savoir.) But both are labored, and the latter, clearly intended to be a howl, is desperately unfunny. Colbert plays the daughter of a bankrupt French marquis (Edward Everett Horton, the best thing in the picture) who agrees to his pleas and marries a rich American businessman (Cooper), then tries to get him to divorce her so she can get a $100,000 settlement. The refined Colbert isn't impressed with Cooper's brusque Yankee manners—which, unlike *Desire*, this movie uses against him (and Cooper has none of the charm he showed two years earlier in *Desire*). But finally she prefers him to her other suitor, a young count (David Niven) reduced to working as an underpaid clerk in one of Cooper's banks. Wilder and Brackett get in a few laughs at the expense of the fallen royalty, but they don't seem to like either of the two protagonists very much, so the romantic-comedy scenes, like the one where she staves off his advances by stuffing her mouth with scallions, feel both stale and sour.

*Bluebeard's Eighth Wife* isn't of much interest; *Angel* is an intriguing fiasco. What's oddest about it isn't Dietrich's flatness (as compared to her work in *Desire*) or even Raphaelson's, but the fact that Lubitsch, of all directors, can't get the tone right. Dietrich is the neglected wife of a British diplomat (Herbert Marshall) who meets Melvyn Douglas at a Paris house of assignation and permits him to take her to dinner. He figures her for a high-class whore, but their evening together reveals her refinement and depth, and he falls hopelessly in love with her. When she vanishes at the end of the night, he vows to find her. He doesn't expect she'll turn up in London as the wife of a distinguished man who's invited him home for dinner. When he gets a moment alone with her, she denies that she's "Angel"—his term of affection for her—in one of those theatrical truth-or-illusion exchanges that seems to have been borrowed from the latest Theatre Guild presentation of a European import. Eventually she owns up, and though she says she won't imperil her marriage for an *affaire de coeur* with him, she does show up in Paris to see him again. So does Marshall, who's figured out what's up. While Douglas waits for her in one room, she encounters Marshall in another, and to him she claims she's come to see for herself Douglas's "Angel," who's supposed to look so much like her. When Marshall makes a move toward the door, she warns him that if he leaves the room it will mark the collapse of their marriage: Either he'll discover that she's telling the truth (but she'll no longer want to remain married to him) or he'll discover she's lying (in which case *he'll* want a divorce). She proposes instead that he remain in doubt—which, for the future of a union that has become tedious and stagnant, might be wonderful. The high-comic solution would be for him to stay, but instead he goes (melodrama). Then the film opts for a *third* resolution: he comes back to her anyway (melodrama with a happy ending stuck on). The botched ending is merely indicative of everything else that's wrong with *Angel*. The plot suggests high comedy, but it's played for melodrama throughout.

What makes *The Shop Around the Corner* at least a borderline comedy of manners has a great deal to do with its style, which is muted, embroidered, and lyrical—trademarks of Lubitsch's movies, of course, but hardly of the other great romantic comedies of its era. The setting is a community of shop clerks, and it's the Depression, but since they're in Budapest and the store that employs them is a *parfumerie*, their interchange is gentle and their venue quaint—this is one of those Hollywood movies set in a painterly, fairy-tale Europe. Even the title suggests the difference. James Harvey points out that "if this were a more American sort of comedy—like *Bachelor Mother* [a 1939 comedy starring Ginger Rogers as a department store clerk opposite David Niven as the owner's son]—they would hate their jobs, but as it is they are merely trying to rise above them."[7] In the delightful musical-play version produced in the sixties, *She Loves Me*, by Jerry Bock and Sheldon Harnick, the employees seem more discontented, but the grousing that can distinguish a hard-boiled comedy from a high one—and that filmmakers often borrow to fill out the edges of romantic comedy—is minimized in *The Shop Around the Corner*. You wouldn't call the ensemble of characters an aristocracy, but unlike their American counterparts they have intellectual interests—art, music, literature—that suggest a longing for a more cultivated life. (This may be partly what Harvey means when he writes that they're trying to rise above the ordinariness of their workaday existence.) What draws the protagonists, head clerk Alfred Kralik (Stewart) and new employee Klara Novak (Sullavan), to each other is a common passion for the arts, which they discuss in the anonymous letters they send back and forth, addressed to "Dear Friend."

What makes the film a romantic comedy is that, in their everyday interaction at Matuschek's store, unaware that they've in fact fallen in love through their letters, the two clerks appear to detest each other. The arc of a romantic comedy traces the movement of a man and a woman who begin in an adversarial position toward a recognition that they belong together—confirming our own instinct about them—and toward a maturity, the point at which they deserve each other's love, just like the characters in a Shakespearean forest comedy or a traditional fairy tale. Raphaelson and Lubitsch came up with the brilliant idea of establishing the parameters of that arc right at the beginning by showing us, on the pages of Klara and Alfred's unsigned letters to each other, what they can't see when they're face to face—and what they must learn in order to get their happy ending. The high-comic element is the device of using their love of art and music and especially books to express the finer feelings that they're willing to share, initially, only in the safety of anonymity and the intimacy of letter writing.

On its most basic level, the movie is about how perspective alters everything, and about how very kind and sensitive people can sometimes behave very badly when they become preoccupied or insecure, and their perspective is clouded. Alfred and Klara meet under unfortunate circumstances: When she approaches him in the store, he's charmed until he finds out that she's only after a job. Then when he puts her off, she impresses his boss (Frank Morgan) by selling a sample of some new musical candy boxes. But Alfred and Matuschek have been squabbling over those candy boxes, which Alfred warned him wouldn't sell, so Klara is making him look bad in his boss's eyes. And he's too self-absorbed to take note of her desperation to find a job during the Depression. So they start off on the wrong foot, and everything they say to each other confirms in their own minds their initial impressions of each other. It's only when Alfred finds out that Klara is "Dear Friend" that he adjusts his impressions—and then he spends the rest of the movie winning her over. The subplot built around the relationship between Matuschek and Alfred cleverly parallels this idea of the danger of misperceptions. The quarrel over the music boxes demonstrates that in his dealings with his employer, as in his dealings with Klara, Alfred is unable to back down; his pride gets in the way, and Matuschek, who thinks of him as a son, is hurt by his obstinacy. These men have such obvious love for each other that they ought to get through these little crises. The problem is that Matuschek has received an anonymous note to the effect that his wife is sleeping with one of his clerks, and he makes the mistake of thinking it's Alfred. He doesn't suspect the true culprit, the ass-kissing weasel Vadas, played by Joseph Schildkraut, a man who uses an air of refinement as a façade for an essential dishonesty and ruthlessness. You can see why Matuschek never considers Vadas, whose existence he barely notices: It would be an insult to his wife to imagine she could be swept off her feet by someone so insubstantial. (He's paying Alfred a compliment, in a way.) This error has to be corrected before he and his head clerk can be reconciled.

On a deeper level, *The Shop Around the Corner* is about the dual nature of human beings—about the tension between surface and depth, which is reconcilable only when we see how they mirror each other. (To pick a comic example: Once Alfred knows Klara is "Dear Friend," he begins to hear in her insults the same deftness of expression he's read in her letters.) What each of them is attracted to in the other is the flip side of what each thinks is offensive about the other. Alfred's blustering and arrogance are the unappealing side of his assertiveness and self-confidence, and his stubbornness is the unappealing side of his straight-arrow quality—his inability to compromise himself, whatever the stakes. (And it turns out he's dead right about those damn music boxes.) Klara's pretentiousness and willfulness and obstinacy are the unappealing side of her intellectuality and her individuality; even the fact that she takes Alfred's boss's part against him masks—for him, if not for us—that she's perfect for the job, a gifted salesperson. (No one else manages to sell a music box.) At the end, just before revealing himself as "Dear Friend," Alfred sets a final test for her, pretending that he's met her suitor and that, physically, he's not all she dreamed about, and Klara tells him, ruefully, that she's built up an illusion about this unseen lover of hers. That's true in a way, but she's got it backward. His letters haven't disguised his true nature, but they've made it difficult for her to see the possibility that he has other qualities, too. Through their correspondence she's constructed an ideal lover whose real counterpart she was unable to perceive in the real world—even when "Dear Friend" himself stepped into her life.

Lubitsch, who died in 1947—in the middle of directing Betty Grable in *That Lady in Ermine*, which Otto Preminger finished—made two more comedies of manners, *Heaven Can Wait* (from a Raphaelson script) in 1943 and *Cluny Brown* in 1946. Neither illustrates the fluidity and light handedness of his earlier movies, but then it was another era, a more stiff-backed one, and Hollywood wasn't making comedies in the loose, ineffable style that bespoke the thirties. Still, these movies are charmers. *Heaven Can Wait* is framed by the appearance of one Henry Van Cleve (Don Ameche) in the meticulously appointed study of the devil (robust Laird Cregar, with a curled shoe-polish mustache and goatee, smiling to the whites of his eyes). Henry believes he has behaved like a reprobate all his life and expects to be sent to hell. But when Satan asks him to recount his life's adventures, the flashbacks indicate an earnest and essentially innocent Lothario whose entire adult life unfolded in the light of his love for his wife Martha (Gene Tierney); her death in middle age provides the high comedy's requisite touch of melancholy. James Harvey suggests that Van Cleve's innocence of any real wrongdoing is a consequence of the restrictions of the Hays Code, and he points out plot gaps that might have been filled in by Henry's infidelities. Harvey's argument is hard to refute. Still—and despite the infelicity in the casting of the two leading actors—the movie makes skillful use of the Shavian moral reversal it invokes in the opening scene (and Cregar's mannerly devil is surely derived from Shaw's *Man and Superman*). In that scene the high-society Edna Craig, used to the best accommodations, is astonished to find herself whisked away by elevator into hell, while Satan listens politely to Van Cleve's case.

Their styles couldn't be more different, but at times Lubitsch's depiction of the American nouveaux riches suggests a whiff of Preston Sturges. Henry comes from a rising Fifth Avenue family: when he wants to run around with showgirls, his mother (Spring Byington) reminds him quietly that the most beautiful roses grow on the most cultivated bushes. But Martha's parents, the Strables, are ignorant midwestern dairy millionaires (played by Eugene Pallette and Marjorie Main) with a statue of their company's mascot, Mabel the Cow, in the front yard of their mansion, and a patient black servant (Clarence Muse) who plays middleman at the breakfast table when they're too sore to communicate with each other directly. It's a wickedly funny satirical depiction of a distinctly American sort of aristocracy, though the filmmakers don't quite portray the Strables as monsters. The Strables' disapproval of Henry estranges them from their daughter (who was supposed to marry Henry's insufferable cousin Albert, played by Allyn Joslyn), but when she and Henry quarrel and she comes home, their hearts melt.

Shaw's influence can be felt in *Cluny Brown*, too, which is set in 1938 in London and its environs. Cluny's plumber uncle, Arn (Billy Bevan), who raised her, is a composite of those ornery characters in Shaw's plays who proudly embrace their working-class origins while articulating sophisticated ideas about class, and Cluny (Jennifer Jones) embodies the trademark Shavian reversal when she gets excited about the challenges of unclogging a sink—a verboten subject for the well brought up. In another reversal, it's the middle-class characters in this picture, Cluny's shopkeeper swain (the hilariously adenoidal Richard Haydn) and his snooty mother (Una O'Connor) conveying her disapproval through loud clearings of her throat, who exert the most rigorous and intractable standards for conduct. When Cluny gets down and liberates the choked drain during tea, mama is so unsettled that she has to retire to her room, and after the tea guests have departed the shopkeeper tells Cluny ominously, "I'd rather not have seen what I saw." Lubitsch and the screenwriters, Samuel Hoffenstein and Elizabeth Reinhardt (adapting a Margery

Sharp novel), essentially transplant a Victorian joke to a contemporary setting, implying that English manners haven't changed very much since the
nineteenth century—they've simply been inherited by the lower classes. The
true aristocrats (Reginald Owen and Margaret Bannerman), who employ
Cluny as a domestic, are nowhere near as inflexible as the housekeeper (Sara
Allgood) and butler (Ernest Cossart) who supervise her.

These aren't the first movies to spin off from Shaw's dramatic notions.
The 1933 Hollywood version of the Marcel Pagnol play *Topaze*, with John
Barrymore in the title role, is midway between a boulevard comedy and a
satirical farce with Shavian overtones. It's about a private-school teacher
with a child's faith in the triumph of industry over dishonesty, and in the essential goodness of the world, who's hired by the aunt of a boy he tutors and
her corrupt councilman lover to serve as the phony director of a company. It
never occurs to him that he's being asked to break the law; when he learns
the truth, he moves from shock and shame to a recognition that money is the
power that governs the world. The discovery doesn't embitter him; he puts
his brain to work to outsmart his boss. He figures out how to build a better
illicit mousetrap. In the American movie, though (one was made in France
the same year, with Louis Jouvet, and there were two later ones), the director, Harry d'Abbadie d'Arrast—working from a Ben Hecht script—lays a sort
of fluffy lyricism on top of the material, slowing down the rhythms artificially
by building retards into them, and lingering on the visuals (some of which
are quite special). I think it's the combination of d'Arrast's style and the
highly verbal quality of the play and Barrymore's marvelous high-style performance that makes the movie a high comedy.

And *Cluny Brown* isn't the first Hollywood comedy to adapt English ideas
about class. You find them as early as 1931, in *The Devil to Pay*, based on a
play by Frederick Lonsdale, where the hero (Ronald Colman) is an affable
ne'er-do-well who, having lost all his money in East Africa, returns home to
London to reconcile with his aristocratic father (Frederic Kerr). And after a
decade of furnishing expensive, sometimes star-studded versions of a number
of classic novels, including several by Dickens, M-G-M finally got around to
Jane Austen's comedies of manners in 1940, with Robert Z. Leonard's *Pride
and Prejudice*. Austen usually doesn't adapt well to the movies; there was a
craze for Austen films in the nineties, but the results were mostly disap-
pointing. The most popular one, Ang Lee's *Sense and Sensibility* (1995), tries
to convert a high comedy into a romantic comedy and succeeds only in sen-
timentalizing the material. Perhaps *Pride and Prejudice* works because there's
a *true* romantic comedy embedded in the high comedy: Elizabeth (Greer Garson) and Darcy (Laurence Olivier) have to overcome his pride and her prej-

udice to fall into each other's arms. (Note that M-G-M selected a pair of Brits to play the leading roles.) And oddly, Leonard, working from a skillful adaptation by Aldous Huxley and Jane Murfin (via Helen Jerome's stage version), makes the material rather Dickensian. (The aura is confirmed when Edna May Oliver, with her long, expressive face, famous with audiences as Aunt Betsey Trotwood in *David Copperfield* [1935], shows up as Darcy's aunt, Lady Catherine de Bourgh.) The novel is tamed down, its edges hemmed. Lady Catherine turns out to be an old softie, and the satirical thrusts Mr. Bennet (Edmund Gwenn) aims at his ridiculous wife (Mary Boland) are gentled by his transparent fondness for her; he's more of a likably distanced commentator than the antisocial wit Austen wrote. Jane Austen is perhaps too sharp-witted an observer of the social scene for the deluxe M-G-M treatment, but the movie is genial, and the actors seem to be having a grand time—especially Boland and Melville Cooper, who plays Mr. Collins, Elizabeth's erstwhile suitor, as a kind of sycophantic moth fluttering around the snooty Lady Catherine, thrilled by her condescensions. But the only real high-stakes high-comedy player in the cast is Olivier, tracing lines as delicate as smoke rings in the air with his hands and coloring his limpid line readings with the subtlest of modulations.

In 1937, RKO made a pass at another Brit with a specialty in comedies of manners, James Barrie, when George Stevens directed a misbegotten adaptation of his play *Quality Street*, set in the very early nineteenth century. The (farce) plot revolves around the disappointment of Phoebe Throssel (Katharine Hepburn), who loves Dr. Valentine Brown (Franchot Tone): apparently unaware of her as more than a friend, he goes away to war, and when he returns ten years later, she's already a spinster. In a last-ditch effort, she dresses up for a ball, looking younger and fresher than she has in a decade, and he doesn't recognize her, so she pretends to be her own niece. The outcome is obvious, but the emphasis is as much on manners as on romance. When Brown enlists, Phoebe confesses to her sister (Fay Bainter), that she let him kiss her: "I could bear all the rest, but I've been un-ladylike." That's the world of Barrie's play.

Stevens never finds his tone, but Hepburn gives a miraculous performance as Phoebe, getting scene after impossible scene to work. She's as inherently a high-comic performer as Ina Claire or John Barrymore—not only in her Philip Barry movies, which are written to be played in that style, and in Stevens's *Alice Adams* (1935), based on a novel by Booth Tarkington, who dealt in social comedy, but also in Tennessee Williams (*Suddenly, Last Summer* [1959], where she mixes high comedy with high camp) and even Eugene O'Neill (*Long Day's Journey into Night* [1962], where she mixes it with tragedy). She's so eccentric and gigantic on camera that you always get the intensity of her emotion through the medium of artifice. One of the weirdest movies she made in the thirties—weirder even than *Quality Street*—is *Sylvia Scarlett* (1936), for George Cukor, one of four movies that cast her opposite her perfect stylistic match, Cary Grant. (Cukor directed three of the four.) Based on a Compton Mackenzie novel, it's the story of a young woman, half-English, half-French, who helps her widowed English papa (Edmund Gwenn) escape from Marseilles before he can get caught for embezzlement. In league with Grant's Cockney swindler Jimmy Monkley, whom they meet on a boat to England, they have a brief career as con artists and then, unaccountably, become strolling players in Pierrot costumes; Monk's sometime girlfriend Maudie (Dennie Moore), whom they steal out of domestic service, makes a fourth in the troupe. They're mock aristocrats, like Astaire and Garland performing "A Couple of Swells" in *Easter Parade*, though they get mixed up with a real one, a moneyed artist played (unfortunately) by Brian Aherne, with whom Sylvia falls in love. It's mostly the presence of Hepburn—who plays half the role in drag—that gives *Sylvia Scarlett* the air of high comedy. I'm not sure what you'd call it, really—it's a mishmash of several genres, and even the parts of the plot don't fit together comfortably. But Hepburn's stylized impression of romantic longing isn't quite like anything the movies had ever seen. If anyone captured the spirit of high comedy in the thirties, it was Katharine Hepburn.

# Notes

1. Anthony Lane, "Master of Ceremonies: The Films of Max Ophüls," *The New Yorker*, July 8, 2002, 78.
2. Harvey, *Romantic Comedy*, 69.
3. Harvey, *Romantic Comedy*, 53.
4. Harvey, *Romantic Comedy*, 50.
5. Pauline Kael, *5001 Nights at the Movies*, 2nd ed. (New York: Henry Holt, 1991), 531.
6. Kael, *5001 Nights at the Movies*, 764.
7. Harvey, *Romantic Comedy*, 401.

~

# CHAPTER TWO

# High Comedy, American Style

Salted among the stage-to-screen European high comedies in the early days of the talkies were a few adaptations of American plays, directed either by Edward H. Griffith (*Holiday* [1930], *Rebound* [1931], *The Animal Kingdom* [1932], *Paris Bound* [1929]) or by George Cukor (*The Royal Family of Broadway* [1930], with Cyril Gardner listed as codirector, and *Dinner at Eight* [1933]). These two groups of films identify the main Broadway sources for homegrown comedies of manners in the thirties. Philip Barry wrote *Holiday* and *The Animal Kingdom*. He also authored *The Philadelphia Story*, the 1940 Hollywood version of which—along with an infinitely superior remake of *Holiday* in 1938—featured Katharine Hepburn and Cary Grant, working under Cukor's expert hand. This extraordinary pair of pictures, perhaps the best known and most adored high comedies ever to come out of Hollywood, had another collaborator, too, the screenwriter Donald Ogden Stewart, working in tandem with Sidney Buchman on *Holiday* and solo on *The Philadelphia Story*. Stewart was himself a refugee from the Broadway stage; *Rebound* was among his handful of plays—and the only one to be filmed. *The Royal Family of Broadway* and *Dinner at Eight*, like the later *Stage Door* [1937], began life as plays by George S. Kaufman and Edna Ferber.

Barry's plays may call up comparisons to Noël Coward, but they're highly distinctive, and his three best, all of which made it to the movies, follow a similar narrative pattern. The hero or heroine begins on the verge of matrimony with the wrong person; in the wings waits a far better match, temperamentally and philosophically, but for reasons that vary from play to play, the protagonist is unaware of the dangerous mistake he or she is making and doesn't discover it until close to the end of the last act. This scenario sounds like the plot of a romantic comedy, and these plays could be considered romantic comedies except for certain significant elements—the focus on class, the slightly artificial Park Avenue language (the sole quality that pulls against an essentially naturalistic style), and Barry's trademark, the seriousness at the core.

If the main character in a romantic comedy is attached to the wrong lover, like Irene Dunne in *The Awful Truth* (1937) or Rosalind Russell in *His Girl Friday*, the happy ending can occur only when she realizes it's Cary Grant (in both cases) she really loves. It's more complicated in the Barry plays. Here the reversal of the protagonist's expectations (if not the audience's—the mistake is apparent to us pretty much from the outset) arrives only after some combination of personal reassessment and a recognition that the intended partner represents misbegotten values. So in *Holiday*, when Johnny Case (played by Robert Ames in the first version, Grant in the second) finds that Julia Seton (Mary Astor, Doris Nolan) doesn't want him to pursue his dream of travel but prefers him to settle down in New York to make more money, her attitude reveals that she's inextricably tied to the dull, soul-destroying world of high finance for its own sake that her stuffed-shirt father represents. And once the romantic mist around Julia has cleared he can see that his real soul mate is her sister Linda (Ann Harding, Katharine Hepburn), the family misfit who shares his nonconformist vision. In *The Animal Kingdom*, Tom Collier (Leslie Howard) abandons his painter lover, Daisy Sage (Harding), for a high-society beauty, Cecilia (Myrna Loy), who wants—like Julia Seton—to drain all the unconventionality out of him. His choice of Cecilia and a proper married life over living with Daisy removes him from the bohemian world of the heroes of Coward's *Design for Living*. Eventually, though, he realizes that Daisy is his true kindred spirit. Contrary to conventional society's ungenerous characterization of a woman who agrees to live unwed with the man she loves, it's his legal wife Cecilia—who uses sex as a reward when Tom gives her what she wants and withholds it when he doesn't—and not Daisy who's the real whore. (You can see why *The Animal Kingdom* could only be made in the freer atmosphere of pre–Hays Code Hollywood—and also why it's never revived: the Shavian moral reversal would hardly operate for an era that places no social stigma on unmarried cohabiting couples. *The Animal Kingdom* is a very good play, but now it's irrevocably a period piece.) And Tracy Lord (Hepburn) in *The Philadelphia Story* rejects her fiancé, George Kittredge (John Howard), moments before their wedding when she suddenly discovers that the qualities she wants to develop in her own character—understanding rather than judgment, broad-mindedness over prejudice, the capacity for love and not the habit of self-righteousness—are out of tune with Kittredge's personality and perfectly in sync with that of her ex-husband, C. Dexter Haven (Grant).

The Cukor movies are far more interesting examinations of Barry's ideas because they're far better movies. Griffith is a stolid director; it's particularly depressing to watch his 1930 *Holiday*, where the stage pauses keep letting the air out of the high comedy, and the performances lack nuance so the terrific dialogue sounds stilted. The striking Ann Harding, with her golden hair and long-legged stride, specializes in a breathy, searching-for-the-muse kind of acting that feels like it belongs to another century. Hollywood had to invent the right style, both of performance and of direction, for Philip Barry. Clearly he knew it—he wrote *The Philadelphia Story* for Hepburn, who starred in it on Broadway in 1939, the year after she filmed *Holiday*, and its success marked her triumphant return to Hollywood, where RKO had terminated her contract.

Both *Holiday* and *The Philadelphia Story* are premised, at least partly, on the apparent intrusion of an outsider into the sheltered circle of old money. Julia Seton is the younger daughter of a Manhattan banking family, while Johnny Case comes from (relative) poverty. But he's a Horatio Alger hero: not only did he work his way through Harvard, but with ingenuity and industriousness he's landed in a top-drawer law firm and made himself a bundle on the stock market. And once Julia's father, Edward (Henry Kolker), gets over his initial nervousness about handing his daughter over to a young man of no background, he comes around to Julia's way of thinking. She thinks she recognizes in Johnny the fiber that drove her grandfather, the original author of the Seton millions, up the mountain of financial success. But Julia's effort to sell her fiancé to her cautious, conservative papa isn't the conflict of the play. Even with the price of admission to the Seton club in his pocketbook, Johnny is no ordinary swell. What he has in mind for himself (and Julia) is a holiday, to "try to find out who I am and what I am and what goes on and what about it—now, while I'm young, and feel good all the time." And when Edward balks at this scheme, Julia sides with her father. It's Linda who recognizes its beauty—Linda, who has always felt like the black sheep, who finds the air of their uptown mansion suffocating, who realizes, with intensifying fervency and certainty as the movie goes on, that she'll never discover who *she* is until she can get away from her family. Barry and his adapters draw the lines very clearly, but they're not precisely class lines—they divide those with positive (life-affirming) values from those with negative (life-denying) ones. So the elder Seton, who not only lacks the imagination to see the benefit of an unconventional lifestyle but is essentially corrupted by greed for money, and Julia, who can only admire Johnny as long as he's adhering to the Seton standards for how to conduct one's life, are carefully distinguished from Johnny, Linda, and their common friends the Potters (Jean Dixon and Edward Everett Horton), academics who are witty and wise (but by no means rich).

What *Holiday* does here is very unusual—and it's what makes this a quintessentially American version of a high comedy. Barry sets up a conventional aristocracy at the beginning, tricks us into thinking that he wants Johnny to gain entrance to it, and then creates a *second* aristocracy that is identified not by money, but by wit, intelligence, education, culture, playfulness, liberality, flexibility, and discrimination. It's an aristocracy of the spirit. And we know it's worth belonging to—and that it is indeed a highly selective club—because it boasts Cary Grant and Katharine Hepburn among its members. At the end of the movie, after Julia has given up on Johnny, Linda, who values him for the very qualities that, ultimately, Julia despises, determines to take her sister's place on Johnny's holiday. Of course, the future they're tumbling into may be full of adventure, but it's unlikely to encounter much hardship. Remember that Linda is an heiress and Johnny has just made a killing on Wall Street. It's a romantic-comedy finish in a high-comedy world.

The most intriguing character in *Holiday* is Ned Seton (Lew Ayres), Julia and Linda's brother. Ned wanted to become a musician, but as the only Seton son he's been forced to enter his father's business, and his hatred of it has driven him to drink. The closest the play comes to a tragic figure, he's Barry's example of what happens to a young man or woman of spirit who assents to being cowed by the cultivated bully Edward Seton; he also provides the touch of melancholy that appears in many modern high comedies. Ned claims the right to drink as much as he likes—which is, he explains, as much as he can stand—at any party he chooses to attend; he says it's his protection against the world he's stuck in and abhors, whereas poor Linda, he observes, has none. Drunkenness can be therapy and represent rebellion in a high comedy, but not when it's all a character has to fall back on. (When she awakens to her love for Johnny on New Year's Eve, Linda flirts with the idea of getting plastered too, but it's not for her. She doesn't have the capacity to turn to it in desperation, like Ned—the Seton world hasn't sapped her spirit.) But it does allow Ned to play the role of teller of unhappy truths. He tells Johnny that his mother "tried to be a Seton for a while, then gave up and died" (it's the movie's most bitter note). And he's the one who observes that when Edward and Julia rob Linda of her gift to her sister—an intimate New Year's Eve engagement party, which they convert into a huge black-tie affair—they turn her hoped-for "little shindig" into "a first-class funeral."

Before running off to join Johnny on the ship to Europe, Linda turns to Ned, whom she adores, and invites him to join them. He's tempted, but too weak to defy his father. When Linda promises she'll return for him, he answers, "I'll be here"—it's the best he can manage. (No viewer of the movie is likely to forget the expressiveness Ayres, a most affecting Ned, brings to this exchange.) Ned is the movie's most serious claim to being a critique of the aristocracy. We can't really count the Seton Crams (Henry Daniell and Binnie Barnes), the dreadful, condescending cousins we meet at Johnny and Julia's engagement party: Cukor has great fun with them, especially Laura, who talks through clenched teeth and wears her hair curled around the edges like frosting on a birthday cake, but they're far too easily pinked (by Linda, who can always paralyze Seton with a reference to their childhood battles, and by Susan Potter, who exposes his fascist sympathies with little effort) to be taken very seriously. Except for the woebegone example of Ned, the film, wonderful as it is, ends up finessing what seems at first like an American/democratic assault on the traditional/conservative stance of high comedy.

*The insiders (Lew Ayres, Katharine Hepburn, Edward Everett Horton, Jean Dixon) cavorting in the playroom: George Cukor's film of Philip Barry's play* Holiday *(1938). Credit: Columbia/ The Kobal Collection*

Julia behaves so badly in this movie that you might wonder why Ned and the Potters are the only ones among the likable characters who see through her. (Nick Potter suggests that maybe she loves herself more than she loves Johnny; Ned argues that "most people . . . make a big mistake about Julia. . . . They're taken in by her looks. At bottom she's a very dull girl, and the life she pictures for herself is the life she belongs in.") We can see from the beginning that she's not right for Johnny: When he's amazed to find out how rich she is and wants to talk about it, she's uncomfortable both with his levity and with his insistence on putting the subject front and center. (He doesn't believe there's anything sacred about money. Why would he? He's had to work his ass off for it.) She scolds him about his tie and his hair; she can't understand why he'd want to keep their engagement a secret for a little while, so that the world doesn't get at it. A romantic comedy is a series of liberating compromises, but in this *high* comedy he's expected to make all the sacrifices, and every one seems like a little defeat, and Grant makes us feel how much each costs him. (Increasingly, his Johnny is like a man trying to smile despite the chain around his neck.) And the distance between these two is just as clear when they're on the same side—when they try to get Ned to tone down his drinking at the party. Julia is insistent, rather imperious, while Johnny is concerned for Ned's welfare, and, drunk as he is, Ned can hear the difference in their tones. I think Johnny can't see Julia for what she is not only because he's blinded by a romantic vision of her, but also because he's projected his own wishes and desires onto her—precisely what she's done with him. Each sees in the other what he or she wants to see. And Linda's blindness to her sister's true nature—until the very end of the movie—is the result of a combination of factors. She's always romanticized Julia, seen her as a reflection of her own values as well as through the haze of her own generous love for her, and Julia hasn't corrected her—because she didn't want to start an argument, she *says*, but it's more likely that she enjoys Linda's adulation of her. Julia is honest about her attitude toward Linda only in private conversations with their father, and their conspiratorial dismissal of her is a little sickening. Ironically, Julia has always viewed Linda through *her* values, but as a rejection of them, and as a kind of broken toy that maybe she and Edward can fix. Linda is so lacking in confidence, so unaware of her own worth, that she could never see what Ned has always seen—that she's a better woman than the younger sister she's always adored.

Cukor makes a lot of the huge, pillared house with its twin staircases, which startles and dwarfs Johnny on his first encounter with it: when the valet takes him up to the second-floor parlor by elevator, Johnny looks down on the main floor below and mutters, "I could have walked that." The house is the embodiment of Edward Seton—except for the playroom, Linda's refuge, where she hides after her father wrecks her engagement party and where she ends up entertaining the people she cares about: Johnny (until his obligations return him to his fiancée), Ned, and Nick and Susan Potter. Along with Linda's party plans, it's the best example in *Holiday* of the high-comedy convention of a serious attitude applied to a seemingly trivial subject. The playroom has tremendous symbolic status: Warm, cheery, homey, it's a contrast to the rest of the mansion. When Johnny steps into it, he announces, "This is *quite* different," and we can hear the relief in his voice. It's the only room Linda feels drawn to, because here she can feel the spirit of her mother, who designed it. The games she and Johnny and the Potters play in this room on New Year's Eve, while the stuffed shirts are at the "adult" party downstairs, release their true, young, vital selves. It's a kind of enchanted forest where they're protected from the tyranny of the life deniers. Our litmus test for the characters is how they respond to the playroom. Edward is uncomfortable in it, Julia basically ignores it, Seton and Laura Cram bring a chill to it when they peep in but finally they just look ridiculous in it, while Johnny and the Potters are instantly at home in it. Ned has a more complex response: At first he finds it creepy, because the ghost of his unfulfilled composer past is hovering in it; but when he sits down at his instruments and, at Linda's invitation, plays some of the Gershwin-like concerto he never completed, he comes back to himself, and we see how happy he must have been there when he was younger, before he became a slave to his father's demands.

Cary Grant is so sensational as Johnny Case (it may be his best performance) partly because he embodies the contradiction in the character: humble roots, aristocratic style. Grant was born Archie Leach, a poor Cockney, and his career began in English music halls (*Sylvia Scarlett, Gunga Din*, and *None But the Lonely Heart* are the only movies in his career that evoke those origins), but in Hollywood he recreated himself and invented "Cary Grant." Actually, his style and Hepburn's are quite eccentric—no one in the real world talks like Katharine Hepburn. But they're so specific and elevated that American audiences have always accepted them as the personification of American aristocracy. (Hollywood's other ideal of high style is, of course, Fred Astaire, whose physical grace and elegance elevate him above the rest of us.) Hepburn is equally remarkable in *Holiday*. Her greatest moment is the one where, sitting on the steps with Julia, she begs her sister to let her organize the engagement party, and admits that even she doesn't know why it's so important to her. In fact it's a kind of rebellion; more than that, a kind of self-identification, on the way to finding out who she is. When she announces, "If anyone touches my party, then I just won't come to it, that's all," the intensity of feeling is so strong that she's a little embarrassed by it. That's Hepburn's specialty.

*The Philadelphia Story*, which takes place in the world of Philadelphia high society (which has its origins in the Quakers), introduces two outsiders. Tracy Lord is about to marry for the second time. Her first husband, C. Dexter Haven, was an aristocrat like herself; she's known him all her life. The second, George Kittredge, comes from humbler roots, but like Johnny Case, he's pulled himself up by his proverbial bootstraps. But Kittredge is no Johnny Case—a point that the movie makes immediately when we see Cary Grant as Dexter and the bland M-G-M contract player John Howard as George. Case deserves to belong to the finest club he can find. George is a social climber and a snob whose vision of Tracy, as it turns out, is as a symbol of virtue rather than as a partner: "We're going to represent something, Tracy—something straight and sound and fine. You're like some marvelous, distant . . . queen." More than that, she's meant to reflect his image of *himself* as a member of the ruling class; with her on his arm, George believes, a man like Haven will no longer be so condescending to him. He's wrong, of course—Dexter sees right through him. When Dexter suggests that Tracy is marrying beneath herself, she's shocked that he should make so classist a remark, but it isn't George's class Dexter cares about—it's his character. (This is the moment when he embraces Mac the night watchman—a man of unassailable character and instincts who detests George—as a perfectly acceptable husband for Tracy.) Dexter is the Philip Barry sort of aristocrat: the world he travels in runs according to a set of values, just like the one Linda Seton chooses in *Holiday*. He's a man of liberal imagination, whereas George has no imagination at all—except, as it turns out, the sordid, backstairs kind.

Kittredge is rather a straw figure—more so than Julia Seton, though they occupy the same position in Barry's narrative schema (and though she's more horrifying). The likable outsider in *The Philadelphia Story* is Macaulay (Mike) Connor (James Stewart), the tabloid journalist who, along with his photographer girlfriend Liz Imbrie (Ruth Hussey), crashes Tracy's wedding weekend. Mike has taken this loathsome job merely for pay; he's really a fiction writer with an undersold book of stories to his credit. His point of view about the moneyed classes, which is indicated by the epigraph of one of his stories, "With the Rich and Mighty always a little Patience," is that they're inherently foolish, living according to a worldview that's hopelessly out of date. He appears to challenge the high society of the play in a way that Kittredge, who courts that society until he feels he's being rejected by it—at which point he reverts to form and insults it—could never plausibly do. And the challenge seems to complicate the issue, because the Lords' world isn't like that of the Setons: it's embodied in Dexter, and by Tracy's parents, Seth (John Halliday) and Margaret (Mary Nash), both of whom are presented sympathetically, even though a sexual indiscretion on Seth's part has temporarily unsettled their marriage. The world of *The Philadelphia Story* is liberal in attitude, and though everyone who lives in it has money, they don't *worship* money as the Setons do. So if the play is going to take Mike's objections seriously, then its portrait of the aristocracy will have to be more complex and surprising than we're used to in high comedy.

But though the movie loves Connor, it doesn't embrace his ideas about the rich—it depicts them as biases. Connor arrives prepared to despise his subjects; he refers to Tracy, whom he hasn't met, as a type—"the young, rich, rapacious American female." He winds up not only revising his opinion of her family but actually falling in love with the bride. The movie parallels Mike's development with that of Tracy herself. Though the object of three men's adoration, including her ex-husband's, she is a mass of prejudices. Instead of sharing the blame for the mess she and Dexter made of their marriage, she pinpoints his alcoholism—and Dexter himself—as the villain. She isn't impressed that he's stopped drinking, or grateful that he arranged for Connor and Imbrie to cover the wedding for *Spy Magazine* in order to keep her father's dalliance with a Broadway dancer out of it. His weakness shriveled her compassion rather than engaging it, just as her father's infidelities have turned her against him—even though her mother sees them as Seth presents them, as an understandable struggle against growing old, and she warns Tracy that they're none of her business. "You'll never be a first-class woman or a first-class human being," Dexter counsels Tracy, "till you have learned to have some small regard for human frailty." Accordingly, she has to stumble a little. On the eve of her wedding, she gets drunk—something she's done only once before in her life, and afterward she blocked it out—and she allows herself to probe her attraction to Mike long enough to sustain a late-night swim, a dance in the moonlight, and one passionate kiss. That drunk and that kiss bring her down to earth, while the priggish, intolerant reaction they draw from George demonstrates indisputably that he isn't the man for her. He acts in a way that reflects her own worst impulses, so his response helps to lead her away from them by negative example. "You're too good for me, George. You're a hundred times too good," she explains as she calls off their marriage. "And I'd make you most unhappy, most — . That is, I'd do my best to." Meanwhile, slipping a little softens her toward Dexter and toward Seth: no longer "Justice with her shining sword," as her father called her, she begins to see both these men as merely fellow human beings, capable of mistakes.

And just as Tracy has to find her own humanity by embracing weakness, growing into the "first-class woman" and "first-class human being" Dexter has been waiting for, so Mike has to grow past his prejudices. He has to learn to follow his own proverb: "With the Rich and Mighty always a little Patience." Fascinatingly, even booze is class-related in this movie. Champagne is the drink of the rich and mighty; Mike remarks, "Whiskey's a slap on the back and champagne's a heavy mist before my eyes." Mike, the working-class Irishman, is used to whiskey, but part of his education is learning to love champagne, and it's when he's drunk on it that he learns his own lesson, from Tracy: "The time to make up your mind about people is never."

So once again Barry effectively mutes his critique of the aristocracy, this time by exposing Mike's attitude toward them as snobbishness and inexperience. The spokesman for the outsiders in Barry—those born without money—might be Richard, the composer in his 1927 play *Paris Bound* who, like Macaulay Connor, falls unexpectedly in love with an aristocrat. (Edward Griffith made a film of Barry's *Paris Bound*, but I was unable to find a copy.) He tells her:

> You're the kind of people I've resented all my life. I never expected to believe that you could be so—so damned valuable. I used to curse in my beard whenever I passed a house like this. I used to spit on the pavement whenever a decent-looking motor-car passed me. I don't anymore, because I've found two among you whom I know to be of absolutely first importance in all the ways I value. You're hard in the right places, you're wise with a most beautiful wisdom and for your life as you live it, I've nothing but salutes and cheers. You're a revelation to me, Mary.

"For your life as you live it"—that seems to be the key. The open-ended, exploratory approach to life that Johnny and Linda share in *Holiday*, while Edward and Julia evidently feel threatened by it, is the ethic that both Tracy and Mike adopt by the end of *The Philadelphia Story*, and it's what finally distances Tracy from George Kittredge. Barry may not be able to surmount his own background entirely, even in *Holiday*, where he takes on the Edward Setons in whose drawing rooms he must have spent many youthful hours. But he does promote an ideal aristocracy of the mind and the heart, and its prime virtue is the ability to shake off prejudices. "I don't know.—Oh, I don't know anything anymore!" Tracy moans to Dexter as she considers the wedding she's just botched. "That sounds very hopeful," Dexter replies.

My most gifted student at the College of the Holy Cross, Jonathan Hastings, pointed out in an undergraduate thesis on modern comedy the significance of the opening images of *The Philadelphia Story*: "Seen behind the credits is a perfectly symmetrical mansion, a symbol of old monied aristocracy. The next image is the Liberty Bell, an icon both of Philadelphia and of the ideal of American democracy and individuality. The film tries to reconcile these two images."[1] The commonality Mike discovers with Tracy and the Algonquin Club banter he and Liz have perfected—every inch the equal of Tracy and Dexter's exchanges—are largely how it meets that agenda, and there's a marvelous comic sequence where Tracy and her kid sister Dinah (Virginia Weidler), forced to endure the presence of reporters but not to like it, demonstrate how unaffected they really are by impersonating the daffy, precious, ivory-tower heiresses they know Mike and Liz expect them to be. (Hepburn burlesques her own Bryn Mawr style; it's one of her most joyous and freewheeling moments. And Weidler's precociousness is the movie's best running gag.) But much as we love Connor (and much as we love Jimmy Stewart, who took home the 1940 Oscar for his performance), he and Tracy can't end up together. They might if this were a romantic comedy, since, as she discovers when she reads his stories, she turns out to be as wrong about him as he is about her. But in a high comedy their romance is an illusion—it's all moonlight and champagne. Mike falls in love with her beauty and vivacity and, I'd say, with his own surprise at having discovered that a millionairess can be magnificent. And she falls in love with his vision of her. After being told by all the other men in her life that she's an icy goddess—by Dexter and Seth because they want to shake her up, and by George, who's such a dolt he thinks he's giving her a compliment—Mike declares that she's flesh and blood, "lit from within," with "fires banked down in you." *Of course* she responds to him. But in the light of the morning, she sees that it's Liz he belongs with. Mac the night watchman be damned; all the heroes in *The Philadelphia Story* seek out their own kind in the end (though Mike and Liz get to serve as best man and maid of honor to Tracy and Dexter when Dexter replaces George at the altar).

The one element of the movie that doesn't sit well is its handling of the Seth–Margaret subplot. The problem isn't so much that Seth gets forgiven so easily for adultery as that the movie lets him get away with blaming Tracy for his succumbing to the temptation to philander. He suggests that a man who can rely on the unquestioning love and support of his grown daughter as he ages isn't as likely to seek it with a younger mistress, an argument that not only is unconvincing in itself but also compounds the battering Tracy is already getting from Dexter for denying *him* love and support in the face of his drinking problem. The movie is at its shakiest when it tries to blame Tracy for everything that's gone wrong. For all his unconventionality, Barry has an old-fashioned male view of what makes a woman an ideal mate. He admires

Liz, who hasn't pressured Mike to marry her because she wisely thinks that he has a lot to learn first and she doesn't want to get in his way while he's learning it. Though it breaks her heart, she hangs back and lets him get Tracy out of his system—and then it's *Tracy* who sends him back to her arms. Liz is a helpmate, as Linda wants to be with Johnny (her exit line in *Holiday* is "If he wants to sell peanuts, Lord how I'll believe in those peanuts!"), and as Tracy learns she was wrong not to be with Dext.

It's not, however, entirely an unreasonable expectation; *The Philadelphia Story* isn't *The Taming of the Shrew*. If the playroom is the central symbol in *Holiday*, here we get the model Dexter gives Tracy, as a gift on the occasion of her second wedding, of the *True Love*, the boat he designed and mostly built himself for *their* honeymoon. "My, she was yare," Tracy reminisces as she turns the model in her hand. "Yare" means quick and bright and flexible— "everything a boat should be," she explains to George, "until she develops dry rot." Though Tracy later confesses to Dexter that *she* wasn't yare, the image suits their first marriage better than it suits Tracy herself. At its most generous, *The Philadelphia Story* implies that both Tracy and Dext were at fault. More than once, a character comments that these two grew up together, but the fact is that he's grown up—which came along with sobering up—and she hasn't. But by the end of the picture she has, and she joins him to make right the union they *both* screwed up the first time around.

The class-bound pairing-off at the end of *The Philadelphia Story* distinguishes it from the romantic comedies of the period (and since), where class divisions only seem important and are easily overcome. In fact, the convention of thirties screwball comedies matches an heiress (Claudette Colbert in *It Happened One Night* is the prototype) with a working-class or solidly middle-class partner (Clark Gable as a reporter in the same movie), or maybe the reverse (Ray Milland, the son of a rich man, romances working girl Jean Arthur in *Easy Living*). It's interesting to note, however, that in the early-talkie romantic comedies, the ones released before *It Happened One Night*—and before the Hays Code came into effect, determining the narrative shape of screwball comedies—class distinctions are invariably honored. That's the convention that gives a movie like Harry d'Abbadie d'Arrast's *Laughter* (1930) or Frank Capra's *Platinum Blonde* (1931), both essentially romantic comedies (and both supreme among the movies of their era), a high-comic patina. In *Laughter*, Nancy Carroll, the paragon of a flapper, with her porcelain-doll face and tiny waist and bobbed blonde hair, is a former *Follies* girl who wound up with a rich husband (Frank Morgan). But her old beau (Fredric March), a composer who's been working in Paris, shows up and reminds her of what she's lost in this passionless marriage—

laughter. "You can't go on with this," March counsels her. "You're dying for lack of nourishment." In *Platinum Blonde*, a hard-nosed reporter (Robert Williams) wins the heart of an heiress (Jean Harlow) when he returns some love letters his paper got hold of rather than publishing them and embarrassing her family. But when he marries her and tries to settle down to a life of ease in her mansion, he's miserable, and they discover they have no affinity for each other's lifestyles or friends. He walks out on her and into the arms of a fellow reporter (Loretta Young). (Pauline Kael points out the amusing casting error: Harlow and Young should probably switch parts.[2] Young is awfully charming, though.) It may be more accurate to call these pictures reverse high comedies, since they stack up against the aristocrats; James Harvey connects *Platinum Blonde* to the movies from the same period "which get a lot of their laughs from noting . . . such futile attempts to cross [class lines] as Cagney having high tea or Harlow meeting 'the ritz.'"[3] Harlow's character doesn't come off very well in *Platinum Blonde*, and the way *Laughter* is conceived, Morgan has the bum role—we have to see just why Carroll leaves him for March. But *Laughter* (which was cowritten by Donald Ogden Stewart) has a strangely ambivalent ending. Back in Paris with March, to whom she's now married, Carroll sits at a café listening to him describe the latest changes in his symphony. She notices a lady with an expensive bracelet at the next table with a rich older husband, and Paul notices her noticing. "I didn't say anything," she insists, and they laugh. It's a wonderful finish, but the tone is mixed: We know that Carroll has made the right choice—laughter and love over wealth—but she's too honest and down to earth not to admit that some part of her misses the wealth.

If most romantic comedies from 1934 through the end of the decade present class boundaries only to mock them, a few find other ways of leveling the playing field between a hero and heroine who seem to come from different worlds. In *Thirty Day Princess* (1935), for example, a Manhattan newspaper publisher (Cary Grant) falls in love with a woman he believes to be the visiting princess from a tiny European country—the dilemma Gregory Peck finds himself in with Audrey Hepburn in William Wyler's *Roman Holiday* (1950), one of the few great romantic comedies of the fifties. But in fact the woman he takes for the princess is an out-of-work actress impersonating the *real* princess, who's come down with the mumps. (That marvelous proletarian icon of the Depression era, Sylvia Sidney, plays both roles; it's perhaps the only movie that allows her to flirt with an aristocratic role, and she looks like she's having the time of her life.) The dénouement reverses the pattern of those eighteenth- and nineteenth-century plays where the maid turns out to be her own mistress. There's a kicker, though—Grant is a Yankee aristocrat, one Porter Madison III, but the script (which Preston Sturges had a hand in) dismisses the *new* inequality between the lovers when Sidney reminds Grant, "I fell for you just as you were. You didn't need a title." In *My Man Godfrey* (1936), the distance between Carole Lombard's pixilated heiress and William Powell's "forgotten man"—the homeless gent she picks up at a riverside Hooverville because she requires one to win a scavenger hunt, and then hires on as her family's butler—is a sham. Godfrey is really a Back Bay blue blood who went down to the river to drown himself after a love affair went sour and liked the folks he met there so much he decided to stay. (The forgotten men are a witty and articulate group temporarily downed by the Depression; one of them is an ex-banker who gave up everything he had in the crash so his depositors wouldn't suffer. This vision of urban life in the Depression is about as convincing as the depiction of the Central Park community in the 1933 operetta *Hallelujah, I'm a Bum!* but without the justification of the earlier movie's wish-fulfillment-fantasy stylization.) The joke in *My Man Godfrey* is the same as in *Tovarich*: a true aristocrat makes the best butler. Of course, no one could buy William Powell as a hobo anyway: As naturally aristocratic as Cary Grant, he makes even rumpled besottedness elegant. When he returns drunk from an afternoon off, he moves like a dancing marionette as he whips up a tray of cocktails for his employers.

Among the American playwrights of the twenties and thirties we associate with high comedy, Philip Barry was the only one who fared well in the movies. Donald Ogden Stewart's *Rebound* was filmed early on, as a vehicle for the ineffable Ina Claire, but it was no better than the Barry movies Edward Griffith directed, and it isn't a very good play to start with. The most interesting thing about it, besides Claire, and Robert Williams in a supporting role, is that its plot about a man and a woman who marry on the rebound from the people they really love is so much in the Barry mode that you can see why Stewart ended up adapting Barry's plays for the screen.

S. N. Behrman wrote such famous comedies of manners as *Biography* and *End of Summer*—two of Claire's biggest theatrical successes. But the only one of his plays to be made into a film was *No Time for Comedy*, in 1940. The results are rather fascinating. The play is about the marriage of a playwright with the unfortunate name of Gaylord Esterbook (Laurence Olivier in the original production) and a celebrated actress, Linda Paige (Katharine Cornell), for whom he has written a series of hit comedies. But a self-appointed muse gets hold of him and persuades him that what he ought to be setting his pen to is Art, so he writes a scathing (and highly symbolic) examination of social issues. The results are predictably disastrous, and in the meantime he nearly leaves his wife for the muse. But failure humbles him, and he and his wife make it up at final curtain. Rewriting the script for Jimmy Stewart and Rosalind Russell, Julius and Philip Epstein boil it down to about an hour and frontload a forty-five-minute section covering Gay's and Linda's courtship, which coincides with the production of his debut play. The gag is that the play is a high comedy set on Park Avenue (it has a dreadful title, *Dilemma at Dinner*) but when the playwright, whom no one has actually seen, shows up for a rehearsal, he's a hick from the Midwest; Linda, not realizing who he is, sends him out for smokes. The retooled role suits Jimmy Stewart down to the ground, and he and Russell are (unexpectedly) delightful together in this first half—which is, of course, a romantic comedy and not a high one. It's when *No Time for Comedy* slides into its high-comic second act, which is the *first* act of the Behrman original, that it falls apart. When he's having trouble with a script, Gay tends to imbibe and become nasty and sarcastic. On stage Olivier probably read his stingers with wilting understatement, but we can't accept the unpretentious Stewart of the first half of the movie as the sudden sophisticate of the second half—and we want to pull against his equally sudden unlikability. I'm not sure if the play Behrman actually wrote would ever work on screen; it may be telling that the only part of the movie that *does* work was written by other people.

It's worth mentioning *Idiot's Delight* (1939), as well—another oddball. Robert E. Sherwood wrote both the stage play and the screenplay for this quintessentially thirties comment on war, set at an Alpine resort on the brink of World War II. The main characters are Harry Van, an American vaudevillian traveling through Europe with his band of dancers, and an arms merchant's mistress, Irene, who claims to be a Russian royal but is really a one-time show-biz mind reader who's reinvented herself. Sherwood fashioned the play for the Lunts; their scenes read like high comedy, and if you've seen *The Guardsman* it's easy to imagine that they would have played them that way. But the movie stars Clark Gable and Norma Shearer, and what goes on between these two performers is a lot closer to melodrama, though Shearer tries painfully hard to convey the tension between her character's made-up style and the woman beneath it (an old flame of Gable's). She's agonizing to watch; Gable's rather good—especially when he does a seedy tap routine to "Puttin' on the Ritz"—but he isn't a high-comic performer. The whole project, which Clarence Brown directed, is something of a shambles. The play was written three years earlier and it comes out of the isolationist social-protest theater of that era, but by the time Hollywood got around to making the movie, the fictional war of Sherwood's play was about to become a real one, so the satirical target shifted somewhat from war makers (personified by Irene's boyfriend, Achille Weber), to the Nazis (though the invading country isn't specifically identified). The movie has some of Sherwood's most fearful speechifying, and poor Burgess Meredith, as an Italian pacifist who's eventually executed, gets stuck with most of it.

George Cukor's name is on most of the outstanding stage-to-screen adaptations of the thirties, including *Camille*. Two are versions of plays that novelist Edna Ferber (best known for *Show Boat*) and the prolific George S. Kaufman coauthored—*The Royal Family of Broadway* (known merely as *The Royal Family* on stage) and *Dinner at Eight*. The Kaufman–Ferber plays are ingenious blends of high comedy and melodrama in which the conventions of the two are magically in sync. *The Royal Family* is also a theatrical parody, one of the first in movies. (The very first is probably King Vidor's 1928 *Show People*, a silent comedy about silent-comedy actors.) There have been many such parodies, often delightful and ranging across a variety of other genres. The unforgettable *Twentieth Century* (1934), with John Barrymore and Carole Lombard as show-biz narcissists, was one of the brand-new, post–Hays Code screwball comedies. *It's Love I'm After* (1937), with Bette Davis and Leslie Howard as husband-and-wife thespians—like the Lunts in *The Guardsman*— is also a romantic comedy, and it bears some resemblance to the musical *Kiss Me, Kate*. *Once in a Lifetime* (1932), based on Kaufman's first collaboration with Moss Hart and focused on the transition from silent movies to talkies, is a hard-boiled comedy, and some of its ideas later reappear in the musical *Singin' in the Rain* (1952). *Gold Diggers of 1933* (1933) is equal parts hard-boiled comedy, romantic comedy, and musical comedy. *Stage Door*, also out of a Kaufman–Ferber play, is a hard-boiled comedy cross-bred with a melodrama; Katharine Hepburn is one of the stars, but you can tell it isn't a comedy of manners because Ginger Rogers, as her wisecracking roommate at the theatrical boarding-house known as the Footlight Club, comes out on top in their insult matches. Later on there are, among others, *Hearts of the West* (1975), *Tootsie* (1982), *My Favorite Year* (1982), *Soapdish* (1991), *Bullets Over Broadway* (1994).

The subject of *The Royal Family* is a Barrymore-like family referred to as the Cavendishes. The veteran stage actress Henrietta Crosman is the irrepressible matriarch, Fanny, who uses her walking cane like a prop; Ina Claire is Julie (read Ethel); Fredric March, giving perhaps the funniest impersonation on record of John Barrymore—the fast-talking style, the raised eyebrow, the boyish athleticism—is Tony; and the wan Mary Brian is Julie's daughter Gwen, whose career is just starting. They are theatrical royalty, and just like other kinds of monarchs their lives are defined by a set of inviolable rules. Their private lives take a limp second place to their careers; they spend a part of each day reading telegrams and fan letters and dealing with photo requests; they always travel in style (they recognize only two choices—you travel like a Cavendish or you travel like a stowaway); and they never retire—at least until death forces their hand. Gwen may complain, "I'm sick of being a Cavendish. I want to be a human being," a sentiment her mother echoes later, but her fate is determined, just as Audrey Hepburn's is in *Roman Holiday*. Both Julie and Gwen marry in the course of the movie and try to live private lives, but it doesn't take, because no one can possibly understand them except for each other and the devoted hangers-on they've kept for years, like their manager, Oscar Wolfe (Arnold Korff). Fanny is a comic version of Irina Arkadina, the self-absorbed actress in Chekhov's *The Sea Gull* (one of Fanny's speeches seems to be a nod to Chekhov), who's driven to boredom at the thought of living any sort of life besides that of a traveling thespian. Tony is an inveterate noisemaker, turning every room he enters into a traffic wreck, forever on the run from directors he's walked out on and women he's jilted. His mother adores him (and still treats him like a big baby), though she disdains his Hollywood career, which she protests isn't worthy of a Cavendish. The Cavendishes are always making grand entrances and playing scenes. Claire is brilliant at portraying the sort of actress for whom theatricality and reality eternally overlap. You see it especially in the scenes around her love affair with an old suitor, Gil Marshall (Frank Conroy), who comes back into her life for a time. She plays a lovely farewell scene with him after their first reunion, and the next time we see her, she's holding one of his roses, lingering poignantly at the top of the stairs. "Very good entrance," Fanny says approvingly, and you understand why audiences go wild for Julie: the moment is shaped exquisitely, but the undercurrent of feeling is genuine. Later, when Gil walks in amidst the usual Cavendish chaos, she does a wonderful crumpled pause, sinking at the thought that he's caught her in this madhouse while she plays up her delight and relief at seeing her sane, reliable old swain. Gil tells her that he left her before so she could have the career she wanted, but now he sees she isn't happy with it after all. We know he's wrong, though: Her vaunted sadness at the life she's sacrificed is part of the melodrama she's always engaged in, and it completes her in a way he never could (and in a fact fails to do once she marries him).

The melodrama in the Kaufman–Ferber script arrives on cue in the final scene: Fanny, who's returned to the stage expressly against her doctor's orders, dies in her dressing room in the middle of a performance. When she falls ill, Oscar wants to ring down the curtain, but she insists that a Cavendish always finishes the show, so Julie promises to go on for her. (Of course she knows the role, one of the wives in Shakespeare's *The Merry Wives of Windsor*, by heart.) Fanny dies with her family around her, and Julie just has time to put the finishing touches on her makeup, shed a few hasty tears, and make her entrance. In *Dinner at Eight*, a more accomplished piece of work, the melodrama and high comedy are interlaced throughout. The opening line, delivered by Billie Burke's Millicent Jordan to her husband, Oliver (Lionel Barrymore), is "Darling! I've got Lord and Lady Ferncliffe!" and, in combination with the credits—photographs of the starry cast in the centers of elegant dinner plates—it sets the high-comic tone. The only priority for Millicent is that her dinner party for the most coveted couple in New York, a pair of émigré Brits, be perfect in every detail. Her increasing desperation as she encounters one fiasco after another fulfills the convention about treating trivial matters with absolute seriousness while it functions as a link to the melodrama, because while she's tearing her heart out over her dinner, everyone around her is in a state of *real* crisis. Oliver's shipping company is about to go bust, and he's suffering from a heart condition that his doctor, Wayne Talbot (Edmund Lowe), knows is about to finish him off. Talbot, married to a patient but defeated woman (Karen Morley), is cheating on her for the umpteenth time—in this case with Kitty Packard (Jean Harlow). Kitty's the vulgar, socially covetous wife of an ex-miner, Dan Packard (Wallace Beery), who's made his fortune clandestinely buying up businesses like Jordan's by offering stockholders—like Oliver's old friend, the actress Carlotta Vance (Marie Dressler)—more cash for their shares than they can refuse. And the Jordans' daughter, Paula (Madge Evans), who's about to be married, is carrying on a secret affair with Larry Renault (John Barrymore), nearly thirty years her senior. Renault is an alcoholic actor on his uppers with too much pride to accept the only work his manager (Lee Tracy) can land him, a one-scene part in a new play. Most of these characters are on Millicent's guest list—it's funny, in a *Six Degrees of Separation* way, that when Talbot gets back from screwing Kitty Packard, Jordan, whom Kitty's husband is screwing *over*, is in his waiting room—so their private troubles are brewing beneath the perfect high-society veneer set by Millicent's party.

Whenever we hear Burke's fluttery buttermilk voice, with its absurd candied affectations, it brings us back to the high comedy. It's not the only comedy in the movie; the rollicking Packard squabbles are hilarious, but deliciously lowdown. Ferber and Kaufman—and the amazing team of screenwriters (Frances Marion, Herman J. Mankiewicz, and the ubiquitous Donald Ogden Stewart)—are very clever with the Packards, who supply all the bitchy, downright humor the play needs. And the couple's separate varieties of social climbing—she wants to get into New York society, he wants to get into government—send up high society while satisfying our Yankee-democratic suspicion of the upper classes.

Every high comedy should get a cast like this one. Beery and Harlow are riotous together, and she's never been more sheerly enjoyable than she is here, lathering that ridiculous phony-high-class vocal style (which audiences were supposed to take *seriously* in *The Public Enemy* [1931] and *Platinum Blonde*) on top of her down-and-dirty, slut-who's-landed-in-a-pot-of-cream persona, lounging on her bed (she's playing sick so Talbot will make a house call), munching on chocolate creams, checking her beauty mark and her marcelled platinum hair and bee-stung lips in a hand mirror, trying on a new hat with just a spray of veil. When she sashays into the Jordans' apartment in a skin-tight lamé gown with absurd crossed straps and a white fur stole, you know civilization has gone joyously to the dogs. Dressler makes her first entrance in a full-length mink and a side-worn hat with a feather, jewels at her neck and dripping from her ears. She has a marvelous warhorse style, and she moves her face around as if it were made of plasticene, while she uses her eyes for a silent-movie-star über-expressiveness. Her Carlotta is the image of every grande dame of the theater; what makes her so likable is that her airs—her allusions to Noël and Winston and Wales coming over for luncheon in London—alternate with a down-to-the-ground all-American frankness about who she is and how far she's come in the world. Carlotta is self-centered and greedy, but she can't help herself, and she has enough self-awareness to realize after she's sold her Jordan stock that maybe she's done something she shouldn't, and to come ask for Oliver's forgiveness. (He forgives her, of course; he's devoted to her.) My favorite Dressler flourish is the one where she hears the name of Paula's fiancé, wonders if she might have known his father, and, checking among the jewels she's wearing, settles on a brooch that confirms it. Best of all is John Barrymore, who's more or less playing himself—but with a devastating precision. He has a bitter quality here that you don't see in his other movie performances, a potent, almost crude side, and he may never have had to play an uglier scene than the one in which Mack, his manager, humiliates him after he's forfeited the last job he's ever going to be offered. (Count Lee Tracy among the movie's pleasures.) It's an archetypal scene that shows up again in both the 1937 and 1954 versions of *A Star Is Born*. Here Barrymore is one of the classic movie drunks, gliding around the hotel room he's about to be thrown out of, tossing his few remaining coins, bouncing on the balls of his feet but at a tipped angle, as if it were an athletic feat to keep himself upright. You know just where the performance is going—he turns on the gas. But first he arranges the lamp over the easy chair and places himself, in his dressing gown and ascot, his hair perfect, under it, so the tabloid photographers will capture him at his best.

It's Carlotta who has to tell Paula about Larry's suicide. (Carlotta, of course, has figured out they've been sleeping together.) Then she helps the younger woman compose herself—they mustn't ruin Millicent's dinner, she reminds her, and she must make sure that her fiancé doesn't see how upset she is; he must never know she cheated on him. And in this presentation of an impeccable façade, high comedy and melodrama are once again intertwined.

Cukor also directed *The Women* (1939), adapted by Anita Loos and Jane Murfin from the Clare Boothe Luce stage play. It isn't in the same class as *Dinner at Eight*, but much of it is fun, in a sort of proto–*Sex and the City* style—high comedy meets low comedy. The characters, or most of them, belong to high society (as in *Dinner at Eight*, everyone's connected to everyone else), but their only activities seem to be stealing each other's men and dishing the dirt about each other. There are a few outsiders. One is Crystal (Joan Crawford), the shop girl who sleeps with the husband of the protagonist, Mary (Norma Shearer). The other is Miriam (Paulette Goddard), whom Mary meets in Reno and who winds up with the husband of the cattiest in the group, Mary's cousin Sylvia (Rosalind Russell). The first is a bitch, the second a decent sort, and everyone gets a share of the wealth in the end, either by coming from it or marrying into it. The gimmick of the play and the movie, and it's a clever one, is that we never see the men around whom the women's lives revolve. Those who find *The Women*'s portrayal of the female sex unappetizing (and it is) can take solace in the fact that the men, absent as they are, come off much worse—as needy little boys who get bored easily and have trouble seeing past their erections.

*The Man Who Came to Dinner* didn't come out until 1943, but it also belongs in this group. Kaufman and Hart wrote the play in 1939; it was their last hit, a send-up of their Algonquin Club friend, the critic and radio personality Alexander Woollcott, here called Sheridan Whiteside. Monty Woolley plays Whiteside, as he did on stage, reading his one-liners with high-comic skill though without much invention. (Nathan Lane, who played the part in a Roundabout Theatre revival in New York in 2000, wasn't really right for it, but he was funnier than Woolley.) The movie, adapted by the Epsteins and directed by William Keighley (who also helmed *No Time for Comedy*), feels a little overbaked, but it basically preserves all the aspects of the play, which is a compendium of both the good and the not-so-good aspects of Kaufman and Hart. There are a lot of terrific jokes, the structure is ironclad, the act finales (you can see exactly where they are) are small marvels of orchestrated lunacy, just as they are in *Once in a Lifetime* and *You Can't Take It With You*. But you have to put up with the sentimentality—which isn't entirely justified by Woollcott's real-life sappiness (Kaufman and Hart *could* have burlesqued that rather than taking their cue from it)—and the four-square mid-American stuff, both of which began to enter Kaufman and Hart's plays after the success of *Once in a Lifetime*. It's a good comic idea to plunk the hopelessly cosmopolitan Whiteside down in Mesalia, Ohio, where he's stuck after he breaks his leg on the front stoop of an adoring women's-club hostess (Billie Burke—who else?); the tension between his circle—and the whirlwind of his life—and the besieged midwesterners he imposes it on during his enforced stay spices up the high comedy. But then his indispensable secretary (Bette Davis) falls for the local newspaper editor, who is a genius playwright too, and we're meant to sympathize with *her* when Whiteside pulls out all the stops to prevent her from leaving his employ. Davis gives this drab role much more feeling than it deserves, but you can't help thinking how much more pleasurable it would be to watch her play the venomous Gertrude Lawrence-ish stage-star role. (Ann Sheridan is miscast in it.) Still, the movie contains a lot of snappy dialogue, and it has Reginald Gardiner and Jimmy Durante in characters based on Noël Coward and Harpo Marx, respectively. And Mary Wickes, as the private nurse Whiteside torments, plays her single note—flat-footed terror—in perfect pitch.

The thirties also offered two high comedies that were as distinctly American as *Holiday* or *Dinner at Eight* but didn't begin as stage plays. Since one is also a murder mystery and the other a ghost comedy, they might escape notice, but they're both signal films of their era. The first is *The Thin Man*, which came out in 1934, the same year as *It Happened One Night* and *Twentieth Century*. Adapted by Albert Hackett and Frances Goodrich from the Dashiell Hammett novel, it was so successful that it spawned a breezy series. Some of the later entries had the same writers and the same director, W. S. Van Dyke, and they all featured William Powell and Myrna Loy as Nick and Nora Charles, the laid-back ex-Pinkerton gumshoe and his high-society wife Hammett based on himself and his lover, playwright Lillian Hellman. (And they all featured the irresistible wire-haired terrier Asta.) But only the original *Thin Man*, with its sophisticated, tossed-off banter and its famous climax—Nick and Nora throw a dinner party and invite all the suspects— is bona fide high comedy. Powell and Loy were an inspired match (they made many other films together), and in this movie their easy rapport makes the marital state look pretty damn good. This is one of those movies that could never be made today: you couldn't show a couple drinking so many martinis without having to editorialize about their alcoholism. It's a blessing that the movie doesn't have to. In their first scene together, Nora discovers Nick at a club, six martinis to the good; he's boiled, and swaying gently as he shakes up another to the rhythm of the band. She orders a half-dozen herself to catch up. Waking up with a hangover, she ties an ice-filled water bottle on like a bonnet, as if it were the latest fashion. Later she sports a full-length fur, and when Nick asks her if she isn't hot inside it, she answers yes, she's stifling, "but it's so pretty." The duplicitous, self-adoring Mimi Jorgenson (Minna Gombell), whose ex-husband's disappearance leads off the mystery, is a faux aristocrat, all affectations; Nick and Nora are the real thing. (The real-life Hammett and Hellman were a different brand of aristocrat—Algonquin Club wits.) Powell's little brush of a mustache completes his aloof, philosophical roué's face, and he can read a line like "I'm very interested in that body" (to the coroner) as if he were expressing a desire for a rare brandy or an expensive Cuban cigar. And Loy finesses lines like—at the dinner party, where the cops guard the suspects—"Waiter, would you serve the nuts? I mean, would you serve the nuts to the guests?"

The other signal American high comedy of the era is *Topper* (1937), also based on a novel (by Thorne Smith). Cary Grant and Constance Bennett play George and Marion Kerby, who crash their car and end up as ghosts, and Roland Young is Cosmo Topper, the banker they haunt until he gives in to his natural inclination to loosen up and his corseted wife (Billie Burke) stops taking him for granted. (This movie, too, initiated a series, but a brief one—two sequels.) *Topper* is a lark without a single serious moment, but like the Philip Barry comedies it juxtaposes two kinds of aristocrats—the fussy, conventional sort and the fun-loving, generous-spirited, free-wheeling sort. *Topper* is premised on a splendid joke: that the only difference between the Kerbys alive and dead is that, as ghosts, they can pull a disappearing act whenever they like. Otherwise they're exactly the same, done up in the same evening clothes, imbibing the same highballs, and just as troublesome and appealing as they were in life. They're joyous, benign poltergeists. Grant and Bennett have a classic scene early on—while the Kerbys are still breathing—with Hoagy Carmichael, as a club pianist. All the other patrons have gone home, and the maître d' looks worried about the time, but when Carmichael performs "Old Man Moon" and the Kerbys join in on the chorus, the dry, hoosier vernacular of the lyric—Carmichael's trademark—strikes the perfect after-hours mood.

Constance Bennett has mostly been forgotten now (Turner Classic Movies is almost single-handedly preserving her memory), but God, she's good. The way she dances across a line may make you think of Ann Sothern, but her voice is both darker and more silvery, and the line swings back unexpectedly like a yo-yo. She holds her arms stiff but droops from the waist, so she always seems gracefully sloshed. I think there are musical numbers—and especially in thirties movies—that embody high comedy in the same way the

*The perfect after-hours mood: Cary Grant and Constance Bennett sing "Old Man Moon" with Hoagy Carmichael in Norman Z. McLeod's* Topper *(1937). Credit: MGM/The Kobal Collection*

song "All in Fun," quoted in the introduction, does, or the Rodgers and Hart song "It Never Entered My Mind," or just about anything by Cole Porter: the emotion is concealed just behind the cocktail-party style. Bennett has one in the 1934 movie *Moulin Rouge*, and though she isn't really a singer, it's a classic—"The Boulevard of Broken Dreams" by Al Dubin and Harry Warren. "The joy that you find here you borrow," she sings, tossing off her perfectly achieved melancholy in a simple gesture with black-gloved hands as she sits down at a café table. (*What Price Hollywood?* from 1932, provides an earlier glimpse of what Bennett can do with a number—"Parlez-moi d'amour.")

The best example of high comedy set to music, perhaps, is sung by Bob Hope in his first feature, *The Big Broadcast of 1938* (1938), with Shirley Ross.

(Ross would introduce "It Never Entered My Mind" in the stage show *Higher and Higher* two years later; her smoky rendition of this much-covered ballad is still my personal favorite.) This is a delirious merry-go-round of a movie, but it settles down long enough for Hope and Ross to sit at the bar of a ship and indulge in a musical reminiscence of the topsy-turvy marriage that fell apart when he cheated on her. "Thanks for the Memory," with its bittersweet Ralph Rainger melody and its Noël Coward–ish Leo Robin lyric, is a brittle, weren't-we-fools duet tinged with erotic longing and authentic regret. When Ross sings, in her champagne-and-tears contralto, about "letters with sweet little secrets / That couldn't be put in a day wire," Hope counters, "Too bad it all had to go haywire," just brushing the emotion. He does the same again when, in answer to her "We said goodbye with a highball," he confesses, "Then I got as high as a steeple." Hope has to stretch a little to reach the notes, but it doesn't disturb his composure except for maybe a slight elevation of the muscles in his forehead. By the end of the song—

Strictly *entre nous*,
Darling, how are you?
And how are all those little dreams
That never did come true?
Awfully glad I met you.
Cheerio and toodle-oo

—she can't keep up the easy-come-easy-go performance and she breaks down, unable to finish the last phrase ("Thank you so much"), and he has to console her: "Darling, I know. I know, dear." It may be the only time in his long movie career Bob Hope ever made an audience cry.

## Notes

1. Jonathan Hastings, *Towards a Sense of Modern Comedy in Film and Dramatic Literature* (undergraduate thesis, College of the Holy Cross, 1998), 49.
2. Kael, *5001 Nights*, 586.
3. Harvey, *Romantic Comedy*, 118.

CHAPTER THREE

~

# High Comedy and Social Satire

Though comedy of manners usually embraces the status quo—as we see in the Philip Barry movies—it has sometimes been a convenient medium for social commentary and satire. That's certainly how Molière employed it: He burlesqued his own social circle, just as Paul Mazursky does in movies like *Bob and Carol and Ted and Alice*, *Alex in Wonderland*, and *Blume in Love*. The movies I'm going to examine in this chapter are sharply different in tone from Mazursky's, however; you wouldn't be tempted to think of any of them as comedies. What intrigues me about them—and, I think, argues for their inclusion in this volume—is that the filmmakers are working with some of the conventions of high comedy. And indeed, the tone of a high comedy can be quite serious—think of films like *The Rules of the Game* (1939) and *Jules and Jim*, plays like Chekhov's *The Cherry Orchard* and Schnitzler's *La Ronde*.

The other element the movies in this chapter have in common is their literary heritage. *Dodsworth* (1936) is based on Sinclair Lewis's novel; *Alice Adams* (1935) and *The Magnificent Ambersons* (1942) derive from novels by Booth Tarkington; the two films of *The Letter* (1929 and 1940) are out of a Somerset Maugham story; and *The Heiress* (1949) is a version of Henry James's novella *Washington Square*. (*Dodsworth*, *The Letter*, and *The Heiress* all came to the screen via successful theatrical adaptations.) These fiction writers share a fascination with the way class operates in the societies they observe—Americans at home and abroad, in small and large cities, and in Maugham's case the colonial English. The other writer who's inspired films that focus on class is Theodore Dreiser, but the point of view of the Dreiser pictures (*An American Tragedy* [1931], *A Place in the Sun* [1951]—a midcentury update of *An American Tragedy*—and *Carrie* [1952], William Wyler's movie of *Sister Carrie*) suggests a different sort of genre. The protagonists of these movies start poor and maneuver their way into the aristocracy—successfully in the case of Carrie, who becomes a stage star, but unsuccessfully in the case of Clyde Griffiths/George Eastman, who trades on his relationship with his rich cousins, has a romance with one of their circle, but is doomed by a liaison with a factory girl. *The Magnificent Ambersons, The Letter,* and *The Heiress* are the stories of aristocrats, just as *The Philadelphia Story* is. And though *Dodsworth* satirizes the operations of Americans in Europe, whose manners are in tension with those of the old-world societies they sometimes crave access to, its main characters, Sam and Fran Dodsworth, represent a kind of Yankee royalty. He's a midwestern automobile magnate who, as the movie begins, is handing over his empire so that he can enjoy an early retirement. The borderline case is *Alice Adams*, whose heroine is—like the protagonists in the Dreiser films—on the outs of a high society she is desperate to infiltrate. I've chosen to discuss it here not only because, like *Ambersons,* it reflects Tarkington's acute perceptions of the way class prevails even in the American provinces, but also because, unlike *Carrie* or *A Place in the Sun,* it's a social comedy (albeit a painful and unsettling one) rather than a tragedy. I realize it's a stretch—in ways that even tragedies like *The Letter* and semitragedies like *The Heiress* and *Ambersons* are not. But in my mind it's a close enough call.

Sinclair Lewis has fallen out of favor; three decades ago, students of twentieth-century American literature read *Babbitt* along with *The Great Gatsby, The Sun Also Rises,* and *The Sound and the Fury* as a kind of collective primer, but no longer. (It's to be hoped that the publication of two volumes of Lewis's twenties novels by the Library of America will help to rescue his reputation.) The likely reason for his unfashionability is that the vernacular he replicates with such humor and precision—the language of boosterism, of the endlessly peppy go-getters of the automobile age—now sounds as foreign to our ears as, say, the nursery moralities of an Edwardian children's story. That's a pity, because the early Lewis novels—*Main Street, Babbitt, Arrowsmith, Elmer Gantry,* and *Dodsworth*—present a commentary on social life in the first quarter of the American century that, in its wit and incisiveness, recalls the work of Thackeray, Sheridan, and Twain. Lewis's territory, as distinctive as Faulkner's Yoknapatawpha County, is the prairie state of Winnemac, whose major metropolis is Zenith. Zenith is where Martin Arrowsmith sets up his initial medical practice, where the charismatic preacher Elmer Gantry presides over his first big congregation, and where

Sam Dodsworth makes his millions in the auto industry—the city he and his wife, Fran, their children grown, leave behind for Europe, setting out to create an adventurous new life for themselves. The other Lewis movies from the thirties (*Arrowsmith* [1931] and *Babbitt* [1934], neither of which is much good) don't qualify as high comedies. (Neither does Michael Ritchie's winning 1975 *Smile*, which sets some of the narrative elements of *Babbitt* in the context of a California teen beauty contest.) *Arrowsmith* is a variation on a heroic romance: Martin transcends the small-mindedness and banality of middle-class American society—as well as his own mixed feelings—to become an authentic scientist. *Babbitt* is a social satire in which the title character fails to transcend those obstacles. *Dodsworth* moves outside America to place the Dodsworths in relationship to another lifestyle and social system. As a piece of social commentary on the subject of Yankee Europhilia, the novel is comparable to Twain's *The Innocents Abroad* and James's *The American*, but its focus is, unexpectedly, the disintegration of a marriage. Lewis sets a domestic tragedy inside a comedy of manners—a glittering achievement. And William Wyler's film, adapted by Sidney Howard from his own stage play and starring Walter Huston (recreating his celebrated Broadway performance) and Ruth Chatterton, does the novel justice.

It's Fran's notion to take an extended European jaunt. She feels suffocated by Zenith society, and superior to it by breeding, experience, and instinct (though in fact her father brewed beer, and her only connection to Europe is one adolescent summer she spent there). And she's terrified of growing old. She has a married daughter, yet she insists that abroad a woman of her age—she's in her forties, though she presents herself as nearly a decade younger—is just "beginning to be taken seriously." So she courts the best society she can find, looking down on other traveling Americans who are interested in the usual tourist attractions, absorbing the customs of each new country, persuading herself that she behaves as if she'd been born to them, and constantly correcting Sam. She treats him with an unpredictable alternation of fondness, irritation, and condescension—though she relies on him to pull her out of the romantic messes she keeps getting herself into. She takes on a series of swains whose attentions flatter her delusion that she's managed to stave off middle age. The first is a British captain (David Niven) she flirts with on the transatlantic crossing: When his attentions turn physical, she pulls away in offended confusion, provoking him to snap back that clearly she isn't the woman of the world she wants to pass as. The second is a banker, Arnold Iselin (Paul Lukas). He gets farther than Captain Lockert: Once she's convinced Sam to go home to Zenith for a visit and leave her on her own, in Montreux and Biarritz, she takes Arnold as her lover. Sam breaks up this affair simply by exposing it, embarrassing both his wife and Arnold. Finally she falls for an impoverished Viennese count (Gregory Gaye) who says he wants to marry her, and his stature is too much of a temptation for her to resist. (So is his youth.) But Fran isn't a true aristocrat, however she likes to present herself, and the barrier between her class and Kurt von Obersdorf's is too great for her to cross. His mother (Maria Ouspenskaya) refuses to issue her blessing on the union—both on religious grounds (the family is Catholic, and Fran will be a divorcée) and because she expects Kurt to produce an heir, which, she points out candidly, would be unlikely given Fran's age. Though the countess is also frank enough to acknowledge the appeal of Fran's fortune, this is one aristocracy Fran can't buy her way into.

From the outset, Sam tries to warn his wife that the society she's courting isn't as grand as she'd like to believe. He finds their manners insufficient to conceal their greed, and he's too self-aware to think that genuine European aristocrats would have much of an interest in "hicks" like them. And Fran's misadventures keep proving him right, though she never learns to trust his judgment or to see herself with his clarity of vision. Even after the disaster with Kurt and his mother, when she calls on Sam to rescue her once more, she continues to treat him high-handedly, and it's that refusal to learn from her mistakes that finally costs her a twenty-year marriage. However, Wyler treats Fran more gently than Lewis does. Whereas the novel describes the "glistening shell of sexlessness"[1] that has always imposed a certain distance between her and Sam, the movie hints at a marital warmth that cools only once she insists on comparing him unfavorably to the more exotic men she meets on the trip. She's more loving to Sam in the early scenes than a reading of Howard's play would imply (though Howard's screenplay retains most of his original dialogue). It isn't until she begins to put him down in front of the Europeans she wants to impress that we begin to dislike her—especially when she murmurs to Iselin, while Sam is across the room, that she's "poor so many ways." And even when she's at her worst, Wyler and Ruth Chatterton (in the performance of her career) make her follies touching—her paralyzed response when, having effected a break between her and Arnold, Sam brings her the news that their daughter Emily is pregnant and they're going to become "a couple of old grandparents"—and finally tragic. Of course, there's no doubt that the movie sets up Sam's emotional and intellectual excitement at making this European journey in contrast to Fran's snobby, superficial preference for the best society and the venues in which she's likely to find it. When Sam sees the "Bishop's light" from shore as the ship approaches England, his boyish delight embarrasses Fran (in front of Lockert), and when he insists she join him on deck to view it, she whines about the cold and her mussed hair. But Edith Cortright (Mary Astor), an American divorcée on the same crossing returning to her home in Italy, is swayed by Sam's unapologetic display of emotion. Eventually—after Fran leaves him for Kurt—he turns to Edith for the support and camaraderie that Fran has denied him.

Sam loses his foolish wife in Europe, but until then—and again once Edith steps into his life—he thrives in his new environment in ways he would never have thought possible. Europe becomes the great education of his middle age, and the path to self-discovery. Dodsworth is Sinclair Lewis's idea of the kind of aristocrat America really can produce. "He was common sense apotheosized," Lewis writes. "He had the energy and reliability of a dynamo, he liked whiskey and poker and pâté de foie gras, and all the while he dreamed of motors like thunderbolts, as poets less modern than himself might dream of stars and roses and nymphs by a pool."[2] Philip Barry would class Sam and Edith as the right kind of aristocrats, and their shared values—tolerance, flexibility, broad-mindedness, an interest in intellectual growth—inevitably bring them together. Wyler sees them as natural beings, an idea he points up by framing them repeatedly gainst the open air, while Fran is only comfortable in sedate, composed settings, with the elements at a safe remove, behind windows or balcony railings—the ocean when they're aboard ship, the lake when she entertains Arnold Iselin in Montreux. This is never clearer than in the juxtaposition of the collapse of her romance with Kurt, in a chalet with the snow falling picturesquely outside the window, and Sam's idyll with Edith at her seaside villa outside Naples, where they fish and swim. (The cinematography is by the great Rudolph Maté.)

Sam adores Fran so much that he almost throws away his chance at a new life with Edith; he's at her beck and call when she phones him, miserable and humiliated, after the debacle with Kurt. For Sam, his marriage is the great love of his life. "Did I remember to tell you today that I adore you?" is his trademark tribute to her; the last time we hear him say it, she's just put him on a train after asking him for a divorce so she can marry her Austrian count. And though she's given him up for the life she thinks she wants, Wyler and Chatterton are canny enough to hint—in the way her mood matches his as they make their way through across the platform, and in the look of startled regret on her face as his train pulls away—that she realizes, in some part of her she's trying to repress, that she's made a dreadful mistake. What makes Fran a tragic figure isn't that she displays such poor judgment in her choice of men, when she has Sam Dodsworth (whom we love, just as we love Huston's magnificent performance), but that she's so frantic about her advancing age and so nakedly hungry for the approval of the *wrong* kind of aristocrats that she denies her own best instincts. Her social pretensions replace the sense of balance that—in Wyler's film, if not in Lewis's novel—we feel must have prevailed while she was making a home for Sam in Zenith and raising Emily. The irony is that while she protests that he's "rushing at old age," it's really her nagging and patronizing and undervaluing him that make him prematurely old. After she leaves him, he begins to stoop and his gait slows; only when Edith finds him, a ghost haunting the Italian tourist spots, untouched by what he sees, and resurrects him does he get his snap back. And Fran, in the meantime, looks more and more gilded as the movie goes on; when we see her for the last time, her struggle to make herself look younger has given her a china-doll fragility. *He's* finally the one who walks out on *her* when she stops exerting any power over him—when he realizes that his impulse to protect her from herself has become an old habit rather than a natural extension of the love he once felt for her. "Love has to stop somewhere short of suicide!" he declares, and sails back to Edith.

Booth Tarkington was a social critic, like Dreiser and Lewis, and *Alice Adams* (a very good novel) and *The Magnificent Ambersons* (a great one)—the Pulitzer Prize was awarded to both of them—view the hierarchy of small-town America with an acute critical eye, though from opposite points of view. The 1918 *Ambersons* is an ironic elegy for the departing aristocracy who ruled before the advent of the automobile, while *Alice Adams*, published four years later, is the story of a young woman's failed attempts to gain entrance to the most desirable social set in town. Both movie versions are largely faithful to their sources, though *Alice Adams*, directed by George Stevens, adds an unconvincing romantic ending (Alice winds up in the arms of her high-toned suitor, Arthur Russell), and *Ambersons*, the film Orson Welles chose to make immediately after his debut with *Citizen Kane* (1941), was notoriously slashed by RKO behind Welles's back while he was out on another shoot; the forty purloined minutes have never been recovered. Robert L. Carrington's invaluable *The Magnificent Ambersons: A Reconstruction* restores the original shooting script, so readers can see, on the page at least, the full-length portrait Welles intended. But what remains—except for the compromised ending (which, curiously, alters Tarkington's much less than the one Welles shot)—is extraordinary.

In the opening scene of Stevens's splendid *Alice Adams* (which has a screenplay by Dorothy Yost and Mortimer Offner), Alice (Katharine Hepburn) slips out of the local five and dime, covering her face with a veil in the hopes that no one will recognize her. She's been invited to the party of a childhood friend, Mildred Palmer (Evelyn Venable), and she feels she can't impress Mildred's set if they know she's been shopping cheap. But the florist she visits next charges too much for corsages. Alice puts on a show for him, claiming that she wore orchids to her last party, that gardenias are too ordinary and violets will clash with her gown; she saunters out, affecting a carefree air, but then she sneaks off to pick flowers in the park. South Renford, Alice's home town, is proud of its heritage and its economic success, and the florist, with his $5.00 orchids and $6.50 gardenia corsages, is an example of the way it would like to see itself—reflected in the lifestyle of the Palmers and their friends. In truth, though, it's sharply divided into moneyed families like the Palmers and struggling ones like the Adamses. Alice and her mother (Ann Shoemaker) suffer most from the divide, which hasn't always separated them with such finality from people like the Palmers. Alice grew up with Mildred, and they were once good friends—far closer than Mildred now wants to admit, though she feels guilty enough about abandoning Alice that she continues to invites her to her parties. According to Mrs. Adams, a quarter of a century ago she and her husband Virgil (the famous vaudevillian Fred Stone) were on par with the Palmers and their friends, but all the other men got farther ahead in the world than he did. Virgil works loyally and contentedly in the office of the benevolent Mr. Lamb (Charley Grapewin), whom his wife has cast in the role of a tyrannical monster. In her mind, Lamb's insensitive treatment of Virgil and Virgil's staunch refusal to strike out on his own are the twin causes of Alice's miserable exclusion from the town's aristocrats and of the moral disintegration of her son Walter (Frank Albertson), who's never had the company of the right sort of people. (Walter also works for Lamb, in a job he obtained through his father's good graces.) What she'd like Virgil to do is manufacture glue from a formula he developed for Lamb, but Adams believes it belongs to his employer (though Lamb's never used it) and not to himself.

The comedy in *Alice Adams* derives from the contrast between the life Alice wants—represented by Mildred's lifestyle, Mildred's elegant party, and Mildred's cousin Arthur (Fred MacMurray), who shows an immediate interest in Alice—and the unattractive and quarrelsome home she shares with her family. The house itself may have been quite gracious in an earlier era, but Virgil doesn't make enough money to keep it up, and without the softening effects of creative housekeeping, it feels chill and blocky and unpleasantly imposing. And the Adams family is horrid—the whining, infantile papa, the social-climbing mama with her tremulous martyr's voice and her persistent nagging, the self-involved son, a slobby lowlife who's constantly at loggerheads with his father and who begrudges his sister the smallest mercies. Walter seems to take his sister's pretensions personally. When their mother insists that he escort Alice to the Palmers' party, he does so with the greatest resentment, then embarrasses her by vanishing into the cloakroom to shoot craps with the servants. The movie views the family as Alice's cross to bear, but it refuses to romanticize her; it's pitilessly objective about her affectations, which fool nobody—though Arthur, who's fascinated by her originality, sees them in the kindest light. *Alice Adams* is one of those rare portrayals of a sort of achieved femininity bolstered by self-delusion that can horrify you and enlist your sympathies at the same time, and it's Hepburn's performance that makes that intense ambivalence possible. (The like performances that come to mind are Vivien Leigh's Blanche DuBois in *A Streetcar Named Desire*, Maggie Smith's in the title role of *The Lonely Passion of Judith Hearne*, and Agnes Moorehead's as the spinster Fanny Minafer in *The Magnificent Ambersons*.) Everything seems to conspire against poor Alice in her efforts to make a good impression. She refuses to be seen emerging from Walter's shoddy jalopy, so she insists he park it outside the gate, which means that she has to walk up to the house in the rain. Walter isn't willing to conform to her notions of proper etiquette; the only person at the party with whom he admits an acquaintance is the black bandleader. (It's 1935, remember, so his egalitarian notions aren't appreciated.) Then he disappears, leaving her alone, to be laughed at by Mildred's rich friends for her démodé organdy dress and snubbed by every potential dance partner except the overattentive Frank Dowling (Grady Sutton), whose zealous ballroom technique brings to mind the agonies of the narrator in Dorothy Parker's story "The Last Waltz." Then the violets she picked for her corsage die on her breast, and when she tries to cast them away surreptitiously, Arthur gallantly retrieves them for her. Alice's attempts to soldier on through these humiliations—to give the impression that she's having the time of her life—are such transparent playacting that you blush for her (and your heart breaks for her). Unlikable as Walter is, you wish for her sake that she could take his point of view and turn her back on these "society snakes," but her environment has trained her to long for access to a society that's constantly reminding her she's not good enough to join. When, back at home after an evening of social purgatory, she sobs at her rainy window, it's the expression of the disappointment and unhappiness of every young American woman who feels the pangs of social exclusion.

Alice isn't awkward with Arthur because he puts her at her ease; he doesn't look away in embarrassment the way others (like Mildred) do when she makes fluttery small talk or bubbles with absurd little compliments. Alice's eccentricity is a desperate defense: lacking the resources to adopt the debutante lifestyle, she's obliged to design an original style for herself. And to her amazement and delight, Arthur is enchanted by her. But a veritable obstacle course seems to stand between them. The Palmers bad-mouth her family to Arthur, and though she's been carefully keeping him away from them, restricting his courtship to the porch, eventually Mrs. Adams insists on inviting him to a dinner given with a put-on grandeur that's an absurd stretch for their means and their manners. Stevens stages one of the great comic social debacles in the movies of this era, with Hattie McDaniel as the insolent hired help in a frilly maid's cap that wilts so badly she has to keep blowing it out of her eyes, and Fred Stone's Virgil cringing and hiding the caviar sandwich his wife forces him to taste, and the rich meal sitting unappetizingly on their plates while they suffer in their dinner clothes from the heat wave that chose that very day to hit the town. The scene isn't far removed from episodes in other thirties comedies that mean to deflate the pretensions of their characters. The difference is that Hepburn makes us feel how completely this confluence of circumstances (the climax is the noisy arrival of Walter, who's just been caught embezzling from his boss) crushes Alice's moonbeam spirit. At first it brings out her chattery, artificial side, but by the end of the dinner she's sunk. Lifting a "poor, dead rose"—the culmination of the movie's floral motif—off the table, she offers it to Arthur for his thoughts. He declines to answer, but he doesn't have to; she knows that this horror show of an evening has put the finishing touch to what, she guesses correctly, the gossip about her and her family began. She sends him away as the upstairs squabbling between Virgil and Walter drifts onto the porch. "Oh, don't mind that," she tells him sadly. "We have plenty of that in this funny old house." Then she runs inside and shuts the door on him. (His reappearance to restate his affections—RKO's enforced romantic-comedy ending—is so abrupt and ill-fitting that it seems to have been borrowed from some other movie altogether.)

"The magnificence of the Ambersons began in 1873," the voice-over narrator (Welles himself) announces at the beginning of the film named for them, but it doesn't last long—less than half a century. The movie starts by chronicling the lightning shifts in social customs and costumes in the last quarter of the nineteenth century and the early days of the twentieth. These are the outward signs of high comedy, and Welles (who also wrote the screenplay) uses them to prefigure the far deeper changes that modernity, embodied by the automobile, will bring to this society in general and to the Ambersons in particular. These shifts also enable him to provide some offhand exposition. Eugene Morgan (Joseph Cotten), the frivolous young man we see climbing in and out of the latest fashions, is courting the beautiful heiress Isabel Amberson (Dolores Costello), but when he gets so drunk one night that

he steps through a bass fiddle in midserenade, she rejects him for the sober—
and retiring—Wilbur Minafer (Don Dillaway), who moves into the Amberson mansion, along with his sister Fanny, after they marry. Their son George
is a holy terror, the product of his mother's indulgence, the lack of a strong
paternal presence in the household, and the boy's assurance that he's the heir
apparent to the town's royal family. And though he grows out of tantrums
and fisticuffs, as a young man, a student at an Ivy League college (played by
Tim Holt), he's just as arrogant and just as much a bully as he was in his
childhood, when the whole town waited impatiently for the day he'd get his
"comeuppance." That's how the movie finds him when, on the evening Isabel hosts what the voice-over calls "this pageant of the tenantry . . . the last
of the long-remembered dances that everybody talked about," Eugene returns, now a widower (and a teetotaler) with a beautiful daughter, Lucy
(Anne Baxter), who catches George's eye. But George doesn't like Morgan:
George is affronted by Morgan's familiarity with the family, and, very much
the scion of a nineteenth-century aristocracy, he looks down on the widower's livelihood. Eugene is an inventor of automobiles.

The ball in *Ambersons* is far removed in tone from the Palmer party in *Alice Adams*. But then again, it comes at the end of an earlier epoch. The camerawork has the same gliding gracefulness you see in other depictions of
grand aristocratic entertainments—the waltz montage in Ophüls's *The Earrings of Madame de . . .* , the ball that takes up the last section of Visconti's
*The Leopard* (1963), the opera scene near the end of Bertolucci's *Before the
Revolution* (1964). Yet Welles's style is truly eccentric; no one has ever filmed
an aristocratic party with quite the same theatrical self-consciousness. The
visuals are thick, glistening; you're aware of the actors' makeup and costumes,
though not the way you are in forced, misbegotten period pieces like most of
the Merchant Ivory pictures. Welles's pioneering homegrown mix of expres-
sionism and impressionism—his distinctive use of deep focus for expression-
istic purposes (rather than as the liberating realist's tool it is for Renoir and
Wyler), the stark shadow-and-light contrasts borrowed from the German expressionists, and the Gothic elements he brings to bear on the cavernous,
echoing Amberson mansion—deepens the visual presence of Mercury Theatre actors like Cotten, Moorehead, and Ray Collins (as George's uncle, the
Honorable Jack Amberson) in clothes they're a little too modern for and
makeup they're a little too young for. In *Citizen Kane*, the audacious use of
camera and editing is playful—the combination of the theatricality Welles
imported from his Broadway training and the inventive application of sound
he learned on the radio with his zeal for discovering new cinematic techniques. Besides, spectacular as it is, *Kane* is shallow enough that you don't

have to take the aging of the characters all that seriously. (The actors—Welles, Cotten, Moorehead in her brief but memorable stint as Kane's mother—pull it off with panache, but their performances have a greasepaint sheen in close-up.) *Ambersons* has a depth you don't find in *Kane*—even at a truncated ninety minutes, it's the greater of the two pictures—and the playfulness goes out of it as soon as the traveling camera whisks us into the Amberson ball along with Eugene and Lucy, their collars bent back by the wind, and the story proper commences. And Welles makes it work. The Mercury Theatre performance style, with its briskness and outsize quality, and the slightly wasted grandeur of the silent-movie actors Richard Bennett (as the woeful-eyed Major Amberson, the family patriarch) and Dolores Costello (as the delicate, anxious Isabel, fretting eternally over her spoiled son), underscore our distance from these people and this era. So do the echoes in the corridor of the mansion, and the iris shot, also a remnant of the silent era, that closes the scene where Georgie's sleigh-ride date with Lucy is intercut with Eugene's taking the rest of the family out for a ride in his auto.

The ball and the sleigh ride are the symbols of the dying era. The second of these sequences begins with a magical shot of the sleigh reflected in a puddle, its evocative tingle juxtaposed with the chugging and farting of Eugene's horseless carriage. The sleigh is the emblem of romance: George and Lucy tumble out of it into a kiss. So when the world loses all of this—when the horseless carriage takes over—romance, in some measure, dies too. Welles's choice to make this elegiac movie about the passing of the old ways is suggestive of a profound ambivalence about the modern age that's borne out, I think, by his style, which is simultaneously ultra-modern and baroque. Welles is a paradox: an iconoclast with an old-fashioned (that is, nineteenth-century) sense of the theatrical. He wears his conflicted feelings about modernism on his sleeve even in *Kane*, where his hero, while laying claim to virtual ownership of early-twentieth-century America, retreats to a Gothic castle and dies longing for the Victorian childhood he was torn away from. In *Ambersons*, those feelings are at home in Tarkington's depiction of the decline of the family, which both he and Welles treat as tragicomic.

George and Eugene act as foils here. As Eugene deserts his old friend Jack to dance with Isabel, Jack quips, "Eighteen years have passed—but have they? . . . Old times certainly are starting all over again." But Gene contradicts him, laughing: "There aren't any old times. When times are gone, they're not old, they're dead! There aren't any times but new times." And then this man who will help usher America into a new age takes the arm of his old sweetheart and leads her onto the floor, not for a waltz but for a newfangled turkey trot. But Morgan, who is also reflective and philosophical, is aware of the weight of the changes that men like him are initiating: his reply to a dismissive dinner-table comment from George about automobiles is a considered (and beautifully written) speech about the unpredictable—and not entirely favorable—ways in which they're likely to alter civilization.

On the other end of the spectrum is George, who tells Lucy, "Anybody that really is anybody ought to be able to do about as they like in their own town, I should think" and, when she asks what career he envisions for himself, announces that he plans to be a yachtsman and really *enjoy* life. Raised to get his own way in everything, he's baffled when his high-handedness draws anger or sarcasm from other people. Lucy, who sincerely likes him and usually responds to his arrogance with a charming, half-submerged irony, is a little less subtle when he's condescending about her father's motors; but then he thinks *she's* insulting *him*, and he can't see what he's done to invite that sort of comment. He's a mass of prejudices—his unwarranted bias against Eugene causes him to jump to idiotic conclusions about him—and he's incapable of admitting he's wrong about anything because no one's ever taught him that he *can* be wrong. When Wilbur dies and Eugene begins to court Isabel, Fanny, who has always adored Gene, grows jealous and bitter. And those emotions—as well as her fear of growing old alone—prompt her to manipulate her nephew into forcing a wedge between the lovers, and he's so insensitive and blind to anything but his own ego that he allows her to. She hints that the whole town is talking about Morgan and Isabel, the great love that never really died and now has been fanned into flame once more by Wilbur's death, and George is thunderstruck. He's appalled that his mother should be the object of gossip—and beyond that, of course, he resents Gene as a rival for her affections. So he goes around to their neighbors, demanding that they take back what they've said, like a feudal lord setting the rules for the conduct of his vassals. Of course, times have changed; they see him as pathetic and throw him out. His code of honor is hopelessly antiquated, and he's using it, moreover, to protect a stupid idea about his mother, who hasn't done anything wrong and has nothing to be rescued from. George literally tries to turn back time, by acting like his mother's baby all his life and preventing her from pursuing a romantic relationship that would take her beyond him to a new life of her own. When Eugene appears at the door to take her for a drive, George intercedes, telling him he's no longer welcome and sending him home—repeating the treatment Gene received years earlier when he tried to see Isabel after he'd made a drunken fool of himself in her yard. This time, of course, he doesn't merit this kind of rejection. But when she's forced to choose between her son and the man she loves, she chooses George and surrenders her own chance of happiness.

All-sacrificing mother love was a popular theme in movies of the twenties and thirties; *Stella Dallas* and *Madame X* were popular as silents and as talkies. In these melodramas, which reverse the conventions of high comedies, the woman from the wrong side of the tracks who marries the aristocrat (in *Stella Dallas*, 1925 and 1937) or the woman who violates the sexual standards of the upper class and is ostracized for it (in *Madame X*, 1916, 1920, 1929, and 1937) gives up everything for the sake of a beloved child. But *The Magnificent Ambersons* takes a critical view of this kind of sacrifice, showing it in its darker form. We understand not only that George is weak, relying childishly on his mother, but that Isabel is, too, in holding onto George as if he were still an infant in her arms.

George's preposterous behavior has a high-comic dimension, but what happens to him is ultimately a tragedy—a private tragedy that reflects the tragedy of progress. At the outset, the notion of George getting his comeuppance is comic—he's Peck's bad boy, his hijinks relayed to us by a comic chorus of townspeople (including Fanny and Jack). But by the end, he's lost everything: both his parents (Isabel dies soon after giving up Gene), his grandfather, the woman he loves, and his fortune. By the time we see him walk to the old house for the last time, in the shadow of the town that has grown past the Amberson era into a modern (and unattractive) industrial present, the comedy has died away. "George Amberson Minafer had got his comeuppance," Welles's voice informs us. "He got it three times filled and running over. But those who had so longed for it were not there to see it, and they never knew it. Those who were still living had forgotten all about it and all about him." To be forgotten by the town where he'd been raised to believe himself a monarch—that's the worst part. The physical component of his downfall—ironically, he's run down by an automobile and winds up in the hospital with both legs broken—is somehow less awful.

The heroines of *The Letter* and *The Heiress* are, like George Minafer, representatives of an insulated upper-class society, and their stories pivot (in different ways) on their interactions with someone outside their circle. They're vastly dissimilar sorts of women, though. Somerset Maugham's Leslie Crosbie is an Englishwoman, married to a rubber planter in Singapore and highly placed in the white colonial settlement there, who empties a revolver into her lover on a hot, moonlit night. She fabricates a story about an attempted rape, but an incriminating letter, in the possession of the dead man's Eurasian mistress, threatens to explode her defense. Henry James's Catherine Sloper is the shy, socially awkward daughter of a Manhattan physician, and she is courted by a fortune hunter. The dramatic versions of these literary works are melodramas, and—as is often the case with melodramas set within the aristocracy—their structures imitate those of high comedies. Despite the upheavals in the two narratives, in the end both women are reabsorbed into their social classes; what ultimately makes the plays tragic rather than comic is the irrevocable damage that has been done—to Leslie's marriage to Robert in the first case, to Catherine's psyche in the second. (In the second film version of *The Letter*, released well into the Hays Code era, Leslie is punished for adultery and murder in the final reel: the Eurasian woman—a wronged *wife* in this retelling—kills her.)

*The Letter* first appeared in the West End in 1925, with Gladys Cooper in the leading role; Katharine Cornell played Leslie on Broadway. It was one of the earliest plays to be filmed after the advent of talkies: the legendary doomed beauty Jeanne Eagels starred, in 1929. It was her penultimate role—she died the same year, of a drug overdose, so her association with the project gave it an ineffable, extraliterary tragic aura. When William Wyler remade the film eleven years later, Bette Davis took over the role. According to one of Wyler's biographers, Axel Madsen, Davis was fascinated by Eagels; one of her first major roles, in *Dangerous*, had been loosely based on incidents from Eagels's life, and five years after *The Letter* she remade the young actress's final film, *Jealousy*, under the title *Deception*.[3] In both its incarnations, *The Letter* is an examination of the insulated, self-defensive nature of a colonial aristocracy, as well as a psychosexual study of one woman who embodies some of its contradictions. Leslie's tale, that Geoff Hammond came by one evening while Robert was away and tried to force himself on her, satisfies not only her loving, rather stupid husband (Reginald Owen, then Herbert Marshall) but in fact the entire white settlement in Singapore, because Leslie—gracious, witty, composed, a bottomless source of domestic virtues—is a tower of respectability none of her peers would suspect of being less than completely morally sturdy. Maugham writes of her, "She had elegance, but it was the elegance of good breeding in which there was nothing of the artifice of society. You had only to look at her to know what sort of people she had and what kind of surroundings she had lived in. . . . It was impossible to associate her with the vaguest idea of grossness."[4] As the more fleshed-out Wyler version (with its excellent Howard Koch script) shows us in greater detail, from the outset Leslie is treated like a victim and not a criminal—and not only because her story, which she sticks to in every detail, frames Hammond as a potential rapist she shot down like a dog. It never occurs to anyone except her lawyer, Howard Joyce (James Stephenson), who is intelligent and discriminating enough to suspect her version of events from the beginning (though he keeps it to himself), that she might not be as pure as the driven snow. It doesn't occur to Howard's wife Dorothy (Frieda Inescort), Leslie's best friend, who fusses over her when she gets out of jail as if she'd just recovered from scarlet fever and throws a party in her honor. It doesn't occur to John Withers (Bruce Lester), the assistant district officer whose first major case this is, who develops a sort of benign crush on her and comments repeatedly on how beautifully she's conducting herself under these trying cir-cumstances. It doesn't even occur to the women's prison warden, Mrs. Cooper (Doris Lloyd), who declares that Leslie is a pleasure to have around and it's only a pity that she has to stay there at all. (She talks about Leslie's situation as if Leslie were in a sanitarium for her health and Mrs. Cooper were her nurse.) And though Howard has to sacrifice his own integrity in or-der to save Leslie—on Robert's behalf, he purchases the letter from Ham-mond's widow (Gale Sondergaard)—and we see how much this action costs him in self-respect, he does it out of loyalty to Robert and out of an unques-tioning loyalty to the small, ruling white community to which they all be-long, which is premised on the rule that they must stick together. Essentially, he behaves like a colonial gentleman seeking to erase the stain of scandal from his lady client's name.

It's assumed that Leslie has behaved nobly and courageously. Hammond, on the other hand, has violated the rule that forbids social intercourse—let alone intermarriage—with a native. Wyler and Koch emphasize Leslie's dis-gust with Hammond's marriage, and though she's a biased party (Hammond threw her over), still her response to his wife, whom she describes as a hor-rid, bejeweled creature with a face like a mask, conveys the racism of the men and women in her circle. Mrs. Hammond represents a kind of frightening sexual openness to a white Englishwoman like Leslie, whose own passions are hidden behind her veneer of British reserve, her role as the perfect colonial wife. (Throughout the film she knits a coverlet for her and Robert's bed; it's the last thing Wyler shows us, while the party at the Joyces' continues into the night and Leslie's body, still undiscovered, lies outside their gate.) In the 1929 version, directed by Jean de Limur, Leslie tells the court that she and her husband cut off their friendship with Hammond when he began living with a half-caste woman (Lady Tsen-Mei), whom she describes as "common" and "vulgar." And though we see Hammond only briefly—played, as it hap-pens, by a younger Herbert Marshall—the movie's depiction of him confirms the notion that he's given rein to his sensuality—gone native. He looks wasted, like a man who's succumbed to the moist temptations of a tropical climate. (It's the look we see on Mel Gibson's Fletcher Christian in *The Bounty* [1984] once he's taken a Polynesian mistress.) The division between the white community and the Asian one is a strict one, and Hammond crosses it at his peril. On the other side of it, in the Wyler version, are Mrs. Hammond, who is all the more sinister to Leslie and her friends because she herself is the product of a mixed union; Mrs. Hammond's friend Chung Hi (Willie Fung), who runs a shop in the Chinese quarter that seems exotic and mysterious, and who sells the letter for her; and the unsettling Ong Chi Seng (Victor Sen Yung), who works in Joyce's office and, drawing on his English public-school training, acts as a middleman between the two communities. (His subservient smile for his employer hides a deadly racial hatred; at first we only sense it, but we see it for ourselves when Joyce leaves the room and that smile turns poisonous.)

Leslie is as trenchant a portrait of sexual duplicitousness as any character in American movies; you'd have to go back to Ibsen's *Hedda Gabler* and beyond that, to the great Jacobean tragedy *The Changeling* by Middleton and Rowley, to match it. The protagonist of *The Changeling*, Beatrice Joanna, has her fiancé murdered so she's free to marry the man she loves. But because she's kept her chastity, she sees nothing wrong in what she's done, and she's shocked when De Flores, the assassin she hired, insists she's implicated in the act—and demands as his prize a share of the sexual fervor that he rightly believes her desire for the murder reflects. If you know this play, it's hard not to think of Beatrice Joanna when Bette Davis's Leslie, only hours after dispatching Hammond, is amazed to learn that she will have to await trial in prison, or when she fails to understand the lawyer's scruples about risking his reputation by purchasing the single piece of evidence against her. ("What have I ever done to you?" she asks him when he hesitates. "How can you be so cruel?")

Both Eagels and Davis give staggering performances, and it's fascinating to compare the ways in which they handle the scene where Leslie tells her story. Eagels, whose acting has a ragged lyricism, does it on the stand. The pain her Leslie relays at remembering Geoff's advances flames up under her practiced composure. As she speaks the words she's invented for him, you realize with a jolt that she's putting *her* feelings for *him* in *his* mouth. Her description of his lovemaking is even more daring, since it's her own erotic impulses she's reporting, with a displacement that seems a kind of psychosis. Davis's Leslie tells her story the night of Hammond's death, to Robert and Joyce and Withers, and at first her bright-eyed recital is a little entertainment, engineered to please her audience, almost in the polished drawing-room style of a Jane Austen heroine. There's so much disdain, and so much critical distance, in the tone of her narrative that it's as if this incident had happened to somebody else. Then, transported by the high drama of the situation, she begins to act out the crucial scene, passing from ladylike modesty through righteous indignation to sudden desperation and mad, instinctual violence against Hammond's predatory advances. At first Wyler stages Davis with her back to the camera as well as to her listeners, in a strange triple-spectator set-up (we're watching the men watching Leslie, who's looking at—as far as they know—a visualization of a horrific memory). Then the men leave the frame, and she turns to the camera as she reaches the climax of her story; the men (along with us) are the audience for her show. Finally *she* vanishes from the frame, too, and as she describes the shooting, it's the camera that creates the drama, as our minds fill in the outlines of the action she describes. When she's done, the men congratulate her for behaving "magnificently," and she stretches back on her couch, as if she were basking in an ovation. (It's an astonishing moment.) In the de Limur movie, we know Leslie is lying because we've seen the interaction between her and Hammond that led to his death. But Wyler starts with the shooting and provides us with no context for it. So we have to rely on our instincts that Leslie is giving a performance (albeit a superb one)—until Ong tells his employer about the letter and our suspicions are confirmed.

The buzzing white ruling class descends to protect Leslie, and she gets away with murder. There's no other way for the story to go, given the aristocracy it chronicles; and in the Hays Code–approved version, it has to be the Chinese community and not the white one that ultimately punishes her. But both movies do provide a scene where Robert finally sees what his wife is made of. (Marshall, in the Wyler film, shows how the truth chips away at his thick skull, suddenly knocking him sideways like a hammer blow.) Leslie tells him, finally, "With all my heart I still love the man I killed," though her motivation is different in the two pictures. Eagels's Leslie spits it out in revenge against Robert, who she feels has abandoned her in this dirty, foreign place and who intends to punish her for her infidelity by trapping her in the colonies for the rest of her life. Davis's Leslie, who has never wanted to hurt her husband, confesses it because she can't deny the truth any longer; she exposes (as Beatrice Joanna does at the end of *The Changeling*) all the compulsive, masochistic churnings of her secret life, and that line is a cry of horror, the horror of a woman who's seen inside herself for the first time. Another Wyler biographer, Jan Herman, tells us that Davis and Wyler fought long and bitterly over this famous scene. He insisted that she look Marshall straight in the face when she said it, and she protested that it would be too cruel to play it that way.[5] I think Wyler was right; in any case, he won the argument.

The high-comic elements in *The Heiress* are clearer than in *The Letter*; you don't have to see them through the melodrama, because the ironies of the story can be read both comically and tragically (at least, until the bitter final act). Henry James's *Washington Square* doesn't read like a melodrama, but that's because James wasn't a dramatic writer, so the first thing adapters always

have to do with his material is to impose a dramatic structure on it. Iain Soft-
ley's 1997 film of *The Wings of the Dove* does that; by contrast, Agniezska Hol-
land's *Washington Square*, from the same year, returns more or less to the structure of the novella, and the results are disastrous. For *The Heiress*, William
Wyler looked to the terrific stage play by Ruth and Augustus Goetz, and his
movie is extremely faithful to it. (Aficionados of James might like to know
that there's still another movie version, *Masquerade* [1988], which cleverly re-
constructs *Washington Square* as a contemporary murder mystery set in the
Hamptons. Meg Tilly plays the Catherine Sloper role, and Rob Lowe is the
suitor.) Olivia De Havilland plays Catherine, whose father, Austin (Ralph
Richardson), despairs that she has developed no social graces. He constantly
compares her to her dead mother, whom he adored and whose death he has
never recovered from, and though Catherine is intelligent and sensitive—
even witty, when she's alone with her doting, fatuous widow aunt (Miriam
Hopkins), her chaperone—she's so handicapped by the knowledge that she
can never please her father that she can't stop getting in her own way. Wyler
and De Havilland make Cathy's social awkwardness funny. She's so deliberate
that she seems to be going down a checklist in her head whenever she's asked,
in company, for the simplest item—a dance, or whether she'd like a glass of
punch. Her instincts become paralyzed, so she can't move with any fluency
from one action to the next. Yet one night, at an engagement party for her
cousin, she's approached by a handsome and charming young man, Morris
Townsend (Montgomery Clift), who's the cousin of the groom-to-be. His ar-
dor transforms all of her failings into virtues—modesty, superior judgment, a
contemplative nature. And he begins to pay court to her, effortlessly winning
the love of a woman who has never known any.

James set his story in the kind of society—like Jane Austen's—where
everyone is acutely aware of how much you're worth. Catherine has inherited a goodly sum from her mother, but on her father's death she will have
twice as much more. And Dr. Sloper, who is as perceptive and exact as a cat
hunting a mouse, and whose rhetorical gift is to turn elegance of phrase into
irony and sarcasm, spies Morris's motives. When he and Catherine disclose
their intention to marry, Sloper interviews Morris's sister, Mrs. Montgomery
(Betty Linley), a widow with a family, in whose house Morris lives. Her description of him is rendered with sisterly fondness, but Austin sees through
it to a confirmation of his own suspicions—that Townsend is utterly self-
interested, a profligate who, having spent his own meager inheritance on a
trip to the continent, thinks he has discovered a fresh means for his own
comfort. And the doctor is right—damnably right. The Goetzes make Morris's agenda clear enough, and in the marvelous revival of the play Gerald

Gutierrez staged at the Roundabout Theatre in New York in 1995, the actor Michael Cumpsty communicated it pretty much from the outset. Wyler takes a different approach that's manifest in the casting of Clift, an immensely likable performer who can't convey guile. Clift and Wyler don't let Morris tip his hand—not until the scene where Aunt Lavinia, an aide to the romance from the first, entertains him at the Sloper home while Catherine and her father are traveling through Europe (Sloper's attempt at making her forget Townsend), and then his priorities are only hinted at, in the way he admires his absent host's environment while he stands smoking at the fire, or in the maid's assurance, upon bringing him a glass of claret, that it's at the temperature he prefers. So we hope against hope that Morris is all Catherine believes him to be, and we hate Austin Sloper for wanting to deprive her of happiness—even though he persuades himself that it *is* her happiness he's looking out for.

That this tyrant without compassion is right about Townsend is one of the ironies of the film; the other is that his rightness doesn't matter in the end. Catherine reads, at last, the lack of love that makes it impossible for her father to see her as the object of anyone's sincere devotion; and she concludes, with an accuracy as pitiless as his, that a life with Morris, whatever his motives for marrying her, could hardly be worse than a continued life with Sloper, who feels no more for her than Morris does and probably far less. (She points out to her father that, since *he* hasn't been able to love her, he might let someone else try.) By this time, however, it's too late. Naively, she tells Morris, as they prepare to elope, that they will have to live without her father's inheritance, and he fails to show up at the appointed time. So she continues to live under her father's roof until he dies (shortly thereafter), though his unkindness and her heartbreak have drained all the filial affection out of her. After his death, the house in Washington Square, where she has been the prisoner of her father's intolerance and the shadow of her mother's memory—this house that was the real attraction for Morris, and that, despising it and despising Sloper, Catherine longed to escape from—becomes her fate, just as surely as Lorca's house of Bernarda Alba is for the women in that play at the final curtain. Two years after his departure for the California coast, Morris returns to woo her once again. But this time, enticing him to believe she's ready to rekindle their dead romance, she bolts the door against him and retreats, lamp in hand, up the empty staircase, entombing herself forever with her father's bitterness and his merciless justice, which are her true inheritance. (Wyler's version is as much a ghost story as James's *The Turn of the Screw*.)

*The Heiress* has unexpected parallels to *Six Degrees of Separation*, the John Guare play Fred Schepisi brought to the screen in 1993 (and that will be discussed in chapter 6). Both relate the story of how an outsider hungry for entrée to a moneyed society brings something wonderful to a member of it—something that another aristocrat could never offer. In both films, the interaction is initially transformative for the aristocratic heroine. But in *Six Degrees*, the unintended gift removes her in some unspecified but absolute way from the values of that society, whereas in *The Heiress* it is withdrawn, extinguishing her spark and leaving her bitter and irrevocably alone. When Cherry Jones played Catherine in the Roundabout production, she made the character so lovable that the coldness of purpose that permitted her revenge on Morris was heartbreaking. De Havilland's Catherine is just as innocent, but also repressed; her metamorphosis is the playing out of a neurosis that's the flip side of her naïveté. And her dreadful transformation into the hard-hearted spinster who bolts the door and retreats from the world plays out the darkest vision of the aristocracy to which she belongs. Austin Sloper reduces his daughter to the embodiment of her inheritance by insisting that's the only way the world could possibly see her, and in the end she confirms his interpretation.

# Notes

1. Sinclair Lewis, *Dodsworth*, in *Sinclair Lewis: Arrowsmith, Elmer Gantry, Dodsworth* (New York: Library of America, 2002), 983.

2. Lewis, *Dodsworth*, 927.

3. Axel Madsen, *William Wyler* (New York: Thomas Y. Crowell, 1973), 200.

4. W. Somerset Maugham, "The Letter," in *The Great Exotic Novels and Short Stories of W. Somerset Maugham* (New York: Avalon, 2001).

5. Jan Herman, *A Talent for Trouble* (New York: G. P. Putnam's Sons, 1995), 212–13.

~

# CHAPTER FOUR

# The Poison in the Champagne: What It's *Really* Like to Be Rich and Famous

There were no pure American high comedies in the three decades between *The Philadelphia Story* (1940) and Paul Mazursky's *Bob and Carol and Ted and Alice* (1969). The war years coarsened the sensibility of Hollywood movies, which became flat-footed and obvious; only a handful of directors—mainly Orson Welles, John Huston, William Wyler and Preston Sturges—kept them alive as an art form. And even when they became interesting again, toward the end of the forties, when vibrant filmmakers like Fred Zinnemann, Billy Wilder, and Elia Kazan rose to prominence, they moved not toward the delicate stylization that comedy of manners requires but toward a grittier psychological realism, embodied in a new breed of actor (first Dana Andrews, Montgomery Clift, and William Holden; then Marlon Brando and James Dean). These were also the years when American popular culture felt the patriotic need to assert, over and over again, the characteristics that are traditionally assumed to define it. And one of the chief virtues, a distaste for class divisions, bred a suspicion of anything that smacked of privilege, refinement, cultural snobbery. Generically the result was a series of fascinating movies where the conventions of high comedy were crossbred with those of mystery thrillers, film noirs, and show-biz pictures—that is, films that purport to expose the seamy underlayer of celebrity.

The antiaristocratic spirit that governs these films is hardly new in Hollywood, of course. You find it back in the early thirties in comedies like *Platinum Blonde*, where the tough-talking reporter, temporarily lifted above his class by an infatuation with an heiress, has to drop back down to earth and reestablish himself among his own kind. And you find it in melodramas like the oft-filmed *Madame X* (the best version, directed by Sam Wood in 1937, starred Gladys George), where the heroine, driven to adultery by an unhappy marriage and caught in a murder scandal, is humiliated and scorned by a callous, unforgiving aristocratic husband; deprived of her son, she sinks into the depths of poverty and addiction. The difference between these movies and the vitriolic portraits of the moneyed classes in the forties and early fifties is that the latter acknowledge—and trade off—our attraction to the rich and famous. They reel us in by promising us both a glimpse of the high life and all the dirt about the people who lead it.

Perhaps the earliest of these hybrids is *Rebecca*, from 1940. An adaptation of the hypnotic Daphne Du Maurier novel, a combination coming-of-age story and Gothic that (for good reason) has retained its hold on adolescent female readers, it's the first of Alfred Hitchcock's Hollywood pictures, and—as a result of his collaboration with the prestige producer David O. Selznick—it has a creamy, expensive look that isn't characteristic of anything else he ever did. (It's also the only one of his movies ever to win the Oscar.) But though the material has the kind of literary-classic underpinnings you don't normally associate with Hitchcock, the movie he fashions from it is genuinely creepy and engaging. The story scrambles the key parts of *Jane Eyre*—a mousy heroine who overcomes the obstacles of an easily cowed personality and inferior class background to become mistress of a grand estate; a difficult, brooding hero beset by private demons; an earlier wife who's virtually a ghost and whose continual presence threatens the happiness of the hero and the heroine. The gimmick is in the title. Rebecca is the deceased first wife of Maxim de Winter (Laurence Olivier), a famously beautiful and vivacious young woman whose untimely death by drowning is assumed to have almost destroyed her husband. We never see her, but when Max brings a new bride (Joan Fontaine) home to his Cornwall estate, Manderley, she finds herself in competition with her predecessor and bested at every turn, as everyone around her seems constantly to be comparing her to Rebecca, and Rebecca's mark is on everything at Manderley from the stationery to the luncheon menus. The protagonist herself doesn't have a name: the published screenplay refers to her as "I" (as she provides the voice-over narration), and other sources call her "Mrs. de Winter."

In the opening section, set in Monte Carlo, "I," the orphaned daughter of a talented but unsuccessful painter, has the unenviable job of paid companion to a vain, snippy American socialite named Edith Van Hopper (Florence Bates). Mrs. Van Hopper represents our unkindest fantasies of the way the rich behave, and the movie has fun at her expense. She complains constantly about the quality of the service at the hotel, treating waiters and other service people as if they were unsatisfactory beasts of burden, and she's obsessed with social currency. She's bored at Monte because her set has apparently deserted it (the season is past), so when she spots Max, who clearly doesn't remember her, she flatters him and flutters around him. She's too self-involved to see that his only interest is in her companion, who is beneath her notice except when she's the target of Mrs. Van Hopper's irritation or censure. When, over coffee with the two women, Max asks the girl's opinion of her surroundings and she replies, with some hesitation, that they strike her as rather artificial, Mrs. Van Hopper laughs off her comment as fatuous ingratitude ("Most girls would give their eyes for a chance to see Monte"—a proclamation that invites Max's ironic response, "Wouldn't that rather defeat the purpose?"). Then, when they're alone, she puts down her companion's "embarrassing" forwardness and advises her that "men loathe that sort of thing." "I" is so self-effacing and tentative that it doesn't take much to persuade her that she's inadequate and out of place. When she sits down alone for breakfast at the hotel restaurant and knocks over a vase of flowers, she apologizes profusely to the staff; she's too nice, and too unsure of herself, to think she might deserve to be waited on. But Maxim is enchanted by her sweetness and sincerity and unaffectedness—by all the ways in which she isn't like an aristocrat. While Mrs. Van Hopper is laid up in her room with a cold, he takes "I" out on drives, treating her to the only vacation she's ever had. She falls in love with him, but she doesn't imagine that he might feel the same way; she can't help thinking of herself as the object of his charity (an idea that makes him furious), and when Mrs. Van Hopper is suddenly called back to New York, and Max suggests "I" return to Manderley with him instead, she asks, in confusion, if he needs a secretary or something.

Mrs. Van Hopper—for all her money, a vulgarian who extinguishes her cigarettes in her cold cream jar, and as enthralled by old-world class as Fran Dodsworth—is astonished when Max tells her he's going to marry her companion. She offers to put off her travel plans to give this poor motherless child a wedding (a scheme Max politely short-circuits), but she continues to boss her around like a servant, and when Max leaves the room, she turns nasty. "Still waters certainly do run deep," she offers sarcastically, and then insinuates that "I" must have been putting out for De Winter, or why would he look twice or her? Certainly he doesn't love her; the big house must be getting on his nerves after Rebecca's death, and he needs somebody to take care of it, though he's bound to be disappointed, because "I" can have no idea how to be the "great lady" Manderley demands. And that's how "I" approaches her life as the mistress of Manderley, positive that she lacks the resources that her new position calls for. Max tries to reassure her that everyone will love her if she only acts like herself, but it starts to rain on his convertible as they pull up to the estate, and she makes a bedraggled entrance, terrified by the size and elegance of the house (which looks like a haunted castle out of a fairy tale), intimidated by the large staff, whom the housekeeper, Mrs. Danvers (Judith Anderson), has hauled out en masse to meet the newlyweds.

Mrs. Danvers, who worshipped Rebecca and loathes the thought that anyone should try to replace her as mistress of Manderley, becomes the new Mrs. de Winter's special enemy. But even those who are on the bride's side, like Max and his affectionate sister, Beatrice Lacey (Gladys Cooper), aren't much help, because they give her mixed messages and insufficient information. They praise her for her unpretentiousness, but at the same time they expect her to handle the role she's been handed as if she'd been trained for it; born to the life of Manderley, they don't appreciate the boldness and courage it takes to leap across class barriers. (Even Beatrice's affable husband Giles, played by Nigel Bruce, is enough of a snob to assume, until he's met her, that the untitled bride Max has brought home must be a gold-digging chorus girl.) "I" is a working-class heroine thrown into a high-comedy world. When she breaks a china ornament in the morning room, she instinctively hides the pieces in a drawer, as a schoolgirl might, and when Mrs. Danvers accuses one of the other servants of stealing it and "I" has to own up to what she's done, Max is satirical with her rather than understanding, and her terror of facing the housekeeper makes him impatient. (This scene shows up again, in dramatically altered form, in Cukor's *Gaslight* [1944], where Charles Boyer encourages the disdain of the servant girl, Angela Lansbury, for Ingrid Bergman, the wife he's trying to drive into madness.) "I" takes Beatrice's word for it that she has to learn to dress more smartly, but Max isn't pleased with her efforts, and Hitchcock juxtaposes the image of her in home movies of their honeymoon, clad comfortably in modest skirts and sweaters, with her strained self-consciousness in her new gown with flowers at the breast. And she takes Mrs. Danvers's word for it that Max could never love anybody but Rebecca. So she wanders around Manderley, lost, playing second fiddle to a dead woman.

The truth about Rebecca, and about Max's marriage to her, is the secret that ranks the film among other visions of the aristocracy as decadent and evil. It turns out that she was a chronic adulteress who flaunted her infidelities before her husband, sure that he'd never divorce her and blacken the family name. "She was incapable of love or tenderness or decency," Max eventually confesses to his new bride. Rebecca is the dark aristocrat, the worm that ate away at her husband's happiness; their marriage was a sham, a "devil's bargain." She reveled in her brilliant performance as the witty, gracious hostess of Manderley, whiling away her afternoons in a seaside cottage on the estate with a series of men. "Love was a game to her, only a game," says Mrs. Danvers. "She used to sit in her bed and rock with laughter at the lot of you." Her surviving partner in crime is her cousin-lover Jack Favell (George Sanders, warming up for his impeccable high-comic turn as the manipulating theater critic in *All About Eve*), a bankrupt socialite hunting for a pot of cream to land in and happy to stoop to blackmail if the occasion calls for it. These two are even more sinister images of the aristocracy than the mean-minded Edith Van Hopper.

But *Rebecca* is also the story of how a mousy working girl triumphs at last in the high-comic world. When the boat containing Rebecca's body is located, and the evidence piles up that Max murdered her, "I" rises to the occasion. Liberated from her misperception that he's never stopped loving her predecessor, she becomes his true helpmate, his rock in this crisis. He expects her to stop loving him; instead she proves she loves him more deeply than ever. "It's gone forever—that funny, young, lost look I loved," he mourns, but what we see in her is a maturation. From this point on Fontaine (who gives a very affecting performance) looks more at ease in clothes that befit the wife of the most important man in the county, and Hitchcock no longer shoots her so she's foreshortened by the architecture. She's finally become Mrs. de Winter—though not at Manderley, which is forever Rebecca's realm. At the end, it burns to the ground (Mrs. Danvers torches it), so she and Maxim have to construct their life together in some other setting—the unspecified one from which she tells the story that begins, "Last night I dreamt I went to Manderley again."

The resolution of *Rebecca* is satisfying because, while it exposes the dirty secrets of the rich, the heroine we identify with from the outset manages to become one of them without sacrificing her values or the qualities that made Max—and us—fall in love with her. Similarly, the heroine of *Laura* (played by Gene Tierney) is both of the social whirl and apart from it. She's an aspiring career woman working at an ad agency who attracts the notice of a famous columnist and radio personality, Waldo Lydecker (Clifton Webb); he becomes her patron, her social and intellectual tutor, and her constant companion—her ticket to the great social world, though, we're constantly reminded, it's where she belongs by virtue of talent and panache. Lydecker explains, "She had innate breeding, but she deferred to my judgment and taste." When they first cross paths, she's a star waiting to be discovered (and it's her nerve and backbone that impress Lydecker). *Laura*, which was directed by Otto Preminger in 1944, is one of the strangest murder mysteries to come out in the big-studio era, less because of the chic setting—that's a convention transplanted from the

British mystery novels of the twenties and thirties—than because of the topsy-turvy narrative and the peculiarly haunted nature of the romance, at least in the first half. Laura's corpse is discovered at the opening, and at first we see her only in flashbacks, through the narrative Waldo tells the homicide detective, Mark McPherson (Dana Andrews). And through what Mark pieces together while investigating her murder, and through the power of the portrait over her fireplace, he falls in love with her ghost, or so the mood of romantic obsession the movie takes on at this point suggests. When she turns up alive in the middle of the picture, it feels as if he's resurrected her. (On a plot level, the corpse turns out to belong to somebody else.)

Except for his fixation on a dead girl, McPherson is a hard-boiled detective out of film noir. His unimpressed, no-nonsense attitude toward Lydecker and Laura's other high-flown friends—her aunt, Ann Treadwell (Judith Anderson), and the southern pretty-boy football player Shelby Carpenter (Vincent Price), who is attached to both women as well as to the misidentified victim, a model named Diane Redfern—forms the way we see them, as superficial and ultimately worthless. Ann's connection with Carpenter is a little like Rebecca's with Favell; Ann argues, "We belong together because we're both weak and can't seem to help it." She's worried that Shelby might be Diane's killer, because she knows that he, like her, is *capable* of murder. (Without the glowering boogie-lady affect of her Mrs. Danvers, Anderson shows exactly the right clipped-rueful style for this kind of corrupt aristocratic character.) And since the murderer—who meant to shoot Laura and not Diane—is really Waldo, the movie manages to indict pretty much the entire social set (except for Laura herself, who winds up with the detective).

When we see Waldo for the first time, the camera surveys his impeccably appointed apartment, full of priceless objets d'art like an antique clock. It's one of a pair; the other was his gift to Laura. Lydecker receives McPherson seated like a monarch in a marble bathtub, typing up his daily copy, as delectable a high-comic image as the dinner party to which Nick and Nora Charles invite all the suspects in The Thin Man. His affection for Laura is really a kind of psychosis: seeing her as a spiritual twin, and also as his own creation, he's so territorial about her that he forces a wedge between her and every man she goes out with. When it doesn't appear to work with Shelby, he snaps and tries to kill her; when she shows up unharmed but falls in love with Mark, he tries it again. As Webb plays Waldo, he seems clearly gay; but since we never imagine his fix on Laura as erotic but rather as an extension of his narcissism, we don't think about its sexual implications. The script (by Jay Dratler, Samuel Hoffenstein, and Betty Reinhardt, out of a Vera Caspary novel) doesn't have much real wit—that was in short supply in mid-forties

Hollywood—but it does give Waldo the best lines as well as a flamboyant death scene in the last reel. The rifle he used to shoot Diane in error is hidden behind a secret panel in the clock in Laura's apartment; when Mark rescues her from Waldo's second attempt to murder her, the police bullets shoot up the antique. And that image tells us exactly what the movie thinks of the trappings—and the values—of high society.

There's no authentic aristocracy in Charles Chaplin's *Monsieur Verdoux* (1947), but Chaplin, as a Bluebeard who supports a crippled wife and a flaxen-haired son on the money he cadges from the matrons he marries and dispatches, plays him as a parody of refinement, with his little trademark mustache and curled hair, his smoking jacket and roses, and his facetious, mannered style. The contrast between Verdoux's fussy gentility and his homicidal behavior is the main source of the comedy, at least in the early scenes. Verdoux, we learn, lost his job in a Paris bank after thirty years when the Depression hit; these murders are a desperate attempt to ensure the stability the modern world can't guarantee. And to enact them, he's invented a high-class persona that's like the flip side of the parodies the younger Chaplin perfected of effete snobbery. *Monsieur Verdoux* is unclassifiable. It occasionally recalls Balzac (especially in the depiction of the squabbling family of one of Verdoux's victims) and Shaw (the tone), but it's a different animal from either. Neither of those writers could have conceived Henri Verdoux, perhaps the most fascinating by-product imaginable of Chaplin's chilly, misanthropic personality. Verdoux professes to love his wife and son, but he confines them to a cottage with a garden and a whitewashed fence that feels like a mausoleum, and he seems tense and old in their company. He can hardly wait to get back to work—rushing about France, plotting his larcenies, detailing his murder schemes, improvising wittily when he meets an unexpected obstacle. That's when he seems most alive. He picks up a girl (Marilyn Nash), lately out of prison, to try out a new poison on, slipping the fateful glass of wine out of her grasp when he discovers that she isn't the world-weary misery he took her for and in fact, like him, has loved and nursed an invalid. But he finds her optimism somehow threatening. In the movie's most haunting moment, she approaches him innocently in the street later to renew their acquaintance, and he dismisses her coldly with some cash and a warning to "go on about your business." Honestly, I don't know what to make of this movie, which may come across in ways that Chaplin didn't intend. But it's a sort of black comedy and a sort of high comedy, though it fails at both.

In the other dark comedies of manners from the forties and fifties, fame is as critical an aspect of elevated social status as money. The paradigm is *Citizen*

*Kane*, with its fictionalized version of the newspaper magnate William Randolph Hearst, here called Charles Foster Kane and played by director Orson Welles. Though *Kane* contains only one sequence that's in pure high-comedy style—the series of blackouts, set entirely at the breakfast table, that depicts the disintegration of Kane's marriage to his first wife, Emily (Ruth Warrick)—it allies itself with movies like *Rebecca* and *Laura* in presenting Kane's privileged world as simultaneously tempting and hollow. The movie begins with his solitary death—the only other human nearby is the nurse who finds his expired body—on a huge, baroque estate (Xanadu, named after the setting of Coleridge's "Kubla Khan") that's as unwelcoming as a desert. Like Manderley, the main house is a fairy-tale castle, and when we see it for the first time it's shrouded in mist and distinguished by warring elements that point up its exoticism: palm trees, caged monkeys, a beacon light with no evident source that appears and disappears at the window. Kane's story, which is told in jigsaw-puzzle-piece narratives and overlapping chronology by the people who knew him to a reporter who's trying to find out why his last word was "Rosebud," is a cautionary tale of the pitfalls of wealth and celebrity. How we're intended to respond to that life depends on whether we want to listen to the narrator who loved him most, his editor Bernstein (Everett Sloane), who sums him up as a man who lost everything he ever had, or the one who hated him most, his second wife, Susan Alexander (Dorothy Comingore)—who protests in one flashback, late in their benighted relationship, "You never gave me anything in your life! You just tried to—to buy me into giving *you* something." These mirror-opposite perspectives capture the same man, who inherits all the money in the world in childhood but loses his parents as a consequence, and never figures out how a man with all that wealth negotiates love. Certainly Welles's portrait of that paean to conspicuous consumption Xanadu, with its Olympian ceilings and canyon echoes, a showplace for joyless guests who trek out for picnics in cars as if they were driving behind a hearse, is ultimately damning.

*Citizen Kane* is a great movie, but it builds on our prejudices about the very rich, and—especially for 1941 audiences—our curiosity about how a man like Hearst might have lived. (*Might live*, actually, since Hearst, contrary to the death scene at the beginning, was still very much alive when RKO released the movie.) In the opening shots, the camera tracks past the chain-link fence with the "No Trespassing" sign, and intrusion is its chief motif: Welles takes us through locked gates, skylights, phone-booth glass, into the intimate details of Kane's private life. That invasive impulse is always present in this kind of movie, whether it purports to be a *film à clef*—like *Kane* or *Sweet Smell of Success* (1957, where Burt Lancaster's megalomaniac gossip columnist was inspired by Walter Winchell) or *Unfaithfully Yours* (1948, starring Rex Harrison as a conductor based on Sir Thomas Beecham) or *Caught* (1949, where the multimillionaire played by Robert Ryan is director Max Ophüls's version of Howard Hughes)—or whether it makes up a celebrity out of whole cloth, like the tennis star Guy Haines (Farley Granger) in *Strangers on a Train* (1951).

*Strangers on a Train*, directed by Hitchcock, is playful and venomous at the same time. This poisonous high comedy is the specialty of Patricia Highsmith, who wrote the novel on which Raymond Chandler and Czenzi Ormonde based the ingenious script. The murder plot has a brilliant Freudian twist. Guy is approached on a train by a fan, Bruno Antony (Robert Walker), who seems to know everything about him—that he's in love with Ann Morton (Ruth Roman), the daughter of a senator (Leo G. Carroll) in whose office Guy works when he's not on the court, and that he can't marry her unless his trampy wife Miriam (Laura Elliott) gives him a divorce. Bruno hates his father (Jonathan Hale) as much as Guy hates his wife, so he proposes that they "criss-cross" murders. The twist is that though Guy doesn't go along with it—he thinks Bruno is just gassing—Bruno's a sociopath who *does* murder Miriam and expects Guy to reciprocate. The social landscape of the movie is complicated. Bruno comes from money, and he has many of the aristocratic graces, like an easy (if creepy) charm and a talent for languages. He gives off the aura of an expensive education (though he confides to Guy that he was thrown out of several schools). He despises his father because the old man expects him to work for his money, not just sit back and enjoy his inheritance. When he shows up uninvited at a party at the senator's house, he fits in—that is, until his psychosis starts to show and he nearly strangles a benign society matron (Norma Varden) while his gaze is fixed on Ann's kid sister Barbara (Patricia Hitchcock), who looks enough like Miriam to make him relive the experience of choking *her*. There's a good joke here: Walker's sensationally witty performance is a wicked parody of high-class manners, so when he knocks the wind out of this poor, silly woman, no one in the room can figure out what just happened (except Barbara, who's understandably freaked out). Guy is a different sort of aristocrat—a sports celebrity (and in the most gentlemanly of sports). Young, handsome, and famous, he's welcome in any social circle, and he's a cinch to make it in politics after he puts down his racket for good. Bruno both sees in Guy a kindred spirit and envies him ("I certainly do admire people who do things"). And in the movie's (Freudian) terms, he's Guy's alter ego, the id to his superego, with the freedom to act in a way that the conscience-bound Guy never would. The only obstacle to Guy's happiness in Washington high society, with a beautiful, loving wife, is Miriam, who reneges on the divorce at the last minute when she learns she's pregnant and plans to use her marriage to Guy as a blind, lending respectability to her offspring, and as a conduit to the leisurely life he's leading and she isn't. (She's Rebecca de Winter as a schemer from the wrong side of the tracks.) Bruno removes that obstacle, neatly. It's as if Guy had made a pact with the devil—even though, on the narrative level, he never agreed to the murder swap. Symbolically, it's the dark part of him that made the pact, without letting the civilized part of him know about it.

There's nothing hidden about this Freudian level; Hitchcock, typically, puts it right on the surface. And it's amazing that the Hays Office didn't pick up on the homosexual subtext—Bruno's approaching Guy has the earmarks of a gay pick-up, and Walker infuses the role with a silken effete seductiveness. His Bruno is a classic psycho-killer, cultivated and insinuating, attached to his dotty mother (Marion Lorne) but with a hate on for his stern papa. But he plays the heterosexual card, too, coming on to Miriam at an amusement park, on an island that's accessible only via a rented boat from the Tunnel of Love. Miriam's identity is her sexual availability, so when he makes eyes at her she flirts right back, not realizing the stranger she's encouraging brings her death.

You can see the pattern in Highsmith—comedy of manners plus murder— if you look at *Strangers on a Train* side by side with *The Talented Mr. Ripley*, a film of another of her novels, directed by Anthony Minghella in 1999. Minghella (who also wrote the script) makes the sociopathic protagonist, Tom Ripley (Matt Damon)—a chameleon from a poor background who attaches himself to a young aristocrat named Dickie Greenleaf (Jude Law), kills him, and takes over his identity. He is made explicitly gay where Highsmith only hints. (It's hard to imagine filming this material at the end of the twentieth century without doing so.) The movie doesn't work; it isn't unsettling enough, though it's intelligently conceived and elegantly made. But it does have a terrific central joke. Dickie's friends—played by Gwyneth Paltrow, Cate Blanchett, and (in a very funny sketch of a spoiled young American abroad) Philip Seymour Hoffman—keep popping up at inconvenient moments and throwing Tom's schemes in danger. Of course they're everywhere: This social set is so insulated that they're constantly running into each other, because they all go to the same places and collectively they form the group that, individually, they seek out wherever they wind up. (This is part of the joke in *Six Degrees of Separation*, too.) That's the danger Tom has to contend with when he tries to slip into this aristocracy.

The most frivolous of these unflattering high-comic portraits of the aristocracy is *Unfaithfully Yours*, written and directed by Preston Sturges. It's arguably his finest film, though its box-office failure was a disaster his career never recovered from, and though he dismissed the film in his autobiography as a "seven-course special" that left audiences hungry.[1] The genre mix is thick even for Sturges: not only his usual unbalanced screwball farce with slapstick, but also black comedy and high comedy. It's the only one of Sturges's movies that really qualifies as high comedy, though *The Lady Eve* (1941), where Barbara Stanwyck impersonates a titled Englishwoman to avenge herself on the Yankee heir (Henry Fonda) who broke her heart, is a romantic comedy with high-comic filigree. In *Unfaithfully Yours* Rex Harrison, softly mustachioed and thin as a rail, plays an émigré British conductor, Sir Alfred de Carter, who comes from money (his family made it on laxatives—a typical deflating detail in a Sturges picture) and is enjoying a fabulous career as a sexy popularizer of serious music. He believes it should be enjoyed flat on your back, with a sandwich and plenty of pretty girls around. And he's married to a beautiful woman, Daphne (Linda Darnell), whose public displays of affection for him are so syrupy and photogenic that the de Carters always seem to be posing for a spread in *Life* on the happy home lives of the glamorously wealthy. But aside from Sir Alfred, nobody buys into her fidelity—not her hard-boiled sister Barbara (Barbara Lawrence, in an older version of the role Diana Lynn plays in Sturges's *The Miracle of Morgan's Creek* [1944]) or Barbara's pragmatic, humorless husband, August (Rudy Vallee), who, misunderstanding a casual directive of Sir Alfred's to take care of Daphne while he's away on tour, has hired a gumshoe to trail her. What he comes up with seems to implicate Sir Alfred's secretary Tony (Kurt Kreuger, handsome in a bland, operetta-tenor way) in an affair with Daphne. So that night, at a sold-out concert, Sir Alfred, whose glittering, larger-than-life personality includes a high-comic facility with language (Sturges wrote some of his best one-liners for this character) and an explosive temper, fantasizes three revenge scenarios while conducting three famous pieces of music.

To Rossini's *Semiramide Overture*, he devises a plot to murder Daphne and frame Tony, reveling in his own ingenuity and indulging his fantasy to the limit. This is where Harrison's technique really shines: He plays the scene like a Noël Coward farce, shaping the pauses in wondrous ways and twisting the phrase "the purple one with the plumes at the hips"—a description of the gown he encourages Daphne to wear as he sets up her death—so that it sounds increasingly insinuating and ridiculous at the same time. He's eccentrically fervent here, and his homicidal madness is savagely funny— Buñuelian. Sturges uses the Rossini for its speed and its flamboyance, and the climax, where Sir Alfred chortles as the cymbals crash—a flourish in the music he described to the percussionist in rehearsal as the composer's "brazen laugh"—is wickedly audacious. (American audiences in 1948—or any other year—would have found a scene like this one too chilly for comfort.) To the *Pilgrim's Chorus* from Wagner's *Tannhäuser*, with its grandiose romantic melancholy, Sir Alfred plays the noble self-sacrificer, handing over his wife to her lover with a fat check so she never wants for anything as he intones flowery sentiments like "I couldn't understand music as well as I do if I didn't understand the human heart." His melodramatic posturing is priceless as he presents himself, for his own delectation, as generous, wise, and gloriously impaled on his bottomless love for Daphne. Finally, as he conducts Tchaikovsky's *Francesca da Rimini*, he plays the role of the devil-may-care romantic, throwing his fate to the winds as he challenges Tony to a game of Russian roulette—and loses. (Bergman uses the Russian roulette scenario for the climax of *his* high comedy, *Smiles of a Summer Night*, though all his hero comes away with is a face full of soot.) These three sequences, back to back, are among the funniest exploration of narcissism in American movies.

Alexander Mackendrick's *Sweet Smell of Success* is, of these movies, the least like a comedy of manners in style, but it shares with the others a cynical insider's view of celebrity. The protagonist is an outsider who'd give his right arm to be an insider, and who's right on the cusp. He's Sidney Falco (Tony Curtis), a quick-witted, weaselly press agent who courts the monarch of Manhattan night life, the columnist and television personality J. J. Hunsecker (Burt Lancaster). (Curtis and Lancaster give classic performances.) Falco is forever begging for J. J.'s scraps—items in J. J.'s column spotlighting his clients—but when the film begins, J. J. is starving him out as punishment for failing to execute one of the dirty deeds he hands out routinely to his lackeys. The price of readmission to the court of Hunsecker is to break up a romance between J. J.'s neurotic sister Susie (Susan Harrison) and a jazz musician, Steve Dallas (Martin Milner), discredit him by planting marijuana on him (the whitewashed Dallas, who gets to express the movie's outrage with the Hunseckers of the world, appears to be the only jazz musician in New York who *doesn't* smoke weed), and set him up for a beating by a sadistic cop (Emile Meyer) who owes Hunsecker a favor. (Dallas's punishment intensifies after he insults J. J. to his face.) The scheme is heinous, but the reward is irresistible: Sidney gets to write J. J.'s column while the great man is vacationing in Europe.

The movie's film noir credentials come with a fascinating variation. Instead of a traditional femme fatale, it offers Hunsecker as the devil who tempts—and ultimately destroys—the protagonist with a promise that he can abandon his seedy gofer's existence and move "way up high . . . where it's always balmy." (Falco doesn't have principles—he pimps his own sometime girlfriend, a hapless cigarette girl played memorably by Barbara Nichols. But he does have a conscience, and going against its dictates makes him look permanently sour and ulcerated.) And, like that of Waldo Lydecker and Bruno Antony, J. J.'s sexuality is certainly ambiguous. He passes judgment on the sexual activities of others from a great height (he makes a crack about the young woman whom a married senator, a presidential hopeful, is transparently squiring). But in a world where every other columnist seems to walk around town with a twenty-four-hour hard-on, we never see J. J. with any woman except his sister, whom he controls so maniacally that he may possibly have unacknowledged incestuous feelings for her. Or possibly not—Hunsecker seems too prim and slithery for sex, and it's just as likely that his borderline-insane overprotectiveness is simply his way of looking after someone he thinks of as his own property.

Like Waldo, J. J. is pumped up with his own self-importance, but the screenwriters, Clifford Odets and Ernest Lehman, go so far as to make him a demagogue, a homegrown fascist poisoned by power. In this entertainingly exaggerated urban world, a columnist who's syndicated all over the world and has his own TV spot has the clout to close down the career of anyone he has a grudge against. And I guess it's more plausible to devise a gossip columnist who wields that much power than a critic. (Both the architecture critic in King Vidor's *The Fountainhead* [1949], a *film à clef* with a hero based on Frank Lloyd Wright, and the theater critic in *All About Eve* have farfetched sway over the careers of their subjects.) After all, Louella Parsons, Hearst's columnist, managed to do a lot of damage to Orson Welles for the insult of *Citizen Kane*.

*Sweet Smell of Success* is as stylized in its dialogue as any high comedy, though the style belongs to Odets, the gifted playwright whose star rose when he wrote the signature plays for the Group Theatre in the mid-thirties—*Waiting for Lefty, Awake and Sing! Paradise Lost, Golden Boy*. As a dramatic writer, Odets is a weird case, a Chekhov-influenced realist with a taste for florid poetic vernacular. That's a flaw in a naturalistic play like *Awake and Sing!* but in *Sweet Smell of Success*, which is entirely artificial, the preposterously overstated metaphoric-tough language seems right at home. In a Philip Barry comedy, you expect the characters, whose background and education have made them highly articulate, to give detailed verbal expression to their feelings. Here, in the most amusingly low-class version yet of high (celebrity) society, the characters are similarly overarticulate and their language similarly high-flown, though God knows it doesn't sound Ivy League. (J. J. is as proud of his idiomatic column prose as if it were Faulkner.) "I'd hate to take a bite out of you," J. J. comments to Sidney. "You're a cookie full of arsenic." And Falco characterizes Dallas's problem as "integrity—acute—like indigestion."

The most interesting of these films—the one with the most unusual texture—is *Caught*. Max Ophüls, the great German-Jewish director whose international career was the result of his efforts to elude the Nazis, had a miserable sojourn in Hollywood, but two of the four films he made there, *Letter from an Unknown Woman* (1948) and *Caught*, are among the most remarkable of their era. *Letter from an Unknown Woman* seems particularly miraculous: a movie set in turn-of-the-century Vienna that rarely gives the impression of having been made in America. It's of a piece with films Ophüls released in Germany before he had to flee (like his 1932 adaptation of the Arthur Schnitzler play *Liebelei*) and the ones he directed in France after he left Hollywood (especially his masterpiece, *The Earrings of Madame de . . .* )—a delicate intertwining of high comedy and romantic melodrama. The script (by Howard Koch, out of a Stefan Sweig story) takes the form of a long letter written to a thoughtless roué, a concert pianist (Louis Jourdan) who has thrown away both the gifts fate has afforded him—his musical talent and the love of a woman who threw away her *life* for him—because he was too shallow to appreciate either. He's like Marcher in Henry James's "The Beast in the Jungle," but the movie, unlike James's story, isn't from his point of view (though it ends the same way—with his too-late epiphany). It's about Lisa Berndle (Joan Fontaine), whose adoration of Stefan Brand elevates him beyond his worth. She worships him as a schoolgirl would, when he moves in next door to her and her widowed mother (Mady Christians), and she listens to him play. And when Frau Berndle remarries and the family moves to Linz, a garrison town, it's the idea of Stefan that prevents her from getting engaged to the lieutenant (John Good) her parents see as a respectable match. Instead she moves back to Vienna, where she continues to watch Stefan. They meet—he doesn't recognize his one-time neighbor—and become lovers. But then he goes on a concert tour and forgets her. She bears his child, marries a wealthy man (Marcel Journet), and leads a contented life. Then one day she sees Stefan again, at the opera, and realizing that she's never loved anybody else, she gives up her marriage for him. But again he doesn't recall who she is, so she runs away. Only after their son dies of typhus and she herself is on her deathbed does she write to Brand, putting together all the pieces of their story, a great, if one-sided, romance.

The fin-de-siècle Austrian setting, the irony, the candied visual style (the magnificent production design is by Alexander Golitzen) are all trademarks of high comedy, and the contrast of extravagant Vienna high society with the fussy propriety of provincial Linz, where the best Lisa's lieutenant can do by way of musical entertainment is to escort her to the Sunday-afternoon concerts of the local military band, suggests some of the observations in Chekhov's *Three Sisters*. You can't imagine how, in 1948 Hollywood, Ophüls managed to get an ensemble that, with only one or two exceptions, seems so European. A scene in a café where an all-female band bitches that Stefan and Lisa won't stop dancing and let them go home is almost a blueprint for the celebrated waltz montage with Danielle Darrieux and Vittorio De Sica in *The Earrings of Madame de . . .* And one sequence is unlike anything in an American movie post-1940. Stefan takes Lisa to an arcade for a mock train ride, where they sit in a stationary vehicle while the proprietor runs painted dioramas depicting the landscapes of various countries past their window. The theatricality of the moving backdrops is distinctly nineteenth century, and it reminds us of the sublime artifice of the whole film. When they reach "the end of the line," neither emerges from the train compartment at first— they're wrapped in a kiss. When Stefan does, finally, he goes up to the booth to pay for another tour, but they've exhausted all the countries the ride offers, so he opts to start all over. "We'll revisit the scenes of our youth," he quips as he rejoins Lisa in the train.

*Letter to an Unknown Woman* isn't quite in the same class as *Madame de . . .* because Lisa is too single-minded for a great heroine. In *Madame de . . .* a countess (Darrieux) who prizes material things above feelings pawns a set of earrings, a wedding gift from her husband (Charles Boyer), to pay some debts and lies to cover their disappearance. Then, unexpectedly, she finds herself falling sincerely in love for the first time. The experience deepens her, but ironically a lie she tells her lover (De Sica) for the best of reasons—to save his feelings—convinces him, after he learns the truth, that she's really shallow. Both lies focus on the earrings, which wound up in her lover's possession and which once more she receives as a present. Now they mean the world to her, but he can't believe that. The movie is like a Maupassant story, with real emotional depth. You can see how the man who made it would also be drawn to the irony at the core of *Letter from an Unknown Woman*.

By contrast, Ophüls's next picture, *Caught*, broaches an American subject. The heroine is Leonora Ames (played by the gifted stage actress Barbara Bel Geddes—the original Maggie the Cat in Tennessee Williams's *Cat on a Hot Tin Roof*—who never got the movie career she deserved). Leonora lives in a cramped L.A. flat with her friend Maxine (Ruth Brady), gazing at furs and jewels in ritzy magazines and dreaming of the millionaire on a white charger who will rescue her from her drab working-class life. She goes to charm school and lands a job as a dress-shop model. That's where she's spotted by an oily character named Franzi (Curt Bois) who invites her to a party on Smith Ohlrig's yacht. She doesn't want to go—she figures she's being pimped. But Maxine tells her Ohlrig is fantastically rich and persuades her to change her mind, arguing, "Girls like us can't pick the way we meet men like Smith Ohlrig." And she does meet Ohlrig (Robert Ryan), who's impressed with her looks and struck by her unconventional reluctance to go to bed with him. He marries her—mostly, it seems, to piss off his shrink (Art Smith, Stefan's valet in *Letter to an Unknown Woman*), who tells him he doesn't love her and is making a mistake that he and Leonora will both regret. Ohlrig is one of several attempts to put Howard Hughes on the screen. If Jason Robards and director Jonathan Demme capture the lonesome, melancholy Hughes at the end of his life in *Melvin and Howard* (1980), Ryan and Ophüls dramatize the arrogant megalomaniac Hughes at the peak of his power. Pauline Kael reveals in *5001 Nights at the Movies* that Ophüls hated Hughes, who produced his Hollywood pictures, squandering his talent and insulting him into the bargain, and that Arthur Laurents based the screenplay of *Caught* on the director's personal anecdotes about Hughes and not on its official source, a Libbie Block novel called *Wild Calendar.*[2]

Ryan gets Hughes's dark, sleek, confident sexuality; he even looks like Hughes. And in Ohlrig's ruthless, cruelly reductive treatment of not only Leonora but everyone else he comes in contact with, we see an authentic American type: the man of legendary wealth and influence who is so removed, absolutely and irrevocably, from the way other people live that he never seems to have considered them as human at all. Ohlrig is linked to both Charles Foster Kane and the magnate Mel Gibson plays in the kidnap thriller *Ransom* (1996), but he's the most frightening of the three because he's the most detached from softer human needs. All he wants is victory over his enemies, and his vicious gamesmanship has made enemies of everyone. When Leonora walks out on him and he begs her to come back, he thinks he's being romantic, and momentarily he persuades *her* that he is. But he presents even this plea in the form of a demand, unyielding, and his reference to her rented room as shabby reinforces our image of him as disdainful of any lifestyle beneath his own impossibly elevated one. Laurents can't resist overanalyzing this character, but still, Ohlrig is a staggering dramatic creation—and, along with Mama Rose in the 1959 stage musical *Gypsy*, another narcissist—the best character writing Laurents has ever done.

*Caught* is, like *Melvin and Howard*, a treatise on the American dream as a Venus flytrap: Leonora gets "caught" in a web spun by her own dreams of wealth and comfort. Brought up to believe that a poor girl has to make herself charming so she can marry well, she falls in love with Ohlrig's money and then convinces herself that it's the man himself she loves. The movie tries to have it both ways with Leonora—she's a good girl at heart who really cares about Smith, *and* she's seduced by his wealth and can't get shut of her naive dreams of a life of ease, even after she's experienced the hellish side of that life. She's still holding onto those bogus dreams when she runs away from him: Working for a pediatrician named Quinada (James Mason), she observes casually to the mother of a patient that her little girl should enroll in elocution lessons, and Quinada has to lecture Leonora about acting like a Park Avenue hostess rather than a receptionist in a doctor's office.

Ohlrig/Hughes is the American dream as nightmare, and he has to come close to destroying Leonora before she can finally let go of her childhood fantasies about being rich. As Mrs. Smith Ohlrig, Leonora is incarcerated in a crueler and more pitiable existence than Susan Alexander Kane, because Kane at last makes some effort to be kind to Susan. (Her complaint is that he doesn't know how.) Leonora's ironic observation on her life—"That's what everybody wants, isn't it? Well, I've got it"—echoes Susan's "You don't want me, not really—you just want me to want you." In their manse on Long Island, Leonora is dressed up as an ornament to impress Smith's guests, waiting up until all hours for him to come home and then expected to play hostess at whatever hour he chooses to arrive. She barely sees him; she's not permitted to visit her family. She feels both imprisoned and abandoned. And when some little thing she does without thinking arouses his paranoid jealousy, he humiliates her. Maxine can't understand what she has to complain about, and neither can Franzi, but Bel Geddes looks horribly uncomfortable in Leonora's new glittering hairstyle and weighed down by an ostentatious necklace and earrings, prematurely cast as a society matron. Ophüls emphasizes the artificiality of her lifestyle with an image of her in an evening gown—at three in the morning—listening to Franzi play piano, surrounded by décor that dwarfs her, while it snows picturesquely outside the window; the soundstage setting recalls Fran Dodsworth in Austria, pretending she can be a countess. When Leonora breaks free (temporarily) and goes to work for Quinada—Ohlrig's opposite number, whose love for her is true (the script is rather schematic in the division of the leading men up into the selfless, hardworking doctor and the self-absorbed, tyrannical millionaire)—he asks her what she was doing on Long Island before she took this job. She answers that she was a paid companion to a rich person.

Movies about show-business celebrities are a genre to themselves; I discussed some of them in chapter 2. But a film like *The Royal Family of Broadway* treats its theatrical monarchs with a mixture of amusement and affection. Other movies present the same jaded insider's view of Hollywood and other branches of the performing arts as *Citizen Kane* or *Caught* offers of the kind of wealth that myths are made of—though generally they sentimentalize show

biz at the same time as they claim to expose its corruption. Even Preston
Sturges couldn't stop himself from going soft in the second half of *Sullivan's
Travels* (1941), where a successful Hollywood director (Joel McCrea) who gets
it in his head that he should be making socially conscious pictures like *The
Grapes of Wrath* (1940) learns—the hard way, on a chain gang—the importance of laughter. (The first half of the film looks ahead to Paul Mazursky's
satirical high comedies about living well in L.A.) A glossy tell-all melodrama
like *The Bad and Beautiful*, directed by Vincente Minnelli in 1952, sets up the
producer (Kirk Douglas) as a manipulative son of a bitch who sells everyone
down the river, but the flashbacks to the stories of the talented associates who
swore they'd never work with him again—a director (Barry Sullivan), an actress (Lana Turner), and a screenwriter (Dick Powell)—reveal how much he
really helped them get where they are today. (They all change their minds at
the end of the picture and agree to collaborate with him on the comeback picture that will lift him out of the ash heap.)

No movie is more schizoid about Hollywood, perhaps, than *A Star Is
Born*—in both its 1937 and its 1954 incarnations. (The less said about the
1976 version, which transposes the story to the rock-music world and stars
Barbra Streisand and Kris Kristofferson, the better.) Its original and best form
is the 1932 movie *What Price Hollywood?* which George Cukor directed, from
a script a number of writers, credited and uncredited, worked on. The marvelous Constance Bennett plays a Brown Derby waitress named Mary Evans
who's dying to get discovered, so she gets a co-worker to let her serve the famous director Max Carey (Lowell Sherman) when he shows up, plowed, at
the restaurant one night. When Max invites her to the premiere of his
movie—in his drunken state, he's forgotten to pick up his real date—she
quits her job to accompany him, and when she's nice enough to see him
home safely afterward, he shows his gratitude by casting her in a bit in his
next picture. After she becomes a star, she remembers her debt to him, even
when he drinks himself out of his own career. The movie is a hard-boiled
comedy mixed with melodrama—like *Stage Door*—but the late scenes, where
Sherman shifts from merry drunk to washed-up alky, are amazing in the way
Barrymore's are in *Dinner at Eight*. (It's widely believed that Barrymore was
the model for Max Carey. One of the uncredited writers, Gene Fowler, wrote
a biography of him, and Sherman, who gives the performance of his career in
the role, was Barrymore's brother-in-law.[3])

*A Star Is Born* has a built-in masochism that's happily missing from *What
Price Hollywood?* though some heavy hitters worked on the screenplay—
Dorothy Parker and Alan Campbell on the first version (directed by William
Wellman), Moss Hart on the second (directed by Cukor). Its treatment of

Norman Maine, the alcoholic actor whose messy public decline is juxtaposed with the rise of the actress Vicki Lester, whom he loves and marries, is luridly exhibitionistic in the way that Hollywood can be when it thinks it's being honest and stripping itself bare. Everyone who's seen the picture—either version—recalls the scene where Norman (Fredric March or James Mason) shows up smashed while Vicki (Janet Gaynor or Judy Garland) is giving her acceptance speech at the Oscars and, when she tries to intervene, he makes a wild, wide gesture that accidentally hits her smack in the face. Though both March and Mason give splendid performances (especially Mason), in both films this scene is phony, not only because it makes Norman's drunkenness into sensational melodramatic fodder, but because the loving, devoted Vicki, who never considers leaving this man, and who is even willing to abandon her career to take him away from Hollywood and nurse him back to sobriety, is an impossible paragon of virtue.

It's telling, I think, that all the actresses who have played this part, including Streisand, have been veterans, not newborn stars, and that both Gaynor and Garland were staging comebacks. There's something disingenuous about an established star wanting to be seen in this wholesome, self-sacrificing way. It didn't work for Gaynor, anyway, who seems wan and straining next to March, with a tired twinkle in her eyes. Garland's performance is legendary among her fans, but it's so overwrought that you can barely watch it. The material is shaped to contrast blooming youth and decaying, self-destructive middle age, but Garland, whose private struggles were far closer to Norman's than to Vicki's, looks puffy and wasted, the creases in her face sharp and shiny, her hair cut short so that she has a weirdly mannish appearance in some scenes—like a slightly woozy Peter Pan. It hardly seems possible that this run-through-the-mill Judy Garland could have grown out of the auburn-haired ingénue of Meet Me in St. Louis, The Clock, and The Harvey Girls. And her voice has already acquired the ragged, sobbing tremolo at the end of held notes that will be her trademark when she plays to worshipful crowds at Carnegie Hall and the Palace in the early sixties. She puts over her numbers (the 1954 remake is a musical; Vicki is a band singer who ends up making musicals in Hollywood) in what would come to be known as the Garland style: intense, heavily weighted, a disturbing combination of no-holds-barred torch singing and a nakedly eager bid for the approval of her audience. When she sings the Harold Arlen–Ira Gershwin "The Man That Got Away" at an after-hours jazz club, she steps into close-up, gazing past the musicians into a nonexistent crowd of admiring fans, her face scarred yet smiling hopefully, as if she were presenting her own heartbreak for our pleasure. She adds an extra layer of masochism to the movie.

There's real bitterness in the scenes between Maine and Matt Libby (Lionel Stander, in a skillful, stylized performance in the 1937 version, and Jack Carson, in a scathing one in the 1954 retread). Libby is the head PR man at the studio that has both Maine and Lester under contract. Cynical and nasty, he hates his job (this is clearer in the Cukor movie) and he especially hates Norman, whom he has to baby-sit in the days when he's still a valuable studio property. When Norman's career is in the toilet and Libby runs into him at the bar at the Santa Anita racetrack—where Norman, working hard to stay off the wagon, is drinking ginger ale—Libby takes the opportunity to vent his spleen. The ungloved force of his insults leads to an ugly altercation that leaves Norman on his ass on the floor of the bar, and of course everyone assumes he's just drunk again. So he *gets* drunk, and stays that way. Unlike most of the rest of the film, this scene, which Fitzgerald or O'Hara might have written—and which is virtually the same in both versions—feels genuine, not pumped up like the whitewashing of Esther (at one end of the spectrum) or the public striptease of an actor sliding toward his own inevitable destruction (at the other). The 1937 version has a follow-up that's even meaner. Norman, overhearing Esther's plans to give up her career for him, walks into the ocean, and Wellman cuts from the newspaper headline announcing his drowning to Libby asking a barkeep, "How do you wire congratulations to the Pacific Ocean?" while the two men enjoy a pop and a hearty laugh at the expense of the dead man.

The 1954 movie does have a hypnotic fascination, and its contradictions sum up the way Hollywood likes to present itself in a celebrity exposé. Cukor begins with the electric charge of the klieg lights outside a benefit, where the crowds watch for their favorite stars to arrive. The camera work is deliberately rough and restless, newsreel style, and Sam Leavitt's photography is textured and gritty, undercutting the glamour of the occasion. And Cukor takes us into corners the newsreel cameras wouldn't show us. The film is *about* spotlights, of course—about the complexities of the limelight, what it means to be in it and to fall out of it. Visually much of this version, shot in dark, reddish tones, is startling, like the image of Mason alone on an elevator in a dimly lit police precinct after he's been picked up on a drunk and disorderly. The lights here are the harsh, unwelcome flashes of the news cameras, to signal the only kind of fame left for Maine, and we see them again at his funeral, when a grieving Vicki is forced into the spotlight at a time when she yearns for solitude. (The treatment of the fans in the funeral scene is rather frightening—even more so in the 1937 version, where they get close enough to paw her and one woman screeches at her that Norman wasn't "so much"—not worth crying over.) Yet for all its alleged deglamorizing, *A Star Is Born* ends up romanticizing Norman Maine almost as much as Vicki Lester. Alcoholic narcissists like Norman—and that's how Mason plays him—don't end up making sacrifices for the women they love. The thing about the Norman Maines of the world, male and female, is that though they make you feel like a million bucks when they shine the warmth of their personality on you, they leave you in the cold when they turn it off. And they really do, as Norman says of himself in a moment of honesty, wreck everything they touch. The movie tries to have it both ways, but it only succeeds on that soap-opera level where the melodramatic gloss is more important than the suggestion of real life underneath.

I don't think you could make that charge against Billy Wilder's 1950 *Sunset Boulevard*. *A Star Is Born* includes some backstage glimpses of the way actors are screen-tested and the way movies are made (so does *What Price Hollywood?*), but the world Wilder and his coscreenwriters, Charles Brackett and D. M. Marshman Jr. beckon us into in the opening scenes of *Sunset Boulevard* is the workaday one of poor struggling bastards like Joe Gillis (William Holden), the voice-over narrator, who aren't having much luck making a living in Hollywood. The movie both honors and mocks the rules and habits of this strange, insulated community of contemporary (i.e., midcentury) Hollywood—and since it's possible to feel two ways about them, I wouldn't say this is hypocritical, like the exposing and romanticizing of Norman Maine. Examples of *Sunset Boulevard*'s mixed attitude toward Hollywood are the depleted relationship between a borderline down-and-outer like Joe and his golf-playing agent, and the depiction of Schwab's drugstore, which, Gillis explains, "some of us" think of as "headquarters . . . kind of a combination office, kaffeeklatsch, and waiting room." The stories Joe tries to sell to Paramount (where, of course, *Sunset Boulevard* was made) are from hunger; whatever freshness he may have had when he emigrated from Iowa (he's an ex-newspaperman) has been lost over several years of seeing his ideas twisted around by producers and other writers. This movie contains the funniest quips about the treatment of writers in Hollywood until Robert Altman's *The Player* four decades down the road; it may also be the first picture to show audiences how writers pitch their ideas. Joe is a tough cookie who talks in the kind of enjoyably overwritten witticisms you hear from Bogart's Philip Marlowe in *The Big Sleep*—or from Falco and Hunsecker in *Sweet Smell of Success*. But the movie does something unexpected with him, and that's what makes it memorable. When his creditors show up to repossess his car, he gives them chase and finally the slip. (As Pauline Kael writes in her capsule review of this movie in *5001 Nights at the Movies*, L.A. is a city where a young man can lose his honor but not his car.[4]) And the neighborhood where he ditches them is the part of Sunset Boulevard where the huge, baroque mansions bespeak the heyday of the silent stars, the Hollywood aristocracy of a bygone era. The one he wanders into belongs, as it turns out, to one of the biggest stars of them all, Norma Desmond (Gloria Swanson, an old-time star herself—of silents and early talkies—in a big comeback part). But Norma has been absent from the silver screen since sound came in.

This section of the movie begins like a haunted-house thriller, where a stranger's car breaks down on a stormy night and he's forced to knock on the door of a house we know he shouldn't enter. Only it's broad daylight, and sunny; this is L.A. And though Wilder lays on the Gothic elements, beginning with the setting and the occasion (Norma mistakes Gillis for the undertaker she's called to bury her pet chimp), and the script acknowledges its debt to *Great Expectations* in the depiction of a woman for whom time has stood still, it's also a film noir, a black comedy, and—most intriguingly—a hard-boiled comedy played against a high comedy. The carefully crafted contrast in the movie is between the modern Hollywood, where writers like Joe and assistant directors like his pal Artie Green (Jack Webb) struggle to get work and grouse good-naturedly about how tough things are (that's the hard-boiled comedy part), and the forgotten Hollywood of the twenties, which is where Norma still resides (that's the high comedy part). It's canny of Wilder to use the resources of Gothic fiction on the old-world (in the terms of thoughtless, fast-changing Hollywood) aristocracy, not only because it makes sense to see the bizarre narrative through a Gothic lens, but also because, like the iris shot Welles employs in *The Magnificent Ambersons* at the end of the sleigh ride sequence, it underscores the faraway quality of this world.

A particularly eloquent example of how Wilder contrasts the two worlds is the New Year's Eve sequence. Joe has moved into Norma's house, originally as a collaborator to edit the screenplay she's written about Salome as an intended vehicle for her return to motion pictures. Pretty much bankrupt, he pretends to have some sympathy for this impossible project for his own purposes. But he becomes her constant companion and she pays for everything—including a set of clothes far too fancy for the life he led before he began to reside on Sunset Boulevard. On New Year's Eve, she makes it explicit that she thinks of him as a paramour as well. She hires an orchestra and a banquet, but Joe is her only guest. He hides his discomfort with the usual sardonic wisecracks, but she sees through them to his refusal to accept her affections and sweeps out of the room. Craving escape from the suffocating atmosphere of decay and self-delusion, he lands on Artie's doorstep and finds a loud, congenial party in progress. The affable cramped quarters are in sharp contrast to the tomblike ballroom where he and Norma have the tiled dance floor (installed at Valentino's insistence) all to themselves; Artie's punch is a counterpoint to Norma's champagne. Of course, Joe's tux makes him stand out among the other revelers. And Betty Schaefer (Nancy Olson), Artie's girl, the Paramount script reader who wants to be a screenwriter and who's been trying to get Joe to collaborate with her—Betty, who becomes his lifeline for a while, as he slips away from Sunset Boulevard in the wee hours to hammer out a *real* script, and with whom he inevitably falls in love—is Norma's opposite number. (In every way, unfortunately: Olson is as drab and uninteresting as Swanson is colorful and intriguing.)

*Sunset Boulevard* is really Joe's story more than Norma's; it's about his willing submersion into her rotting aristocratic world (though he tries to distance himself from it with irony and wisecracks), then his discovery that it's dragging him down. By the time he has that revelation, however, it's too late for him to retreat. He calls the mansion from Artie's to ask Norma's factotum, Max (Erich von Stroheim), to pack his things, and finds out that "Madame" has tried to kill herself by slashing her wrists. And his compassion for her overcomes his desire to escape from her clutches. He makes love to her (the mixture of pity and distaste on Holden's face, which Kael notes,[5] is the most amazing moment in an altogether remarkable performance). Once he's become her kept man in every sense of the term, he's doomed. The only escape possible to him is the one we see in the movie's opening images of him (though we don't yet *know* it's Joe), dead and floating in Norma Desmond's pool.

Far more remains to be said about this movie than I have space for—a discussion of Max, Norma's one-time director-husband, who now keeps the museum of her life intact and writes fan letters to preserve her illusions about her undiminished stardom; an examination of the way Wilder uses the images of the silent era, like the clips from the one movie Swanson actually did for Stroheim, the notorious, unreleased debacle *Queen Kelly.* I'll restrict myself to a reference to one other scene. When the *Salome* script is completed, Norma sends it to her favorite director, Cecil B. De Mille, at Paramount, then she has Max drive her and Joe there one afternoon to surprise him on the set of his latest picture. Someone from Paramount has been calling her, but she figures it's an underling of De Mille's, so she won't speak to him; she'll only talk to the great man himself. (It turns out the studio just wants to borrow her antique car for a shoot, but Max and De Mille see to it that she never learns the truth.) The guard at the gate doesn't know who she is and is reluctant to let her on the lot, but as luck would have it, an older guard who recognizes her is still on the job, too, and he treats her with the deference she's used to. And when De Mille ushers her onto his set, suddenly she finds there are people who remember her—a grip, a wardrobe lady. It's a very touching moment, and given the unsparing nature of Wilder's movie and our certainty that the story will end in tragedy, a wholly unanticipated one. Norma, with Max's help, lives as if the world had never advanced past the roaring twenties. She entertains old movie friends for games of bridge, she screens her own movies, she entertains Joe with impersonations of silent-era stars. She leaves her mansion only to visit the "waxworks," as Joe calls her friends (among them are Buster Keaton, H. B. Warner, and other veteran actors whom many in a 1950 audience would have remembered), or when, on one occasion, she takes Joe out to buy him clothes. And then the men's shop she patronizes (Max locates it for her) isn't significantly different from one she might have chosen to outfit a lover twenty-five years earlier. But now here she is back at the studio where she had her triumphs decades earlier, and though of course it's changed in a hundred ways (Max points out a few of them to Gillis), the recognition of these old-timers distances her from those changes. It's as if the world had conspired to collude in Norma's delusion—to close the gap between her and the world outside her Sunset Boulevard mansion. In Pirandello's *Henry IV*, a man falls from his horse while costumed as a king from centuries earlier, and the fall damages his brain, freezing him in the role of Henry IV, so his friends furnish a setting for him to live in that allows him to go on believing that's who he is. This scene from *Sunset Boulevard* recalls Pirandello's masterpiece.

The theatrical aristocracy writer-director Joseph L. Mankiewicz portrays in *All About Eve* (released the same year, 1950) isn't as sinister as Wilder's, but it's another—perhaps the most sheerly enjoyable—example of how Hollywood in this period presents an envenomed high-society world. *All About Eve* is the only one of the movies under discussion in this chapter that I would have no hesitation describing as an out-and-out high comedy, largely because of the deliciously artificial, often bitchy banter of the characters, and because of the performances, particularly Bette Davis's as the queen of the legitimate theater, Margo Channing, and George Sanders's as the critic Addison De Witt. Mankiewicz had already tried his hand at banter—and at a blending of comic styles—in the previous year's *A Letter to Three Wives*. That movie has a premise that fits both high comedy and melodrama. In a New York suburb, three women, best of friends, receive a letter from another in their social set, Addie Ross (whom we never see, but who, in the person of Celeste Holm, provides the occasional voice-over narration). The letter informs them that she's run off with one of their husbands. They won't learn which one until the end of the day; meantime each thinks back on the problems in her own marriage. The three flashbacks are in different styles and tones. Deborah (Jeanne Crain) recalls the night Brad (Jeffrey Lynn), whom she met in the service during the war, first took her out to meet his friends and she felt shabby and inadequate. Rita (Ann Sothern, whose sophisticated, slightly theatrical style is fitting equipment for comedy of manners), who writes for the radio, invites her sponsors (Florence Bates and Hobart Cavanaugh) to a dinner party, where their rudeness and self-absorption brings out the most caustic side of her English-teacher husband, George (Kirk Douglas). And we see how Lora Mae (Linda Darnell) got her boss, Porter (Paul Douglas), the owner of a chain of highly successful department stores, to marry her and rescue her from the wrong side of the tracks—but still can't convince herself that he really loves her. The sequences are of variable quality: The dinner party, though it bears some resemblance to the one in *Alice Adams*, is the most strained and overwritten; Porter's and Lora Mae's courtship is the most sharply observed and most touchingly acted. But they all flirt with high-comic concerns—class, social rituals—and they provide an intriguing study of the social life of a suburban town.

Mankiewicz's love of jigsaw-puzzle flashbacks and shifting point of view runs in the family: His brother Herman was the major force behind the script of *Citizen Kane* (though its structure was borrowed from Preston Sturges, who, as a young screenwriter, had introduced it in *The Power and the Glory* in 1933). You find it in *A Letter to Three Wives*, in *All About Eve*, and again in *The Barefoot Contessa* (1954), a purplish, fairly ridiculous purported exposé of Hollywood venality. In *All About Eve* several voice-over narrators share the task of telling us all about Eve Harrington (Anne Baxter) as she receives the Sarah Siddons Award, the movie's version of the Antoinette Perry (Tony) Award for outstanding leading performance in a Broadway play. They are Margo Channing, Addison De Witt, and Margo's closest friend, Karen Richards (Celeste Holm), whose husband, Lloyd Richards (Hugh Marlowe), wrote Eve's play and most of Margo's successes. The other major character, Bill Sampson (Gary Merrill), is the director and Margo's longtime significant other. These characters, in addition to the producer, Max Fabian (Gregory Ratoff), and Margo's maid, Birdie (Thelma Ritter), a no-nonsense retired vaudevillian, represent the theatrical aristocracy at the heart of the film. And the movie has the usual Hollywood ambivalence toward it. We're meant to enjoy the squabbling and the flamboyant outbursts, high on emotional octane, and the behind-the-scenes backbiting and underhandedness, while participating in the movie's adoration of these people. Or most of them: There's no affection for Eve, a schemer who reinvents herself to become a star and stops at nothing, including adultery and blackmail, to get there. And there's no affection, exactly, for De Witt, though his acerbic bons mots are among the movie's great pleasures—and though it's his intervention (for entirely selfish reasons) that ultimately prevents Eve from absconding with Karen's husband.

Taking our cue from Mankiewicz, we love the others as much because of their insecurities and obstinacy and self-centeredness as because of their talent and depth of feeling, their literacy and wit. Ultimately they're benign monsters; all the malevolence is housed, conveniently, in Eve and Addison. And the characters' devotion to the theater is as amusingly self-important and affected as it is in *The Royal Family of Broadway*, though Mankiewicz isn't as conscientiously parodic as Kaufman and Ferber. "It is very important that you know where you are, and why you are here," begins Addison's pompous voice-over, and he goes on to explain that the Sarah Siddons is "the highest award our theater knows." The "our" is telling: De Witt considers himself as essential a part of the legitimate theater (as it used to be called) as Margo or Bill or Lloyd. Naturally it is De Witt, whose weekly column chronicles the careers of these lords and ladies, who identifies each one for us—Karen, educated at Radcliffe (where she met Lloyd when he came to lecture), is "of the theater by marriage," while Margo, who made her debut at the age of four, is "a great star and a true star, and she will never be anything else." Note that

*The outsider who'd do anything to get into the theatrical aristocracy: Anne Baxter as Eve (back to camera) with Celeste Holm, Hugh Marlowe, and Bette Davis in Joseph L. Mankiewicz's* All About Eve *(1950). Credit: 20th Century Fox/The Kobal Collection*

the theatrical royalty doesn't require Karen's social credentials; in fact, when she's drunk and belligerent, Margo burlesques them. Margo's proud of her working-class origins—and she doesn't treat Birdie, a lifelong pal, as a servant, but as a sort of live-in companion. Membership in this exclusive club is a consequence of talent, though everyone in it has a broad knowledge of the other arts and speaks as eloquently as the characters in a Philip Barry play.

The movie makes much of the difference between Margo and Eve, though we have to take everyone's word for it that Eve is a first-rate actress who deserves praise for her performances, if not for her humanity. (If I sound a mite unconvinced, it's because Anne Baxter is *not* a first-rate actress, and in fact, as Pauline Kael points out, the movie's flaw is that though it's premised on the threat Eve poses to Margo, both professionally and personally, you can't take seriously the idea that Davis would have anything to fear from Baxter.[6] This is Davis's best performance, which is saying a lot.) Even though Margo goes in for big scenes—which are shaped by her impeccable style and sharpened by her withering way with a putdown—we're never cued to think that anything about her is the least bit phony. A possible exception is the great-lady performance she puts on when Karen first introduces her to Eve, her most dedicated fan, who has attended every performance of Margo's hit, *Aged in Wood*, and hung around the theater afterward for a glimpse of her idol. (Birdie punctuates Margo's airs neatly on this occasion with a crack about her playing Hamlet's mother.) The old idea—we saw it in *The Royal Family of Broadway*—that the theater gets all mixed up with real life if you're a veteran actor is alive in Margo, but that doesn't mean that the feelings she expresses in her big scenes, her terror of growing old and her insecurity about holding on to Bill (who is eight years her junior), are trumped up. Eve, by contrast, is insincere. You can't trust any emotion she floats in any situation, except on the rare occasions when she strips off her mask and exposes the nakedness of her ambition—as she does when she blackmails Karen into agreeing to get Lloyd to star her rather than Margo in his next play.

You can hear how much less respect the movie has for Eve in the difference between her language and that of the other characters. "You can breathe it, can't you? Like some magic perfume" is the best Eve can do, describing the atmosphere when Karen takes her backstage. Even Bill's windy lectures about the theater (which the movie—and the other characters—make fun of) are pithier, and Addison's speeches, pumped up as they are with his self-aggrandizing self-delight, are at least as much fun as Sheridan Whiteside's in *The Man Who Came to Dinner*. (De Witt is Whiteside without the sentimentality—thank heaven.) And when the *real* aristocrats get going, their exchanges can be juicy, their language marvelously artificial and epigrammatic. Here's my favorite exchange, an argument between Margo and Lloyd when he dares to praise Eve's performance, in Margo's role, when an aspiring actress (Marilyn Monroe) reads to replace one of the supporting players:

> Margo: All playwrights should be dead for three hundred years.
> Lloyd: That would solve none of their problems, because actresses never die. The stars never die, and they never change.
> Margo: You may change this star any time you want, for a new and fresh and exciting one. . . .
> Lloyd: I shall never understand the weird process by which a body with a voice suddenly fancies itself as a mind. Just when exactly does an actress decide they're her words she's saying, and her thoughts she's expressing?
> Margo: Usually at the point when she has to rewrite and rethink them to keep the audience from leaving the theater.
> Lloyd: It's about time the piano realized it has not written the concerto!

The shifting points of view and the use of flashbacks are meant to serve the same purpose here—and in *The Barefoot Contessa*, and in *The Bad and the Beautiful* (not written by a Mankiewicz, but borrowing heavily and ineffectually from both *All About Eve* and *Citizen Kane*)—as they seem at first to serve in *Kane*. And, come to think of it, Joe Gillis's voice-over has the same purpose in *Sunset Boulevard*. Gillis begins by assuring us that the story we're about to hear, which will explain how a body wound up floating in the pool of some forgotten silent-movie star, is the unvarnished truth, before the gossip columnists have glamorized and distorted it. *All About Eve* makes a claim in its title to tell us truths that the newspaper coverage of her award—and Addison De Witt's much-read column—won't reveal, and the multiple points of view are a way to assure that those truths are complete, that we get everyone's point of view. It's the promise of any show-biz movie: to provide an insider's view, however unpersuasive that view may sometimes be (*The Bad and the Beautiful*). But all the perspectives *Citizen Kane* gathers on the life of its famous dead protagonist don't really add up, the way they do in *All About Eve*; if the movie called itself *All About Kane*, the title would have to be ironic. For all the reporter Thompson's intrusion into the life of his subject, what we come away with is his line, when nobody is able to tell him what "Rosebud" means: "I don't think any word explains a man's life." That said, however, it's important to point out that though Thompson never finds out the meaning of "Rosebud," we do. Welles shows us Kane's childhood sled burning up in the furnace along with other useless acquisitions buried for years in the basement of Xanadu. We're in on the dark secret. That's the appeal of these poison-pen comedies of manners.

## Notes

1. Preston Sturges, *Preston Sturges by Preston Sturges*, adapted and edited by Sandy Sturges (New York: Simon & Schuster, 1990), 307.
2. Kael, *5001 Nights*, 126.
3. Kael, *5001 Nights*, 830.
4. Kael, *5001 Nights*, 729–730.
5. Kael, *5001 Nights*, 730.
6. Kael, *5001 Nights*, 16.

# CHAPTER FIVE

~

# The Aristocracy of the Hip

The only American movie between 1950's *All About Eve* and the very end of the sixties that you might be tempted to call a high comedy is Stanley Kubrick's adaptation of Vladimir Nabokov's *Lolita* (1962). Generically it's a black comedy mixed with sex farce, with a startlingly varied tone—sometimes broadly comic, sometimes tragicomic, sometimes satirical, melancholy, or (particularly in the opening scene, where Humbert Humbert confronts Clare Quilty and murders him) enigmatic. If anything qualifies it as comedy of manners, it's the style of the performances of James Mason (as Humbert) and Shelley Winters (as Charlotte Haze, whose house he boards in and whom he eventually marries as a way to get to her pubescent daughter, Lolita). Mason plays Humbert, a British émigré—an academic, a translator of French poetry, who has landed a gig teaching English at a school in a privileged small community called Ramsdale—as a silky roué who executes every scheming step to bring Lolita (Sue Lyon) closer; he brings to the role the self-delighted spring of a Noël Coward hero. Mason glides freestyle over some of the funniest lines in American movies, like his begging off from a late-night tête-à-tête with Charlotte because he fears "my neuralgia is about to strike . . . with heartburn, an old ally." One of the elements that make *Lolita* so entertaining is the contrast of Humbert's manner with the flat American suburban setting (which the movie sends up). And Winters's Charlotte is a faux aristocrat with a cigarette holder and a society laugh who boasts about the cultivated plane of the Ramsdale country-club set, interpolating French phrases into her chatter. She plays the role in tragicomic high style. Her pretentiousness is hilarious—she gives herself away every time she opens her mouth to say something like (to friends at a school dance) "Your Mona looks simply enchanting in that cloud of pink," in a breathy, affected voice. But her desperate yen for Humbert gets to you. (The movie is much more sympathetic to her than Nabokov is in his novel.)

But it wasn't really until Paul Mazursky's 1969 *Bob and Carol and Ted and Alice* that high comedy made a triumphant comeback in American movies. A new era was beginning in Hollywood. The big studios, having lost their shirts on too many antiquated, misbegotten projects (mostly gargantuan musicals nobody wanted to see), and suddenly alert to the fact that old-style studio thinking didn't take into account a new-style audience, opened their doors to long-haired young producers willing to gamble on talented, inventive writers and directors. Thus the counterculture invaded the film industry. And by chance, the most gifted generation of filmmakers since the silent movies—directors like Robert Altman, Sam Peckinpah, Francis Ford Coppola, Martin Scorsese, Irvin Kershner, Bob Fosse, Arthur Penn, and Hal Ashby, writers like Woody Allen, Robert Towne, Buck Henry, David Newman, and Robert Benton—were already at work in Hollywood. Some of them had been trained on the fly in live television, so they knew how to improvise; all of them were influenced by the Europeans (especially the French New Wave directors) and by revue-sketch comedy, as well as by the political and social concerns of the day. So they brought a contemporary sensibility to their films, as well as an inclination to experiment with new styles, unconventional stories, mixed tones.

Paul Mazursky was the clown prince of this "American renaissance" epoch. A natural comic who trained with Method acting teachers in the fifties (he played a punk in *The Blackboard Jungle*), he drifted into writing in the sixties, and with his first partner, Larry Tucker, he turned out *I Love You, Alice B. Toklas*, which was released in 1968. A revue-style comedy about a lawyer (Peter Sellers) who meets an ingenuous young hippie (Leigh Taylor-Young), gets high on her brownies, and drops out, it doesn't have much style—Hy Averback directed it—but it does have zing and a fresh perspective, and it made enough of a showing at the box office to land Mazursky a job directing his and Tucker's next screenplay. *Bob and Carol and Ted and Alice* caught both audiences (who adored it)—and critics (many of whom were snobbish about its appeal)—by surprise. It was the first attempt to create a high comedy with the new young California hipsters as the aristocratic heroes. Like their precursors in the Philip Barry movies, Bob (Robert Culp), who makes documentaries, and his wife Carol (Natalie Wood) enjoy a privileged lifestyle (in Beverly Hills), but the code of manners they embrace is the code of the sixties counterculture. That means that their sartorial style is contemporary (love beads, miniskirts, and leather jackets from the most expensive shops), their language is peppered with the latest youth vernacular ("man" as a term of affection), their politics are progressive (war toys are forbidden in their household, and Carol speaks Spanish to their housekeeper), their stimulant of choice is weed rather than alcohol, and their philosophy elevates the virtues of absolute honesty and broad-mindedness. Mostly, though, what makes this code so different from the one in *The Philadelphia Story* is that the rules the Philly upper classes adhered to were set and had been for generations, whereas here—and this is part of what's so much fun about Mazursky's movie—the characters are just discovering them, inventing them as they go, though they're doing it collectively, as a culture of like-minded young Americans. The characters in *Bob and Carol and Ted and Alice* are the upper echelon of the counterculture, with the money to implement their impulses. And like Barry, and like Sheridan before him, Mazursky is writing about them from the inside. These characters—like the ones in his other early high comedies, *Alex in Wonderland* (1970), *Blume in Love* (1973), and *Next Stop, Greenwich Village* (1976), and the ones in *Down and Out in Beverly Hills*, which he made later, in 1986—are his people. So even when he satirizes them—unlike Barry, he is a satirist, and an acute and precise one—he does it lovingly. That tone is his trademark.

The movie begins with Bob and Carol driving north to spend a weekend at the Esalen Institute (known in the movie simply as "the Institute"), where the latest group therapy theories are put into practice. Bob is there to do research for a documentary, he explains to the others in the group, adding, "At least I *think* that's why I came." He's open to new experiences, and so is Carol, though she's shyer and more tentative at first, preferring to follow his lead. The weekend alters their perspective dramatically. When they return, they go out for dinner with their best friends, Ted (Elliott Gould), an attorney, and his wife, Alice (Dyan Cannon), and begin to inculcate them with their new point of view that complete honesty is beautiful and that it's vital to acknowledge your feelings. Shambling, banal Ted is susceptible, at least to the sensual temptations of these new ways—he likes to smoke grass with Bob and Carol, and he's turned on by the promise of sexual freedom—but uptight Alice stands outside the social revolution, a little patronizing, more than a little disapproving. She's a southern California princess who isn't comfortable with anything that threatens the behavior she's accustomed to, and beneath her cute debutante manner beats a puritan heart. Marijuana has no effect on her; it's as if she'd willed it not to alter her. And when her husband indulges at dinner with their friends, she points out, quietly but insistently, that he's breaking the law he's sworn to uphold and calls him "junkie," with pretend good humor, as she hoists him up at the end of the evening to go home. He's restless from the dope and dying for sex, but she isn't in the mood, and she makes her sexual reluctance into a moral prerogative. She doesn't want what she doesn't want, but she wants what she wants: If Ted can't get laid, he needs to walk off his energy, yet she expects him to stay in bed with her for comfort. This argument over sex is one of the funniest marital squabbles ever put on the screen, and you can hear in the banter the influence of Mike Nichols and Elaine May, who practically invented the revue-style humor that writers and directors like Mazursky shepherded into the movies in the late sixties and early seventies.

Bob and Carol's reverence for feelings and honesty is tested when he comes from a shoot in San Francisco and, unable to make love to her, confesses to her that he had a one-night stand with another woman. He's guilty and he expects her to explode, but, careful to articulate exactly what she's feeling as she's been trained to, she says she's not upset or jealous or even surprised, and when he pushes her, sure that she's hiding her true emotions, she repeats that it was only a physical thing and it doesn't imperil their loving relationship. The tension between his insistence that she *should* be jealous and her hippie acceptance is hilarious, and so is her instinctive maternal response: she cradles him and tells him he's an attractive man who hasn't done anything wrong. Finally she wants him to *describe* the sex; it turns her on. Sometime later, he returns a night early from another shoot and she meets him at the bottom of the stairs to warn him that she's got another man in their bed—a burnished blonde tennis pro named Horst (Horst Ebersberg). Bob's initial reaction isn't as generous as Carol's was—he takes her sexual indiscretion personally before he realizes he's behaving like an asshole and invites Horst downstairs for a drink. "You are one hell of a guy," Horst says with awe. "You've got a lot of class."

One of the key appurtenances of the new aristocracy is therapy; *Bob and Carol* is one of the earliest analysand comedies (a genre that Woody Allen would make famous). It's Alice who goes to a shrink (Donald F. Muhich), who claims he never makes judgments even though his muted surprise at her pronouncements makes it clear that he's judging her all the time. (What he *never* makes is a helpful suggestion.) But it's hard *not* to respond to her tight, princessy tone. Carol confides in Alice and Ted that Bob was up-front about his San Francisco affair, and Alice is appalled to the point of nausea. (It's her response to this news that chills her to the notion of sex with her husband that night.) It takes a while for her to get over it, and by the time she has, and the two couples are weekending together in Las Vegas, Ted, encouraged by his friend's carpe diem approach, has also strayed (on a business trip to Miami). Alice's response to his admission of infidelity, in front of their friends, is to strip off her dress and demand that the four of them have an orgy. It's a fascinating moment. Too much focus on sex has always made Alice uncomfortable; she thinks it can't be healthy. So when she bullies Bob and Carol into taking this radical step by challenging their trumpeted sexual openness, she's being nasty and mocking, intending (though she may not be conscious of it) to expose the limitations of that openness. They want to see sex as clean and wholesome and therapeutic; she restores its mean, dirty, sluttish side. And though she's working off her anger, they're naive enough to see it as insight. So the four wind up in bed. The sexual experiment doesn't succeed, of course; there's a psychological wall that none of them can break through—an essential unease that they're not hip enough to ignore. We've seen the limits of Bob and Carol's broad-mindedness.

One of Mazursky's satirical strategies is to keep us aware, in some scenes, of the perspective of outsiders. The cashier at Bob and Carol's favorite Italian restaurant, where they tell their friends about the Esalen experience, is clearly amused by their conversation, and when Carol, trying out their new honesty, cross-examines the waiter (Lee Bergere) to get beneath his superficial inquiries about the quality of the food and the service, she makes him comically uncomfortable; he figures there must have been something wrong with the wine. Another night, after Bob and Carol have sent their other dinner guests home and taken out their stash and their pipe to share with Ted and Alice, Mazursky keeps the housekeeper in the back of the frame, so we're aware that someone outside this exclusive circle is watching their behavior. It's a reality check; we wonder how these rich young hipsters with their dope might strike a working-class immigrant. But Mazursky himself makes no moral judgments on their behavior, even though he may laugh at the follies he recognizes in them. This burlesque of people who feel a moral obligation to say what they're feeling at every moment recalls Molière's *The Misanthrope* (which argues that though courtly flattery is artifice, an excess of honesty screws up social intercourse). But Molière, like most satirists, is cold; Mazursky's warm—an odd duck, really. It would be more accurate to compare him to Chekhov.

Mazursky's favorite movie subject in this era is his own contemporary social set. The exception is *Next Stop, Greenwich Village*, made in 1976, which is a memoir of his twenties, when he lived, for the first time, away from his Brownsville family. It's a high comedy, too, set in a club of hipsters, but they're an earlier variety—young intellectuals in the early fifties who hang out in Greenwich Village cafés; their favorite, the Caffe Reggio on Macdougall, where Mazursky shot many of the key scenes, is still operating. They argue about art (they're high on Chaplin) and politics (the Rosenbergs and Joe McCarthy) and each other's sex lives (which occasionally overlap); they hold rent parties; they use language that would no doubt shock their parents almost as much as their sexual freedom; they celebrate an experimental, antibourgeois existence. Larry Lipinksy (the gifted beanpole Lenny Baker, who died young), Mazursky's stand-in, has a girlfriend, Sarah (Ellen Greene, who suggests Barbra Streisand in her best dramatic roles); she still lives with her folks and has to lie to her mother when she sleeps over at Larry's. Her last boyfriend was an abstract expressionist. Their friends include Robert (the remarkable young Christopher Walken), a brilliant, articulate aspiring writer who argues over the precise meaning of words but seems to have no real feelings beyond them—he's a narcissist and a compulsive womanizer. Anita (Lois Smith), a depressive, is chronically unlucky in love, and her periodic suicide attempts are a rallying point for the group. Bernstein (Antonio Fargas) is a gay black man with an invented past and a penchant for sailors. And then there's Connie (Dori Brenner), who mothers them all. They're endlessly self-dramatizing, and with Anita and Bernstein, drama and reality blur into each other. The collective style of these friends is argumentative and vaudevillian; they conga in the streets or waddle down them pretending to be the Little Tramp, and the Jews among them—Larry, Sarah, and Connie—are always doing shtick. They smoke constantly (especially the women—it's a sign of rebellion against the old-fashioned propriety of their upbringing), and Larry's beret and the scarf flung around his neck, Isadora style, are in lieu of a pin confirming his membership in the beat Greenwich Village fraternity.

Mazursky depicts the Village of this bustling, colorful period with the same mix of humor and affection that characterizes his contemporary comedies. Larry takes classes from a large, imposing Method acting teacher (Michael Egan) who censures him for distancing himself from his feelings by horsing around. This teacher is smart about what's wrong with his students' work, but he misses the boat about Larry's joking; it's the special quality that takes him—Mazursky, that is—beyond his *Blackboard Jungle* days. (Mazursky is, by the way, a wonderful actor who appears in small roles in most of his own movies.) Inside and outside class Larry argues with his classmates about the merits of Hollywood as an outlet for young actors (just like the theatrical aristocrats in *All About Eve*). His day job is at a tiny health restaurant whose owner (Lou Jacobi) berates his regulars for the "poison" they eat when they're away from his establishment. In the bars and cafés he runs into Barney (John Ford Noonan), a bearded painter who has a hundred pick-up lines and makes a commission if he steers business toward an abortionist friend.

There's also an old poet (Joe Madden) who peddles his wares for a quarter, exclaiming merrily, "In the winter I'm a Buddhist, in the summer I'm a nudist!" It's a vivid panorama.

And, for Larry, it's fraught. Larry is the grandson of Polish immigrants, and the subway ride from Brooklyn to downtown Manhattan is, in his own mind, his journey to freedom. The source of his misery is his overbearing, possessive mother (Shelley Winters, never greater than here), who stages a hysterical scene when he departs and another one every time she and his quiet, pragmatic papa (Mike Kellin) show up in his apartment—usually unannounced and sometimes at embarrassing moments. Larry longs to shake off his Brownsville world and immerse himself totally in his Greenwich Village one. He's too young to realize that the Village is only a stop along the journey, and too stubborn to admit that, along with the *tsouris* his mother gives him, she's also bequeathed him her humor, her smarts, her talent, her passion, and her devotion to the arts. (She cries over Jussi Bjoerling's recordings.) Obviously, *Next Stop, Greenwich Village* is also a coming-of-age picture, and we know Larry has reached adulthood when, signed to appear in his first movie, he goes back to Brooklyn to say goodbye to his folks and we can see he's made peace with his roots. "Remember your grandmother . . . she had to sneak across the border in a wagon covered with potatoes," his mother exhorts him. "And the guards, they stuck bayonets into the sacks. That's where you came from." (The famous improv teacher Viola Spolin plays an earlier version of Mazursky's mother in *Alex in Wonderland*, but not memorably.) He walks toward the subway, listening to the violinist playing in the street, eats the strudel his mother gave him for the train ride, and looks at the place that shaped him. I'd say this is the most poignant scene Mazursky has ever shot, but the glories of *Enemies, A Love Story* still lay ahead of him.

Both *Alex in Wonderland* and *Blume in Love* are about Angelenos in the early seventies. Alex Morrison (Donald Sutherland), the protagonist of the first, is another version of Mazursky. He's a movie director who has just had a big commercial hit; he can pretty much sign his own ticket with M-G-M, but he's paralyzed by success and can't figure out what to do next. Mazursky himself shows up in a cameo as a hip young producer named Hal Stern. Stern offers a trip to Paris to Alex and his wife, Beth (Ellen Burstyn, in her brief affecting, sad-eyed period, before she became hard edged) to provide an ideal setting for him to read a novel Stern hopes he might want to film, and before Alex leaves his office, Stern tries to press on him a Chagall lithograph he's admired on Stern's wall. This may be the only portrait in American movies of the hipster producers of this era, with their leftist-flavored acquisitiveness (and it's a classic). Stern's ideas are uproariously dopey—*Huck Finn* as the tale of a modern revolutionary, with Brechtian songs; a love story about a black girl who gets a heart transplant from a white donor; an American version of Dostoevski's *The Idiot*. But you look up at him, and you think about the movie he's in the middle of, and you have to marvel. *Alex in Wonderland* is a rambling shambles of a movie, with Felliniesque fantasy sequences (Fellini himself appears, as does Jeanne Moreau); it's very likable, but who the hell would ever have green-lighted it except a producer just like Hal Stern?

What makes it interesting are the glimpses of Alex's lifestyle and the pals who form the unofficial club to which he belongs—loud, contentious, leftist, and well on their way to amassing the money that will allow them to live far better than their parents did. They stroll on the beach, passing a joint and arguing racial politics; the only one among them (Michael Lerner) who doesn't think it would be such a great idea if rioting African Americans took over L.A. is branded a bigot. *O tempora, o mores*. Alex frets over the idea that his financial success seems to demand a bigger house; he and Beth quarrel over whether her sister would be the best guardian for their kids if something happened to Beth and Alex. He insists that the sister is a square whose children live in front of the TV set. The argument anticipates the scenes in Irvin Kershner's *Up the Sandbox* (released two years later) that showcase the kinds of tension caused by intellectual Manhattan parents (Barbra Streisand and David Selby) who, in the spirit of the new tolerance and communication, relax the rules for their children. *Alex in Wonderland* isn't quite as good as *Up the Sandbox* at evoking lyrically the feel of this now-faded time—the messy romanticism of candles around the bed, the granny nightgowns, Streisand's Madonna glow and her hair trailing down her back—but they share, in their best moments, a comic delicacy and a respect for naturally shifting domestic moods that it's almost impossible to get at the movies anymore. (*The Secret Lives of Dentists*, from 2003, provided it; before that, you'd have to go all the way back to the 1982 *Shoot the Moon*.)

Though no one made films about Vietnam in the late sixties and early seventies, the atmosphere of a country engaged in an unpopular war and undergoing dramatic social changes on the home front was everywhere present in American movies. The combination of talent and license in Hollywood enabled filmmakers to get the changing tide on the screen as Americans were experiencing it, and three and a half decades later that still seems like an astonishing achievement. And though no one could have expected that the genre of choice for these expressions of the national mood would be high comedy, in fact many of the finest reflections came in precisely that form, or at least had one foot firmly planted in it—Mazursky's *Blume in Love*, Arthur

Penn's *Alice's Restaurant* (1969), Hal Ashby's *Shampoo* (1975), and *The Long Goodbye* (1973) and *Nashville* (1975) by Robert Altman.

*Blume in Love* is about an L.A. lawyer named Stephen Blume (George Segal) whose wife, Nina (Susan Anspach), walks out on him when she finds him in bed with his secretary. In narrative terms, the movie chronicles his attempts to win her back—even after she's moved in with a druggy musician named Elmo (Kris Kristofferson), whom Stephen befriends. Stephen's motives are not always pure—his friendship with Elmo is a case in point—and his behavior is not always admirable, but his commitment to this romantic mission makes him the indisputable hero of the picture. Through Stephen and Nina's story, Mazursky (sole author of the screenplay for the first time) further explores the world of the hip in early-seventies L.A. There's the usual cast of wild supporting characters and cameos—the deep-eyed bearded waiter at a vegetarian restaurant who describes the Zen stew; the bouncy blonde who thinks swinging will cure society of its sexual hang-ups; the yoga instructor, who patiently lectures her students, "Stop the thinking, which is *about* reality but *not* reality"; the girl at a party who says L.A. is the center of the universe but you can't breathe the air; the man with the Old Testament beard who talks about God's owning land in Turkey; the woman who describes a film she saw about bread rising; an acquaintance of Blume's—we hear about him from his grown son—who flipped out, dropped a lot of acid, and moved to a commune.

Mazursky also uses the tensions between the Blumes to show what's happening in America as the war drags on. In a flashback, we see how Stephen and Nina met—at a benefit for the farm workers, where they dance to "Mr. Tambourine Man." It's only six years earlier, but it's a different and breezier time—pre-Nixon, pre-Altamont, pre-Manson. Nina is a tuning fork for the national impulse toward experimentation, and as the country gets weighed down, she conveys its restlessness and depression. She holds down a gloomy welfare job out of a desire to be of service; she tries yoga, weed, psychotherapy; she gets involved in leftist causes because she feels most Americans are uncommitted ("The whole country is full of shit," she complains to her husband); she contemplates adopting a baby of color, going to Esalen, sampling encounter-group therapy; she takes in Elmo, who's blasted all the time. She tries to find words for the nameless longing she feels ("I want to be free and open and clear about all my relationships. I don't want to have hatred for anyone if I can help it. I want to be my own person"); she tries to be completely honest about what she feels, like Bob and Carol. But how can she be, when she doesn't always *know* what she feels, and when her feelings keep shifting on her? In the end she tries motherhood and a return to Blume.

The main problem with their marriage—even before the infidelity—is that though Stephen is the first one who's ready to get married (Nina, who's seen bad matches, is more wary), once they are he can never really commit himself to the kind of experimentation she's willing to throw herself into. While she takes them to meditation classes, or talks about adopting a child of another race, he maintains an ironic distance, making jokes. He isn't a joiner by nature. He humors her because he loves her, but of course she knows he's humoring her, and it makes her angry; she feels his distance—she feels condescended to. She accuses him of "playing games," "putting people down"—familiar charges in this era, and familiar to us, too, from *Bob and Carol and Ted and Alice*, though the tone of that movie is much lighter. When Nina walks out on her marriage and hooks up with Elmo, you see why—he glides through life, refusing to define anything (like his relationship with Nina: "She makes me feel good. I make her feel good. Is that love?") or to linger on anything that brings him down. (There's one notable exception: He breaks down when he comes back to the house to find Stephen, in an act of desperation, has forced himself on Nina.) To Nina, who is having such a hard time when she meets him, Elmo's lifestyle and attitude are very appealing—as they are to Blume, who's in the throes of his own misery when he meets Elmo. But Stephen can't take on Elmo's vision of the world, any more than he could get into Zen or the farm workers. He gets stoned with Elmo and Nina, he sits around and sings the silly song Elmo's made up, but you can see by Segal's eyes (it's a splendid, unheralded performance) how removed he is. He has to remain who he is and what he is—ambivalent about everything. The movie is as much about ambivalence as the national mood of the early seventies as it is about the nature of love.

It's easy to dismiss Blume (after he rapes Nina)—especially in a self-righteous culture like ours, which tends to forget Yeats's credo that art is forgiveness for sin. And it's easy to dismiss Nina, who speaks in the now affected-sounding lingo of her time. But a whole generation said and did the kinds of things Nina does, and Mazursky appreciates that her desperation to find happiness—and Blume's, and that of Blume's client Mrs. Cramer (Shelley Winters), who's dumped by her husband for a younger woman—is both funny and moving. Stephen's shrink, who later becomes Nina's, too, carefully refrains from telling him what to do, just as Alice's does, and they're both very funny characters (and played by the same actor, Donald F. Muhich). But the shrink in *Blume in Love* is also affecting, because we see he doesn't know how to help his clients, who have come to him all messed up. The movie tells us that life is too complicated and too full of obstacles and changes and wildly different people for anyone to devise a cure-all for its difficulties. The psychiatrist admits that sometimes what he advises his clients to try doesn't work. So Stephen asks him why he goes on, and the psychiatrist answers, "Sometimes it does. And until we can find something better, what else is there to do?"

Arthur Penn's *Alice's Restaurant*, made four years earlier, also chronicles the sea change from the sixties of the Beatles and the Peter Max posters and the Summer of Love to the era of anomie and disillusionment. The script by Penn and Venable Herndon spins off the popular talking blues by Arlo Guthrie, who plays himself in the movie, but the story of Arlo's experience at the draft board is only one episode in the film, and its lightheartedness doesn't suggest the tone the movie shifts to in the last section. The movie is structured as a coming-of-age story for Arlo, who drifts away from college, makes small inroads toward a music career, deals with the deterioration of his father, the famous singer-songwriter Woody Guthrie (Joseph Boley), from Huntington's chorea, and—after a few stumbles—finds his soul mate, a beautiful Asian potter named Mari-chan (Tina Chen). But the main characters are really Alice and Ray Brock (Pat Quinn and James Broderick), who create a commune in the Berkshires in a bankrupt church, supported by the restaurant Alice manages and made up of young people, some of whom met her when she worked as a librarian at the local high school. This is a progressively downbeat comedy of manners where the hippie aristocracy defines itself in contradistinction to the uptight, intolerant straight world, which preaches war instead of peace and love. Except for a few rednecks and cops in Arlo's college town, though, the filmmakers don't vilify the straights; they poke fun at them. In fact, the movie is more interested in the commune, which is fragile—too fragile to survive because, like the post–Civil War commune John Guare portrays in his play *Lydie Breeze*, in its out-and-out rejection of the values of the world beyond its borders, it refuses to acknowledge that the people within are merely human beings with the same flaws.

Traveling east from the college he's dropped out of, Arlo stops to watch a tent meeting that culminates in the singing of "Amazing Grace." "Seems like Woody's road mighta run through here one time," he muses—and indeed it does seem like a scene out of Guthrie's memoir *Bound for Glory*. But though Arlo appreciates the revival meeting, it isn't his scene. He follows a religion that's more personal and quirky and improvised, and it finds its place, for a short time at least, in Alice and Ray's church, where he feels accepted for who he is. Ray promises it will be "a place to be what we want to be," and Arlo, the true believer, adds, "Amazing grace." And at first it does seem like a wonderful place. Everyone joins in to put it together, or to play music to inspire the construction work—the commune is full of artists, visual ones like

Shelly (Michael McClanathan), musicians like Arlo and his buddy Roger (Geoff Outlaw), who doesn't stay long.

But Ray deludes himself—and them—about what the community can achieve. He thinks it will solve all their problems and provide a permanent home for kids whose age—as well as the social realities of the era they're living through—prompts them to uproot themselves from any sort of home. As played by the ineffable Pat Quinn, Alice is the angel of the place, its embodiment of amazing grace. She represents the gentle, loving spirit of the sixties while it was still generous and sweet. There's more to her, of course—she's restless and moody, with blue spells when she feels overextended in her role of mother to all these kids (including Ray, who's an overgrown kid), exhausted by their sometimes stupid and irresponsible antics. She and Ray are supposed to have an open marriage but she gets angry when he beds someone else; she palms one of his lovers off on Arlo. The free love philosophy doesn't work easily on human beings, who have a tendency to get jealous and possessive, and we see its limitations here. And Alice doesn't always exercise good judgment. When she sleeps with Shelly, a not-very-reconstructed heroin addict who's always on the verge of a breakdown, she's following her inclination and probably giving him the love she thinks he needs, but she forgets for a moment how delicate he is. He falls in love with her, he's driven crazy by her ongoing relationship with Ray (who constantly competes with him), and the emotional pressure of his feelings for her becomes one element in his self-destruction. (We shouldn't blame Alice entirely: We take one look at this kid when he walks onto the screen and we know he's a walking time bomb, and so blocked up he can't express what he's feeling.)

Ray and Alice talk a lot about their "beauty," and the beauty of those around them, but they're not *always* beautiful. Generous as Ray is, he's also a sore loser; he horses around and doesn't know when to stop; he makes promises and extends invitations he relies on Alice to make good on. He doesn't appreciate how hard she works, or how she holds the place together. He doesn't get why she can't just leave the customers at the restaurant to fend for themselves and go swimming with him and the kids; he thinks every day should be a holiday. When Alice runs away to New York, he chases her down, vowing things will be different from now on. And indeed the Thanksgiving dinner they put on is the most upbeat scene in the movie—a true communal feast, staged in a mock-Puritan, true-hippie style. Grace before dinner begins, appropriately enough, "Grace be to Alice," their angel, and when they pass a joint around while singing (of course) "Amazing Grace," you feel this could be the religion Arlo and indeed all the alienated, disenchanted youth of America are looking for. But then you see Shelly's face when Alice goes upstairs to make love to her husband, and you know this mood can't last. And it doesn't: Shelly goes back to heroin, and Ray's reaction is bullying and accusation; he acts like the bull-headed papas that many of the kids were rebelling against.

By the time Shelly kills himself on his motorcycle and Arlo goes home for his father's funeral, the mood of the film has become mournful and elegiac. And though the Brocks try to bring back the old spirit with a big wedding to renew their vows, and the sequence begins by echoing Thanksgiving with a mock-yet-genuine religious ceremony and a joyous swing, it goes sour once the other guests have left and only the kids, the inner circle, are left with Alice and Ray. Everyone is drunk and high, and almost everyone looks lost and low. Roger plays an acid blues on his electric guitar. If Thanksgiving felt like *Sergeant Pepper's Lonely Hearts Club Band*, this scene is closer to the Rolling Stones' "Moonlight Mile." You feel the hippie legacy has faded, grown distended, and that everyone has been hanging around too long. And then Ray overdoes it, as usual, racing around the church, liberating the balloons and yelling, "It's up there! It's up there!" promising they're going to fly to heaven on the inner beauty in their souls. We get a very bad feeling, as we realize he hasn't changed. He still expects Alice to take charge—to fix them all something to eat, in her wedding gown. And now he has a *new* dream—a farm where they can grow their own food and have all the space they need. If they'd had a farm, he theorizes, "I bet what happened to Shelly wouldn't have happened." He's said this sort of thing before. So Arlo and Mari-chan pack up and hit the road, while Penn's camera follows their car, gazing back at Alice in the doorway of the church, as Arlo might—Alice in her wedding gown, the mysterious emblem of an era ("Grace be to Alice") that's already vanishing before our eyes. The camera returns to her as Arlo's mind will undoubtedly return to her through the years.

The high comedies of this era are perhaps the saddest American movies have ever given us. They seem more acutely conscious of evanescence than even Noël Coward was, and where the thirties high comedies kept the Depression magically at bay, the anguish of America at war in Vietnam, moving toward a deeper and deeper pessimism, hangs in the air in these films. Hal Ashby's *Shampoo*, with its extraordinary script by Robert Towne and star Warren Beatty (Towne is the real creative force behind the project), is a case in point, though it's often very funny too. Here's another movie about the shift toward the end of the sixties, though the filmmakers locate it at a specific point in time. *Shampoo*, which came out in 1975, is set on the day of the 1968 presidential election, when Nixon's arrival in the White House and the foreign and domestic policies he pursued turned hippie hopefulness into disenchantment and defeat. But the setting isn't a commune in the mountains; it's Paul Mazursky territory, aristocratic L.A. And the protagonist, George (Beatty), is the most popular hairdresser at the most exclusive salon in Beverly Hills, a joyous womanizer who often services his clients— as a hairdresser and as a stud—at their homes. Standing on his hippie prerogative to be independent and fly in the face of nine-to-five convention, he sets his own hours (to the exasperation of his employer, played by Jay Robinson) and treks across L.A. on a motorbike. He's the closest this movie comes to the spirit of the Brock commune: though he wants to open his own place, he's so inexperienced in the ways of the straight world that when the bank he visits to secure a loan demands references, he gives the name of a movie-star client.

Everyone is linked in this picture, as in the later *Six Degrees of Separation.* George's current girlfriend is Jill (Goldie Hawn), a model who's so naive it never occurs to her that he has other lovers. Her best friend, Jackie (Julie Christie), is George's favorite ex. She left him to seek financial security, and found it in Lester (Jack Warden), a wealthy businessman who keeps her while remaining married to Felicia (Lee Grant). Lester has no idea that George does Felicia as well as her hair; he assumes that, given George's profession, he's probably gay, and it's to everyone else's benefit not to disabuse him of this error. When Felicia's late for her home appointment with George, her daughter Lorna (Carrie Fisher) entertains him in her bed. Lorna hates her mother; it's an act of revenge. But when Felicia comes home and finds her lover stumbling out of her daughter's bathroom, her realization that they've had sex doesn't make her angry and jealous; it turns her on, and she wants George right away.

*Shampoo* is a sex farce, a roundelay like Renoir's *The Rules of the Game* (its unofficial inspiration), which is also set in an aristocratic world where everyone seems to be sleeping with someone else's partner. And like *The Rules of the Game*, as well as Bergman's *Smiles of a Summer Night*, Ashby's movie culminates at a big social occasion—two, in fact, that are set up in contrast to each other but where the guest lists overlap. Lester holds a Republican party at a restaurant to celebrate Nixon's expected victory, and when Jackie insists on an invitation, he asks George to escort her—in effect, to be her beard. They arrive in tandem with Jill and Johnny (Tony Bill), who's trying to hire Jill for a shoot and has a romantic interest in her too. Felicia, who's no fool, figures out immediately who Jackie is, and when Lester doesn't pay her enough attention, Jackie gets smashed and tries to go down on George in the middle of dinner. Still, no one—not Lester, or Felicia, or Jill—realizes that there's a genuine erotic spark between George and Jackie. It shoots up at the next party, on a large estate, where the guests (except for a transplanted Lester) are liberals, smoking dope and listening to the Beatles and Buffalo Springfield and cavorting naked in the hot tub. These are representatives of the era to which Nixon will bring an abrupt end. When George and Jackie make love in a guest house at the edge of the estate, and Lester, Jill, and Johnny happen upon them, the last erotic secret is uncovered.

George is a compulsive Don Juan, but he's also a true innocent, while everyone around him—except for sweet, clueless Jill—is corrupt in some way. So in the movie's terms, what makes them corrupt isn't their sexual conduct but the baseness of their motives. When George lashes out at Jackie, "I don't fuck for money, I do it for fun," he's holding up his irrepressible love for women in contrast to her bid for security. And really she *is* a high-class hooker selling her favors for Lester's money and his lifestyle—though at the end, when Felicia insists on divorcing Lester, Jackie makes the leap to the coveted position of his new wife. (Lester, who's actually one of the more likable characters in the picture, forgives Jackie her indiscretion with George; he doesn't want to lose her and Felicia in the same twenty-four-hour period.) By contrast, George is a romantic, a Don Juan who's utterly lacking in venality. He doesn't mean to hurt Jill; he doesn't want to hurt anybody. But he's like a little kid who wants all the candy in the store.

The morning after the election, George walks into the salon to find everyone in a state of grief and confusion, because Norman, his boss, has just learned his son has been killed in a car crash. Here's Pauline Kael on the significance of this scene:

> Was it Osbert Sitwell who said that life might be considered a comedy only if it were never to end? *Shampoo* tosses the fact of death into the midst of the beauty shop. . . . It's an artifice—reality intruding upon the clowns at their revels, death as an interruption to the babble and trivial bickering of the beauty-salon world. But it's needed, and it's the right death—the accidental death of someone young, the only event, maybe, that can't be converted into gossip.[1]

This scene also clinches the melancholy, longing tone of the movie, which is aided by Paul Simon's plaintive soundtrack, with its hummed solo vocal, and which derives from the subject beneath its subject. *Shampoo* is about a kind of spiritual emptiness (I mean "spiritual" in a broader sense, not in a conventionally religious one), and George has the worst case of it. Some of the characters are so at home in the material world that they don't seem to notice what they're lacking (Felicia and Lester; Lorna's anger and venom suggest that she knows she's lacking *something*). But the fact that, as Jill points out, George is always moving indicates that he senses the void at the center of his life and he's desperately circling it. And I think it's his sense of that emptiness in his own life that makes him finally such a sad character, and makes us empathize with him. George says he wants to settle down, but he seems terrified to, as if he'd fall into that abyss if he did. At the end of the movie, when he asks Jackie to give up Lester and marry him, and she tells him he's too late, he implores her, "Please, honey, I don't trust anybody but you." But she's made her choice, and we realize it's the only one she would ever have made. From a hill above her house, George watches while she drives off with Lester, the distance accentuating the sadness of the scene. The film ends with a fade-out—no closure, just this retreat and abandonment. And the soundtrack returns to the opening song, the Beach Boys' "Wouldn't It Be Nice?" which is the sweetest, most innocent sexual proposition imaginable—and which harks back to the brief, candied period whose death knell we've already heard.

Robert Altman's vision of the L.A. wealthy in *The Long Goodbye* is less indulgent than Ashby and Towne's—it's sinister, curdled. Of course, that's how Raymond Chandler, who wrote the 1953 novel and several other Philip Marlowe mysteries, always sees the rich; think of *The Big Sleep*. But Altman and Leigh Brackett, the screenwriter (who also worked on the script for Howard Hawks's 1946 film of *The Big Sleep*), update the material to the present, with surprising results. The protagonist, Marlowe (played this time around by Elliott Gould, intentionally a far cry from Bogart), is the outsider, though it takes him almost the entire movie to realize just how outside he really is. The city seems friendly and inviting in that superficial southern-California manner, even the gated Malibu colony. Terry Lennox (Jim Bouton), the old friend who shows up at Marlowe's pad one night, bruised, and begs a ride to Tijuana, is a resident of the place, along with his wife Sylvia, who turns up dead; Lennox is the chief suspect, until word arrives from the Tijuana police that he's dead too. And the hard-drinking Hemingwayesque writer Roger Wade (Sterling Hayden) lives there, too, along with his wife Eileen (Nina Van Pallandt), who hires Marlowe to hunt Roger down when he disappears—because, she tells him, she heard about how loyal he was to her neighbor when the LAPD assumed Lennox was responsible for Sylvia's death. (Marlowe sat in jail when he refused to play nice with the cops.) The other figures in this labyrinthine mystery are all connected to these two couples—the Jewish gangster Marty Augustine (played by film director Mark Rydell), who has both Wade and Lennox in his debt, and the creepy, bullying Dr. Verringer (Henry Gibson), who gives Roger sanctuary in his expensive sanitarium (that's where Marlowe tracks him down) and then shows up in the middle of a barbecue on the beach to humiliate his patient publicly into paying his bill. The affability of this milieu is deceptive; it disguises adultery, alcoholism, and murder. It's as much a façade as Augustine's stand-up-comic style and joshing attitude, which hide a sociopathology, a penchant for truly shocking outbursts of violence.

Gould is a scruffy, shambling comedian with a sad-sack face who typically plays luckless *schlubs*, and his hilarious seventies revue-style parody of Bogart is as bizarre in its way as Woody Allen playing Bogart in *Play It Again, Sam*, which came out the previous year. Altman wants to trick us into thinking he's making the same kind of joke Allen did, but he's not, and Gould's Marlowe, for all his funny, oddball variations on forties mannerisms (like the way he smokes a cigarette), isn't kidding. (Gould gives an astonishing performance.) This Marlowe is a chain-smoking hipster in a coat and tie; he never removes it, not even to relax when he's drinking aquavit with Roger Wade, whom he likes. He bebops through his low-rent existence (he charges only fifty bucks a day plus expenses, exactly double what Bogart's Marlowe did two and a half decades earlier), meeting adversity with an insouciant demeanor. His cat refuses to eat a new brand of cat food, obliging Marlowe to head for the supermarket in the middle of the night? "That's OK with me," he mutters. Terry wants a lift south of the border, no questions asked? "That's OK with me." His gorgeous topless neighbors are so high on hash brownies and yoga and California sunshine that they don't even hear him when he asks their help to find his lost cat? "That's OK with me."

But it's *not* really OK with him. Marlowe gets furious when the cops insist that Terry offed his wife; furious when they dismiss Terry's own death as a suicide; furious when Roger gets hassled by Dr. Verringer. Marlowe's carelessness masks a deep emotional commitment (to his friends) and a righteous anger (against bum raps and any obfuscation of the truth) amounting to a code of honor, an item as incongruous in this early-seventies L.A. setting as a flivver would be—or Bogart's Marlowe. But his moral righteousness doesn't make him sexy. In this setting, it's the hoods like Augustine and the social-climbing killers like Lennox—yes, he *did* kill Sylvia—who get the beautiful women. Marlowe can only act as a sort of clown for them, and he couldn't possibly understand them anyway, because they belong to a world that's run by a code he can't decipher and a set of rules he can't comprehend. The world the rich Sternwoods inhabit in *The Big Sleep* has something to fear from the likes of Phil Marlowe; he makes a dent when he intrudes on it. But what chance does Marlowe have against a Marty Augustine, whose moves are so out of the blue that even his own henchmen are staggered and sickened when he smashes a Coke bottle in his the face of his dumb, innocent mistress (Jo Ann Brody) in order to show Marlowe how scary he is?

And what chance does he have against a woman like Eileen Wade? An other-worldly blonde beauty with an untraceable European accent (it's even stranger and more artificial than Kim Novak's in the first half of *Vertigo* [1958]), clad in sunbonnets and long, flowing flower-child dresses, she's a mystery Marlowe can't solve. When we look into her eyes, all we see is a shimmering blank, and when she runs into the ocean after her suicidal husband (whose death quotes Norman Maine's in *A Star Is Born*), all we see is a blur of flaming orange, like a figure in a Turner canvas. We don't know she's Terry Lennox's lover; Marlowe doesn't even guess.

Marlowe spends the whole movie looking for the truth about what happened to Terry Lennox, but since his straight-ahead vision of the world can't take in the skewed, odd-angled lives of the characters he runs into, he wanders through the movie in a sort of haze, not spotting any of the signs, and his timing is way off. He never seems to be in the right place at the right time. Practically everyone else in the picture seems to be in on some kind of scam he can't get a handle on; rather than being ahead of everyone else, like Bogart's Marlowe was, he's constantly closed out. Dancing with the waves on the beach, he misses the argument the Wades are waging in the house above him, and he's inside the house while Roger is outside drowning himself. What closes him out, of course, are those old-fashioned ethics of his: you give good, honest service to your clients; you don't sell out; you don't cooperate with the cops. Altman and his cinematographer, the legendary Vilmos Zsigmond, suggest his exclusion with a probing, restless camera (an Altman trademark) that implies his quest; and a combination of wavering, distorted lighting and deceptive reflective surfaces—supposedly transparent but really semiopaque—mock that quest. In this paradisal, spaced-out milieu, the reflections the other characters throw back at Marlowe are fakes; the truth is opaque. Some examples of this kind of lighting: the flickering light from the candles on the hippie girls' balcony; the neon light at the Thrifty Mart; the dim lights on the lawn at Verringer's when Marlowe arrives at night; the lights of the car that swerves to avoid Jo Ann, Marty's damaged girlfriend, as she wanders out, moaning, a towel to her face, after his attack; the candles on the table when Eileen serves Marlowe dinner; and of course the shot of her in her gorgeous orange and white dress, running into the ocean, shot from far off so she looks like a flame. Some examples of the not-quite-reflective surfaces: the two-way mirror through which some cops watch Marlowe's interrogation, which Marlowe partially obscures with his inky handprint as a sign of disdain; Eileen reflected in a painting on her wall; the smeared binoculars through which Harry (David Arkin), the funniest of Marty's stooges, looks at the topless young women dancing; the security guard at the Malibu colony reflected in the hood of Harry's car. The Wades' house is all glassed in, as if their lives were an open book, but Marlowe can't see in. He's completely wrong about them: He figures Roger slept with Sylvia and killed her, not that Terry is sleeping with Eileen and killed his own wife. We see Roger reflected in the glass as he answers the door when Marlowe comes by, and Eileen reflected in it when she enters, and in the most visually breathtaking sequence (I'd be tempted to say of this entire period of American film), an enormous picture window cuts Marlowe off from Roger and Eileen as he waits below on the beach, with his own image reflecting off it—two layers of separation. What an image for Marlowe's exclusion from this creepy, moneyed aristocratic world! And after Roger's death Eileen drives away from Malibu to meet Terry, who is still very much alive (though we don't know that until later). As Marlowe chases her car, neon lights melt on the windshield while her gorgeous sapphire eyes stare ahead like an automaton's, apparently seeing only some image in her mind. *The Long Goodbye* is a frightening portrait of the L.A. aristocracy that Towne depicts with compassion and Mazursky with affection.

Altman is always intrigued by exclusive clubs, whether they're the more vulgar groups of hard-boiled comedy (M*A*S*H, or his one-of-a-kind gambling movie, *California Split*) or the more haute versions you find in comedy of manners (*The Player*, *Gosford Park*, even some of his abject failures, like *A Wedding* and *Prêt-à-Porter*). He's temperamentally drawn to high comedy, with its complicated texture and its tonal mix and its often mysterious social landscape. And his style, which may be the most sophisticated in the history of American movies, is ideally suited for the kind of demonstration of the complexities of human interaction that high comedy delights in. His techniques are, famously, a multitrack soundtrack; improvisation with the actors; a muted, allusive approach to showpiece scenes; the dramatization of off-center moments; wide, delicately textured settings explored by that unmoored, probing camera. And when he's really cooking he can accomplish on film what Virginia Woolf did in her novels—reconfigure the notion of realism, shifting among individuals to create a patchwork of personalities and perspectives.

In 1975, the year of *Shampoo*, Altman released the film that must stand beside it as the finest example of high comedy ever made in this country: *Nashville*. Yes, it's also a backstage musical and even a kind of political thriller that climaxes in a deftly prepared-for yet utterly unanticipated assassination. What qualifies it as a high comedy is that, like *All About Eve* or *Sunset Boulevard*, it presents an aristocracy of celebrity—the stars of the country and western music industry, which makes its home in Nashville, the location of the densely packed narrative that takes place over five days. It's true that Altman is using the resonant setting of this city and this industry in an election year as a way of uncovering America itself at the approach of the Bicentennial, and it's true that he extends his focus beyond the stars. When Haven Hamilton (Henry Gibson), whose recording session opens the film, explodes at the shortcomings of the pianist, Frog, he orders him to get his long hair cut and snaps, "You don't belong in Nashville"; Altman is more inclusive. (Frog is played by Richard Baskin, who arranged all the songs for the movie and collaborated with the actors to write many of them.) But the code that regulates attitudes and behavior among the Nashville stars and their hangers-on is of special interest to this movie.

So are their paths. Between the airport scene that introduces most of the cast and the rally for the independent presidential candidate, Hal Phillip Walker, that ends the movie, the characters wander in and out of various clubs and concert venues, a hospital, church, the drag races, parties, hotel rooms. Their whereabouts at any given time tell us as much about them as their dialogue does. At the club owned by Haven's girlfriend, Lady Pearl (Barbara Baxley), King of the Road, stars like Haven and Nashville's signal black recording artist, Tommy Brown (Timothy Brown), sit among their fans; at the Devil's Den, aspiring amateurs like the waitress Sueleen Gay (Gwen Welles) get to perform, and others like Albuquerque (Barbara Harris), slipping the grasp of her husband Star (Bert Remsen), come by in search of musicians. Sueleen sings with the choir at her local Catholic church, where the congregation includes her co-worker Wade (Robert Doqui) and Star and Lady Pearl, whose life was defined by her campaign work for the Kennedy brothers and who is as bitter, all these years later, over JFK's poor showing in the anti-Catholic (in her view) state of Tennessee as grief-stricken over their fate. Altman cuts from this service to the Protestant church: Haven sings in the choir while among the deaf children who sign along with the hymns are the two kids of Del Reese (Ned Beatty), Walker's liaison in Nashville. At the Baptist church we find Tommy and his wife, and Del's wife Linnea (Lily Tomlin), who sings professionally with a black gospel group. And in the hospital chapel, Mr. Green (Keenan Wynn), a Nashville native with no connection to the music industry and a dying wife, and the faithful soldier Kelly (Scott Glenn) listen to Barbara Jean (Ronee Blakley, in an ethereal performance) sing a hymn. Barbara Jean is Nashville's most gifted star, who is recovering from a breakdown at the airport. Kelly adores her and hangs around the periphery of her intimate circle.

In Altman's Nashville, the divisions between singing stars and regular citizens are deliberately blurred, or they seem to be. The music is "real folks"

*The country-western stars in performance: Ronee Blakley and Henry Gibson with Barbara Baxley in Robert Altman's* Nashville *(1975). Credit: Paramount/The Kobal Collection*

music, which supposedly dramatizes the conflicts of ordinary people, and the stars play on that invented connection. Haven introduces his son Bud (Dave Peel) to the crowd and talks about giving Bud the breaks that *he* never had (while we wonder what breaks Haven Hamilton didn't have, exactly, since he seems to be as rich as Croesus). Connie White (Karen Black) signs autographs, "Your friend, Connie White," and makes a point of engaging the kids in the Grand Ole Opry audience in conversation. No wonder so many Nashvilleans think that they, too, can be stars. Sueleen can't sing a note but she swears that someday she's going to be as big as her idol, Barbara Jean. Albuquerque is on her way to stardom; if that doesn't work out, she says, she'll sell trucks. In the meantime she steals backstage at the Grand Ole Opry and intercepts Connie on her way to the stage: She's got a song for Connie to record, she says; she'll call her up next day for a little chat. The just-folks approach of the stars is, of course, a veneer beneath which they're just as exclusive as any other celebrities. (They even look down their noses at movie stars; Elliott Gould and Julie Christie appear in cameos as themselves so Altman can make this point.) The only exception is Barbara Jean, who is also the only true popular artist we get to hear, terrific as some of the others are.

The audience loves her in a way they can't love even Haven, though they may fall for his patented mix of sentimentality and show biz. She makes a genuine connection with them, the way Bruce Springsteen was doing with rock and roll audiences at the same time; her love for them is real. And when she sings the soap-opera lyrics of "Dues" or "My Idaho Home," she transforms them. The fact that she's emotionally stunted—still a child who needs her manager-husband Barnett (Allen Garfield) to watch over her, prey to one disaster after another—may be the necessary corollary to what she's able to achieve on stage: a childlike belief in the clichés about home and family, romance and marriage, that are the cornerstones of country music. A singing star like Haven is cynical enough to know the platitudes are bullshit and manipulate them (and his audience) to make commercial hits out of songs like "For the Sake of the Children We Must Say Goodbye" or the patriotic Bicentennial march "200 Years." Barbara Jean doesn't seem to know she's singing platitudes, so she turns what would be fake, programmed emotions in their songs into real emotions in hers.

There's a political element in *Nashville*, more central than it is in *Alice's Restaurant*, *Blume in Love*, or *Shampoo*. But Altman's chronicling a later time, after Vietnam and Watergate have finally made Americans fed up and effectively depoliticized them. The critic Ray Sawhill calls the movie "an X-ray of the era's uneasy political soul."[2] The theme song for the America of the Me Decade is "It Don't Worry Me," which has been a big hit for the Peter, Paul, and Mary–like trio, Tom (Keith Carradine), Bill (Allan Nicholls), and Mary (Cristina Raines). If Barbara Jean is the protagonist of the movie's everyone-wants-to-be-a-country-celebrity theme, the mainstay of its political theme is John Triplette (Michael Murphy), Hal Phillip Walker's front man. In this atmosphere of political apathy and wariness of politicians, Triplette has the unenviable job of trying to persuade a broad spectrum of singers to appear on behalf of Walker, an eccentric who heads something called the Replacement Party. But in fact Walker's platform, "New Roots for the Nation"—a nonsense phrase that nonetheless hooks onto many Americans' dissatisfaction with the roots they have—makes Walker the perfect politico for people who hate politicians: for Tom, who doesn't vote for president, and Bill, who says he doesn't care; for Haven, who refuses to be associated with a political party (he gives sizable contributions to all of them), and Barnett, who won't allow his wife to be identified with a candidate. Walker's campaign is empty but catchy, full of appealing nonsequiturs about the smell of Christmas and the need for a new national anthem, and full of absurdities that sound less stupid than they are ("When you pay more for an automobile than it cost Columbus to sail to

America, that's politics"). And we never see him; we only hear his voice, or some tinny amplified version of it.

Triplette is the ideal representative for this politician without a face. He's the front man as chameleon, preparing a different face for each of the faces that he meets. He tells Del that most Nashvilleans think movie stars are crazy communists, and agrees laughingly that many of them are. He pledges Walker's help if Haven ever decides to run for governor of Tennessee; that's his way of getting the singer to consider appearing at a political rally. But behind Haven's back Triplette makes fun of his diminutive size and flamboyant cowboy outfits, and then, sweet-talking Bill and Mary into joining the bill, he refers to country as "redneck music" and "crapola" and promises them that their hip counterculture sound will naturally dominate the concert. Murphy's such a resourceful actor that he makes the blandness of his own personality work for him here, as he would later as a Democratic candidate in Altman's *Tanner '88* television series. Triplette never seems to be a strong enough presence to impose his own point of view, yet he ends up with a glittering cast of celebrities for his concert.

The outsiders—the manipulator Triplette; the gentle Mr. Green, whose visiting niece, L.A. Joan (Shelley Duvall) is so caught up in the whirl of celebrity that she neglects her dying aunt; the dogged, faithful Pfc. Kelly; the touching, talentless Sueleen; the pretentious Brit Opal (Geraldine Chaplin), who claims to be making a documentary about Nashville for the BBC and who misses the only truly important event that happens in the time she's there; Albuquerque—all help to define what the aristocracy of *Nashville* is. That's particularly true of Opal, a snob who acts like she belongs but doesn't, and is ignored by almost everybody—and of the tirelessly assertive Albuquerque, who actually becomes a star in the last minutes of the movie, affirming the lie that anyone can become a country-western star. (It helps that she's bursting with talent, and that she's in the right place at the right time.) And it's true of one major character I haven't mentioned, Kenny (David Hayward), who walks into the rally with Mr. Green in search of Joan and winds up shooting Barbara Jean, who's on stage finishing up "My Idaho Home." Altman and Hayward quietly build the character of Kenny, the nerdy northerner with the locked fiddle case who rooms with Mr. Green, so that even if we don't spot the sociopath behind his specs and his blank, grad-student looks, in retrospect we can see all the reasons why we should have been sharper-eyed. When he abandons his car, which breaks down on the highway, the back seat is littered with Walker literature, and we see him hanging around Walker headquarters; presumably it was the politician he came to Nashville to shoot. So why does he end up firing on Barbara Jean?

Kenny camps at Mr. Green's because his landlord's homey manner warms him; later we hear him on the phone to an obviously neurotic, possessive mother—he hangs up on her. Kenny's in the audience when Tommy Brown sings, and he hears Connie and Haven, too, but he barely seems to be aware of them; then Barbara Jean gets up at the mike and he's mesmerized. We could use him as an indicator of the distinction between her music and everybody else's; and ironically, it's because she gets at the depth of our longing for the country values her songs espouse that, when she's standing in front of an American flag and singing about Mama and Daddy and her Idaho childhood, he's moved to kill her. It's the pure embodiment of an ideal that has probably eluded Kenny all his life that makes him snap; it's the American family myth he's taking aim at. Barbara Jean is at the highest point on the Nashville celebrity hierarchy, but that's not what gets her killed; it's that she believes with her heart and soul what the others just reflect, and her art is such an untrammeled expression of that belief that Kenny couldn't possibly miss it.

Ray Sawhill writes:

> It's eerie how accurately *Nashville* pointed the way to the future. Here's our coming attachment to the "outsider" candidate, and our tireless hunger for authenticity and sincerity; here's how feeling good about ourselves and griping about taxes came in the '80s to take precedence over everything else political. In the film once the crisis has been reached, every relationship snaps back to its previous state; we're watching the country try to reaffirm its innocence. It rejects what it has seen of itself; the surface closes over again, like ice over a pond. This could almost be an anticipation of how, during the Reagan years, we acted out a manufactured version of normality and cheerfulness for ourselves.[3]

At the end of the movie, after the Parthenon concert ends in disaster and the crowd has watched its idol shot down before their eyes, Albuquerque takes the stage in an impromptu version of "It Don't Worry Me," and, scattering flowers to the audience, gets them to sing with her. This anthem to political apathy rings out like the rousing finale of a community sing, and it's not clear what we should do with this emotionally loaded moment. Sawhill's reading is certainly one response (and a brilliant one); here's another. Altman once said in an interview that what he wanted was for us to think, What the hell is wrong with those people who can sing that song after what's just happened? and at the same time, Look at those people—isn't it great that they can sing in the face of what's just happened? Virginia Woolf wrote in *To the*

*Lighthouse*, "Nothing is just one thing"; *Nashville* takes that dictum as its gospel.

The only other major filmmaker of the late sixties and seventies who ventured into the realm of high comedy is Woody Allen—and not, I'd say, successfully. The Oscar-winning *Annie Hall* (1977), the best movie he made in the first decade of his career as a director, is really a romantic comedy that touches high comedy in the superficial way the classic screwball comedies of the thirties do, by pairing an aristocrat with someone from the working or middle class. In this case, Annie (Diane Keaton), the offspring of an insulated WASP family, falls in love with Alvy (Allen), a New York Jew. But though his self-presentation in these early movies—and not only in them—appears to be self-deprecating, Allen really longs to be thought of as a kind of intellectual aristocrat himself, and his forays into the artsy territory of Bergman (*Interiors*), Fellini (*Stardust Memories*), and the German Expressionists (*Shadows and Fog*), not to mention Ibsen and Strindberg (*September*, *Another Woman*), are embarrassingly pretentious.

*Manhattan*, which he made at the end of the seventies, is more highly regarded than any of these, and it's certainly a high comedy, but I confess to not liking it very much. Allen plays Isaac Davis, a TV writer who quits his job because he's sick of writing crap and sits down to crank out a novel. His best friend, Yale (Michael Murphy), is an academic and a book critic; his ex-wife, Jill (Meryl Streep), who left him for another woman, has just written a scathing book about their marriage. And both Yale and Isaac become involved, at different times, with Mary (Diane Keaton), a high-toned, Radcliffe-educated journalist and culture critic—though when we first meet Isaac, he's seeing a high-school actress, Tracy (Mariel Hemingway). The intellectual and professional credentials of the characters—except for the untried Tracy—are impeccable, and it's clear those credentials are very important to Allen, as are their conversations as they dine at Elaine's (they say things like "Gossip is the new pornography") or as they stroll through the latest show at MOMA. Isaac and Mary seem to be a match for the usual high-comic reasons, that they belong to the same world and are equally witty—and for the modern, analysand-comedy reason that they share a tendency to overanalyze, certain neuroses (they're both afraid of thunderstorms), and overpowering ex-spouses. The problem with *Manhattan* is that, unlike the other movies discussed in this chapter, which adapt the genre to a contemporary milieu and sensibility, it's hopelessly retro. Shot in carefully composed black and white by Gordon Willis, so that every shot looks like a classic photograph, with Zubin Mehta conducting Tom Pierson's arrangements of Gershwin on the soundtrack, it's

Woody Allen's fantasy of what it would be like if you could reproduce a thirties comedy of manners half a century later. The answer is that it would be dead as a doornail.

## Notes

1. Pauline Kael, *Reeling* (Boston: Little, Brown, 1976), 440–441.

2. Ray Sawhill, "A Movie Called *Nashville*," *Salon*, June 27, 2000, at dir.salon.com/ent/movies/feature/2000/06/27/nashville/index.html?sid=859833.

3. Sawhill, "A Movie."

~

# CHAPTER SIX

# The Eighties and Beyond

High comedy reached a peak of achievement under Lubitsch and Cukor in the thirties and early forties, and another one during the late sixties and early seventies. The first coincided with a signal era in Hollywood entertainment, the second with the "American Renaissance" epoch, which equaled and perhaps even surpassed the heyday of silent movies. American films haven't enjoyed an era of comparable glory since. But high comedy hasn't faded out in the three decades since *Shampoo*, *Nashville*, and *Next Stop, Greenwich Village*. It resurfaces occasionally, sometimes in surprising places.

Both Paul Mazursky and Robert Altman continued to produce work in this genre. Mazursky's career has been on the downswing since the end of the eighties; these days he directs only for cable, and not often there. But in the eighties he made three marvelous comedies of manners, each strikingly different from the others—*Moscow on the Hudson* (1984), *Down and Out in Beverly Hills* (1986), and *Enemies, A Love Story* (1989). *Down and Out* is the closest in subject matter to his earlier films. He and his coscreenwriter, Leon Capetanos, adapt Renoir's classic 1931 social satire, *Boudu Saved from Drowning*, setting it among the conspicuously consumptive Beverly Hills aristocracy. Richard Dreyfuss and Bette Midler play Dave and Barbara Whiteman, whose lives are changed when a homeless man named Jerry (Nick Nolte), dispirited at losing his dog, fills his pants pockets with rocks and dives into their pool. Dave saves him and takes him in (over the objections of his scandalized wife), and before he knows it Jerry has forged a link with everyone in the house, including Barbara, the two Whiteman kids (Tracy

Nelson and Evan Richards) and the Latina maid (Elizabeth Peña). He's the outsider as catalyst. The film is *Boudu Saved from Drowning* with a light touch of Pasolini's *Teorema* (1968), and the climax, which takes place at the Whitemans' Christmas party (who's more assimilated than a Beverly Hills Jew?) involves a farcical chase like the one in the last act of Renoir's *The Rules of the Game.*

Since *Bob and Carol* and *Blume in Love*, Mazursky's southern California has become even nuttier—and multicultural. The Whitemans' most vocal neighbor is a black record producer named Horace (Little Richard). When the burglar alarm draws a phalanx of cops to the Whitemans' door, some of them in a chopper, Horace complains loudly that he doesn't merit such service because he's a brother. But he has a gorgeous white trophy wife, and, when Iranians move onto the block, it's Horace who mutters, "There goes the neighborhood." Class boundaries are ever present in this updated Beverly Hills, but they seem more fluid than they used to be: Dave's Asian gardener, observing his employer's stress level, offers him the use of his condo in Hawaii. And the family has a mixture of old and newly refurbished hang-ups. Dave and Barbara don't have sex anymore, so he makes nightly visits to the maid, Carmen. Max, the teenage son, hangs out with an androgynous crowd; Jenny, the daughter, returns from her first semester at Sarah Lawrence with an eating disorder and a rock-manager boyfriend back east (with a drug problem). Barbara has a yogi; it's the dog, Matisse, who sees a shrink (played by— who else?—Donald F. Muhich), because he feels so much hostility toward his masters. The Whitemans are ripe for someone to straighten out their convoluted lives.

*Down and Out in Beverly Hills* is wilder and more satirical than *Bob and Carol*, and though Mazursky has retained his affection for his characters, he's made them more narcissistic. Dave is the only one in the family who could pass for outer-directed. He helps Jerry as much out of genuine compassion as out of a desire to see himself as a generous soul, and he's held onto enough of his Jewish upbringing to believe they ought to feel some guilt at Thanksgiving because of all the starving people in the world, and to feel a slight embarrassment over his ostentatious new car. Barbara, on the other hand, claims—quoting her yogi—that guilt is useless. She finds Jerry's appearance disgusting (though when Dave questions her values, she reminds him, just before whipping off to her aerobics class, that she volunteers three days a week at the local free clinic), and she prefers not to be told anything that might spoil her day. So when Dave goes slumming with Jerry, spending the night with his hobo pals on Venice Beach, he delights in assailing her sensibilities by proclaiming, "I ate garbage last night, Barbara, and I loved it!" The emblem of the Whitemans' solipsism is the life-sized portrait of them that hangs over their bed; it's a mirror that reflects their images back to them. Mazursky gets a lot of mileage out of it: Awake or asleep, they're always positioned in comic relation to that painting.

In the other two Mazursky high comedies from this period, the elite groups are defined by characteristics other than money. *Moscow on the Hudson* (also cowritten by Capetanos) is centered on a Soviet saxophonist named Vladimir (Robin Williams, in one of the sensational performances he gave in his first decade as a screen star) who plays in a circus band. It's the era of *Glasnost*; the circus takes an unprecedented trip to perform in New York. And that's where Vladimir decides, on the spur of the moment, to defect—in that comic emblem of Yankee decadence, Bloomingdale's. Perhaps no one else would conceive of this fish-out-of-water scenario as a high comedy, but Mazursky's temperament inclines that way. In his movie, when Vladimir begins to make his home in New York, he finds himself in a community of immigrants. His girlfriend, Lucia (Maria Conchita Alonso), a Bloomie's salesgirl, is Italian; the lawyer who handles his immigration case (Alejandro Rey) is Cuban. In the defection sequence, we see Japanese tourists snapping photos of the Russians who are grabbing at pants on a rack, and the newswoman who arrives to cover the event is Connie Chung (playing a character named Katy Tong). Later we meet a Korean cab driver, a West Indian immigration official, an East Indian doctor, a pair of Vietnamese nurses. Even Lionel (Cleavant Derricks)—the Bloomie's security guard who protects Vladimir from the petty Soviet bureaucrats trying to snatch him back—is an African American who announces that he can understand how Vladimir feels because he himself is "a refugee from Alabama." Lionel becomes Vladimir's best friend in America.

What defines these characters is, in large part, what they don't have—what they've lost. (In Lionel's case, it's the child he left with his girlfriend down south.) Away from his Moscow family, Vladimir looks for substitutes—he adopts Lionel's crusty old grandfather in place of his own, with whom he shares a special bond. He tries to keep in contact with his kin by writing them regularly, not knowing whether they're receiving his letters. But he feels unmoored in Manhattan; he haunts the Russian community in search of a connection back to his past. Mazursky shows us Lucia's family doing the same: Their home is an effort to create a touch of Italy in the middle of New York—the familial intimacy, the old folks snoozing at midday, the closeness of the water all have the feeling of the old world. But the architecture of the neighborhood reminds us immediately that they're far from the homeland. Lucia, who came to America to escape poverty and other constraints, is having an identity crisis about being Italian American; she tells Vladimir, "Sometimes in the middle of the night I sit up straight and wonder what I am." She loves him, but she rejects him because he doesn't fit into her dream of American assimilation; she dreams of being Katy Tong, who, of course, doesn't have an accent. But Lucia works through her hesitation eventually, accepts her identity as bicultural, and comes back to Vladimir, declaring, "I would love to live with an immigrant." Mazursky brings it all together in a Fourth of July scene where, after Vladimir's experienced the distinctly New York experience of getting mugged, he bitches loudly in a coffee shop about what's wrong with America. Another Russian quarrels about his ingratitude—the two men yelling at each other in public is very Russian, very American—and patrons of different ethnic backgrounds recite bits and pieces of the Declaration of Independence, while a Chinese man floats by with a sparkler. This scene sounds perfectly dreadful on paper; on screen it's enchanting. (The same might be said of almost every scene in Mazursky's 1974 road comedy *Harry and Tonto*; he's a master of the improbable.) Mazursky pulls it off because the movie it's planted in is high comic rather than sentimental.

*Enemies, A Love Story* is set in the various boroughs of New York in the late forties, and what links its main characters is that they're Polish Jews who survived the Holocaust. Herman (Ron Silver) was hidden in a hayloft by the family servant, Yadwiga (Margaret Sophie Stein), whom he's since married and brought to America with him. Masha (Lena Olin), his mistress, was in the camps; so was her mother (Judith Malina), though neither knew the other had made it through the war until it was over. Herman believes he lost his wife as well as his children to Hitler, but it turns out that Tamara (Anjelica Huston) limped away from a mass grave with a bullet in her hip and hid in Russia; eventually she comes to New York too. The story, which Mazursky and Roger L. Simon adapted faithfully from Isaac Bashevis Singer's 1966 novel, is a wondrously rich farce about a man in retreat from the world. "The truth is, you're still hiding in the hayloft," Tamara tells him at one point, and we see it's true: He has nightmares—even sometimes in his waking hours—about the SS hunting him down. So he's always running away, fleeing from one of his three women to another. He retreats from Yadwiga's domestic demands to Masha, from Masha's crazy jealousy to Yadwiga, and from both of them, from the proliferating complications in his life, to Tamara. Tamara tells Herman about Masha, "She's not your lover. She's your enemy," but the real enemy is inside Herman—the part of him that torments him with his wartime past. In the end, Masha is dead but he's still running. Even we don't know where he is, any more than Yadwiga and Tamara, who are left to raise his new daughter together. (They name her Masha.)

When Tamara asks Herman, "Were you always like this, or did the war do it?" the movie doesn't tell us the answer, but we figure it's a little of both. Certainly their marriage was always a troubled one, and he was always duplicitous and unfaithful, but the experience of the Holocaust must have made him more desperately so, more terrified of committing himself and carrying through, more confused about what he wants and who he is. Who are you when you spent years hiding in a hayloft, when your wife returns from the dead, when your children have been murdered by the Nazis? Masha's legacy from the war is a driving, self-tormented neurosis that's most apparent in her relationship with her mother, whom she blames for everything. Yet when her mother dies, Masha kills herself; it's as if the old woman held the scrambled parts of her together somehow and she loses all structure, all purpose, without her. As for Tamara, she considers herself dead, finished off by the Nazis, though Anjelica Huston's eyes are alive with pain, and Tamara can't really be a ghost as long as other ghosts—her dead children— still haunt her at night.

These three characters are intensely intellectual (though Tamara complains that Herman never took her ideas seriously). In bed, Herman and Masha ask each other endless questions: If I committed suicide, how long would you mourn me? Would you sleep with a woman if there were no men left? Did you ever screw a guard? Would you still want me if we were both in the grave? Even when they're making love, they're still challenging each other, battling each other. They argue even in public; they're forever breaking up and getting back together again. Tamara's style is more ironic than Masha's, but she's just as feisty and just as smart. Either woman is a match for Herman, and so, in her nonintellectual way, is Yadwiga. Though she's devoted to him, bathes him, is up hours before him to shop and clean and prepare his food, even polishes his slippers, she has a peasant earthiness and persistence, and when the neighbors tell her that he's cheating on her, she starts fighting back. She doesn't mind being his servant still, his *special* servant, as long as he respects her and remembers what he owes her—as long as he doesn't lie to her. (And he lies to her daily.)

Yadwiga decides to convert to Judaism because she wants to be the perfect wife for Herman. She's grateful to God for sending him to her, and if it's the Jewish God who did that, then she'll be Jewish. And so she observes all the rituals (though, in a supreme comic moment, when Tamara walks through her door one day, Yadwiga thinks she's seen a ghost and instinctively crosses herself). Yadwiga's devoutness is one of the traits that distinguish her from the other main characters, for whom Jewishness is more a matter of culture and experience than of religion. God is something they argue about: Masha says He doesn't care what happens to them, while Herman, as usual, can't make up his mind—he says at different times that God means suffering, that there *is* no God, that if there *were* a God, he would defy Him, and that he can't commit suicide because he's afraid of Him. Tamara lives with her aunt and uncle on the Lower East Side (which resembles an old-world *shtetl*) and works in their shop, selling Jewish artifacts, but the meaning of the artifacts doesn't touch her, any more than the rest of the world does since her children were killed. Both Herman and Masha have mixed feelings about their Jewishness, too (as a cultural identity). Masha wants to be married to Herman, in a Jewish ceremony that she says will (by Jewish law) outweigh his marriage to a *shiksa*, but she claims she's only doing it for her mother. (After the wedding, ironically, her mother still isn't happy; she adores Herman, but she's perfectly aware that, Jewish marriage ceremony or no, he remains a bigamist.) Herman doesn't want to attend temple with social Jews who go only on the high holidays; he'd rather stay away altogether and not be a hypocrite. But when Masha's ex-husband (played by Mazursky) tells him extravagant stories about her infidelities, prompting him to break up with her, he suddenly embraces Judaism, sitting around in a homemade prayer shawl, refusing to answer the phone on the Sabbath. And even when he's not in this phase, he celebrates Yom Kippur, the Day of Atonement, privately, kissing the photograph of his dead children and weeping as we hear the "Mourners' Kaddish" on the soundtrack.

By the time he made *Enemies*, Mazursky had become masterly at tonal shifts—a true Chekhovian. Pauline Kael described *Moscow on the Hudson* as a comedy about a tragedy, and *Enemies* is even more complex: It's a tragicomedy about characters whose tragedies have made their lives into a farce. So though the movie is full of profoundly emotional moments, they're always surprises, like the one where Tamara tells Herman that her children visit her at night and "talk till morning, and when I wake up I don't remember anything," or the one where Masha's mother expresses her disappointment to Herman when it turns out that Masha's announced pregnancy is a hoax: "I wanted so much to have a grandchild—if only someone to name for the murdered Jews." The structure is the purest farce: Herman maintains two completely plausible existences, as Yadwiga's husband and as Masha's, but they keep intruding on each other. *Enemies, A Love Story* is as intricate and delicately balanced as *Shampoo*. It's Mazursky's masterpiece.

Altman's movies often fall into the category of high comedy, even when they also belong to other genres; he's a director who can no more be pinned down to one genre than he can be restricted to a single tone. Films as different from each other as *The Player* (1992) and *Gosford Park* (2001) are high comedies blended with something else. *The Player* is a show-biz film peppered with glimpses of the rich and famous: A vast number of well-known faces (many of them actors who have worked with Altman on other occasions) show up at parties, in restaurants, on the lot of Levinson Studios, where much of the narrative unfolds, or in clips from movies the studio is completing. Making these cameos into a game for us (how many can we identify before they've vanished?) helps Altman and the screenwriter, Michael Tolkin, adapting his own caustic 1988 novel, to make their point that everyone is fixated on celebrity, everyone aches to be invited into that gilded world. Griffin Mill (Tim Robbins), the movie's producer antihero, explains that writers are desperate to make a successful pitch because they all believe it's going to land them that hit movie that will put them on the Aspen slopes with Jack Nicholson. It's the movie's stark reduction of Hollywood greed and competitiveness to that naked desire that makes *The Player* as funny as it is. (The novel is meaner. The way Altman has studded the movie with stars is great fun but mitigates its bite; it begins to feel like a vision of Hollywood that the community itself approves and wants to participate in creating.)

The movie is also a film noir, like *Sunset Boulevard*. Mill wields so much power over the creative life and death of writers (he hears half a dozen pitches a day; writers show up unannounced outside his office and approach him in bars with their latest ideas) that their almost universal hatred for him is only natural. *The Player* builds on the portrait of the needy, struggling writer we saw in Wilder's movie. Joe Gillis wheedles his way into a cushier lifestyle and winds up dead. So does David Kahane (Vincent D'Onofrio), the tactless, embittered screenwriter Griffin goes to see, months after promising to get back to him about a pitch, because an anonymous writer is sending Griffin death threats and he thinks it might be Kahane. Griffin figures that if he dangles a deal in front of Kahane, he'll back off, but when he buys the writer a drink, all he gets back are drunken insults. The Hollywood gossip mill is so active that even this unemployed scribe has heard the rumor about Griffin—that he's due to be replaced at the studio by the obsequious up-and-comer Larry Levy (Peter Gallagher). And he doesn't hesitate to taunt Griffin with it. They fight, and Griffin gets so furious that he drowns Kahane in a parking-lot puddle. What he's angry about is that some "dogshit writer" could threaten a man in his exalted position—especially since he knows how vulnerable that position is. He's half-crazed by the possibility that he might lose his membership in the club.

Griffin gets away with murder; he even lands Kahane's girl (Greta Scacchi), an ice queen far better suited to him than the woman he's been sleeping with, Bonnie (Cynthia Stevenson), a studio exec who makes the mistake of wearing her emotions on her sleeve. He even inherits the throne of the studio head (Brion James) whose demise he's helped to engineer. At the end Bonnie gets fired for objecting to the commercial compromises in a high-profile courtroom thriller the studio is putting out. But though *The Player* presents the producer as king shark, it doesn't sentimentalize screenwriters. At Kahane's funeral, a fellow writer uses his eulogy as an opportunity to rail against producers, but he has no idea Kahane was actually dispatched by one; his anger is generalized, and hilariously inappropriate in this setting. It's also essentially fraudulent. Mill is a bastard, but he's right about the longing at the root of writers' desperation. Kahane has let Hollywood get to him; he's lost the knack of kissing ass (if he ever had it). And he's not the only writer we see up close. The authors of the thriller Levinson Studios takes on, *Habeas Corpus*, are a pair of expert showmen, Oakley (Richard E. Grant) and Civella (Dean Stockwell), who sell the prestige concept of a movie with a downbeat ending and no stars; they're so adamant about the virtues of this uncompromising approach that Griffin, who's seeking a way to make Levy look bad, pins him to the project, figuring it'll blow up in his face and then he can play the hero by saving it at the eleventh hour. That doesn't seem to be precisely what happens (in the final reel, Mill and Levy are thick as thieves, and Altman and Tolkin omit the intervening steps), but when *Habeas Corpus* screens in-house, Julia Roberts and Bruce Willis are in the leads and it's got the cheesiest happy ending imaginable. Bonnie carps, "What about the truth? What about reality?" She was naive enough to buy the writers' sell. But Oakley, who made the original (melodramatic) pitch, snaps back, "What about the way the old ending tested in Canoga Park? Everybody hated it. We reshot it. Now everybody loves it. That's *reality.*"

In *The Player*, Hollywood is made up of enclaves, each one a club that looks down on outsiders. The inner circle at the studio, where flattery and venality are flip sides of the same grasping impulse, is one; the griping writers' pack we see represented at David Kahane's funeral is another. Like David, they're the ones who haven't made it; a little success, we're certain, would turn them into Oakley and Civella. Then there are the actors. Griffin's affectionate, comradely tone when he sees a star at a party or a restaurant gives the impression that he pals around with them, but they hold him at arm's length and he doesn't mind it; he knows he exerts power even over them. Their disdain for him is often quite funny. Running into John Cusack at breakfast with Anjelica Huston and the ubiquitous Larry Levy, he calls Cusack "Johnny" and promises he'll see him at Park City, and we see the wariness in the actor's eyes as he edges away. He gives Burt Reynolds the glad hand as he passes Reynolds's table, but when he's out of earshot, Reynolds mutters, "Asshole!" under his breath. Only Malcolm McDowell speaks his mind: confronting Griffin in a hotel lobby, he suggests that the producer might tell him what he thinks to his face instead of talking about him behind his back. "You guys are all the same" is his final disgusted comment.

The Player is one of several memorable show-biz high comedies of the last couple of decades. Richard Rush wrote and directed one of the finest and most unorthodox ones, The Stunt Man, in 1980. It's set among movie people filming a war adventure with literary-philosophical overtones. There's an outsider, a Vietnam vet (Steve Railsback) who's on the lam (the reason he's wanted by the law isn't made clear until late in the picture). He comes to be known as Lucky when he's hired to replace a stunt man who drowned during the shoot. Actually, Lucky causes the drowning, in the virtuoso opening sequence: Running from the cops, he's almost mowed down by the driver of an antique Dusenberg; he draws on his battle savvy to short-circuit his attacker, and the car ends up in the drink. Lucky's failure to realize that his assailant is trying to execute a movie stunt is an indication of a naïveté about the filmmaking process that the movie director, the formidable and enigmatic Eli Cross (played, in incomparable high style, by Peter O'Toole), trades on when he puts Lucky on the payroll. The movie is dense with illusion/reality gags that wouldn't work if Rush didn't place us repeatedly in the position of someone who can't see how Cross is pulling the strings. In one marvelous, extended action scene, Lucky's attacked by the head stunt man, Chuck (Chuck Bail), with what seems like murderous intent (but the cut he gives Lucky is only a makeup wound) and shoved off a tower (where he lands in a net); then he crashes through a skylight into a whorehouse, where he lands in the arms of a pair of whores (who are really more stunt men in drag). Rush moves between the point of view of Cross's camera and Lucky's own point of view, and since he seems like Alice in Wonderland, unprepared for what he's in for, we're in an almost constant state of surprise. What makes the movie a high comedy is the savvy group of movie pros who manipulate the game of illusion. They include Cross (who suggests both John Huston and Orson Welles); Chuck; Sam, the writer (Allen Garfield); Nina (Barbara Hershey), the star, whom Lucky falls for; and the leading man (Adam Roarke), who makes jokes about the daring feats the stunt team makes it look like he's pulling off. What distinguishes the movie, aside from O'Toole's extraordinary performance, is the Pirandellian style and content. Cross assures Lucky that his new job will give him sanctuary from the cops: "You must have heard, surely, of movie magic. You shall be a stunt man who is an actor who is a character in a movie who is an enemy soldier. Who'll look for you among all of those?"

Identity is a different sort of issue in *Tootsie* (1982). The hero, Michael Dorsey (Dustin Hoffman, in his most appealing performance), is an acting teacher and professional actor fed up with imaginatively limited directors who can't see past surfaces. So he passes himself off as a woman named Dorothy Michaels in order to land a role on a daytime soap. This wonderful movie is an unconventional romantic comedy in which the hero earns the love of the heroine (an actress on the show, played with great comic delicacy by Jessica Lange) by learning, at first hand, how a woman feels. It's also both a parody of the acting process and a loving tribute to it, and its affectionate, inside treatment of the business—which resembles the scenes in *Next Stop, Greenwich Village* built around Larry Lipinsky's struggles to get his career off the ground—is the film's high-comic element. Sydney Pollack does double duty as director and in the role of Michael's agent, George Fields (excelling at both). George tries to tell Michael that his obstinacy—which Michael thinks of as a refusal to compromise—has made him so unpopular with producers and directors that no one wants to hire him. Michael's impulse to go in drag is partly an answer to George's lack of faith, and partly a way of keeping faith with the advice he drums into his students' heads—that it's always been tough to be an actor but that's no excuse for failing to find work somehow. Dorsey is the best acting coach in the history of show-biz movies because of the lengths he goes to in order to live out what he teaches.

Peter O'Toole provides the high comedy in *My Favorite Year* (also 1982), which is otherwise a hard-boiled satirical show-biz comedy with a TV setting (like the later *Soapdish*). *My Favorite Year*, directed by Richard Benjamin, takes place in the days of live TV. Joseph Bologna plays a gifted nutcake named "King" Kaiser—obviously a version of Sid Caesar—whose writing staff is almost as quirky as he is. O'Toole is Alan Swann (read Errol Flynn), whose off-camera hijinks, usually involving some combination of women and alcohol, are almost as famous as his on-screen presentations of various swashbuckling heroes. He isn't, perhaps, much of an actor; Flynn wasn't either. But he's indisputably a star, and he's earned his stardom through bravado and panache. O'Toole, of course, *is* an actor—a great one—so he's able to suggest the insecurities lurking beneath those qualities. The movie puts Swann in the charge of the novice member of the writing team, Benjy Stone (Mark Linn-Baker), who has to make sure the notorious movie star makes it to every rehearsal and stays away from trouble. The script (by Norman Steinberg and Dennis Palumbo) has a sentimental hook: The only way Swann can overcome his private terrors—of rejection by the daughter he's estranged from, of playing before a live audience—is by truly embodying the larger-than-life persona he projects in his movies. O'Toole is so amazing in the role that when this conceit pays off at the end, you don't feel you've been jerked into an emotional response. He makes Swann not just a star but a monarch; his performance may begin as an uproarious impersonation—like Fredric March's in *The Royal Family of Broadway*—but it ends on a higher plane. When, at the conclusion of the dress rehearsal, he tells Kaiser that he hasn't had so much fun since the world was young, tossing off the line but lining it with feeling, you realize you're watching one of the supreme high-comic performers in movie history.

Woody Allen's on firmer ground in the delirious burlesque *Bullets Over Broadway* (1994) than in the affected comedy of manners *Manhattan*. Several social strata collide in this 1920s story of a self-serious young playwright, David Shayne (John Cusack), who's lured away from his Greenwich Village intellectual set (which resembles a jokey version of Larry's crowd in *Next Stop, Greenwich Village*) into the glittering world of Broadway. David not only gets a production of his play, *God of Our Fathers*, he even gets to direct it, supposedly so it won't be wrecked by interfering hands. But the only backer the producer (Jack Warden) can find is a gangster (Joe Vitarelli) whose cash comes at a price: His hilariously untalented showgirl moll, Olive (Jennifer Tilly), has to play one of the parts. The double-tiered central joke is doubly at the expense of the pretentious, nerve-wracked Shayne. He turns out to be both corruptible and mediocre. The famous star, Helen Sinclair (Dianne Wiest, in a prize comic turn), seduces him into shaping her role as she sees fit, while Cheech (Chazz Palminteri), the tough guy the gangster assigns to baby-sit Olive during rehearsals, offers aggressive suggestions about how to improve the play that beat Shayne's own instincts hollow. The aristocracy here, of course, is theatrical, though Allen sends them up (just as Kaufman and Ferber send theirs up in *The Royal Family of Broadway*). Chief among them is Helen, a man-eater with a brass-tinged lower range and a tendency to squint as she intones phony tributes to the ghosts of Broadway history lurking in the recesses of the theater. Then there are the elegantly trained Warner Purcell (Jim Broadbent), a secret glutton, and Eden Brett (Tracey Ullman), who's tirelessly energetic and chatty, like Bea Lillie on amphetamines. This peerless trio represents a parodic version of the high-gloss drawing-room Broadway that the talkies eventually killed off. When he joins its ranks, David begins to smoke his cigarettes through a holder.

Like *The Player*, *I'll Do Anything* (1994), written and directed by James L. Brooks, is a study of narcissism, Hollywood style, but its dramatic strategies are quite different. Nick Nolte plays Matt Hobbs, an L.A. actor who's left his pretty-boy youth and is heading toward middle age without having had many breaks. He lives in a world where it's perfectly acceptable—the norm—to put your own needs before anyone else's, and where insincerity is the hallmark. Nolte gives one of the funniest, most subtly nuanced and most accurate portrayals of an actor on record. In the early scenes, he seems to be parodying his own days as a hunk; later he parodies the Method. It's a loving send-up, like Dustin Hoffman's in *Tootsie*. These are actors whose Method preparation, after all, is famous: Nolte lived among the homeless for a while before shooting *Down and Out in Beverly Hills*, and in the scene where he entices the Whitemans' dog into eating his supper by lapping his food out of his bowl, he's really eating dog food.[1]

Matt's wife, Beth (Tracey Ullman), broke up with him a few years back when she got tired of playing second fiddle to his career, and moved back to Georgia with their daughter Jeannie. He's been too self-involved to make time to see the kid; the distance has made it easy for him, and it's now been two and a half years. He's finally set up a visit, though he tries to get out of it, pleading the primacy of his career once again, but Beth won't let him. And then the visit turns out to be a lot more: Beth has gotten herself arrested, and Matt has to take over custody. Jeannie (played by the one-of-a-kind child actress Whittni Wright) is a handful. She's loony and uncategorizable—damaged, eruptive, hilarious, infuriating, touching. She demands so much attention, and everything she does is so immediate, so on the surface, that Matt can't ignore her, and he can't reason with her. It becomes increasingly difficult for him to coexist in the world defined by her childish needs and the phony world of Hollywood—the neurotic, high-comic world that has dictated his mode of behavior up to now. So Matt has to modify his values to accommodate Jeannie.

Actually, in the Hollywood of *I'll Do Anything* (one of the unjustly neglected—and best performed—comedies of the nineties), Matt resides at the positive end of the spectrum: He may be self-centered, but he isn't insincere. The kindest person we meet is Nan Mulhanney (Julie Kavner), who's in charge of previews for the studio that calls Matt in for an audition. She doesn't have enough self-confidence to take a job in a less insane environment, but she's balanced enough to recognize that Hollywood is peopled by "overprivileged people crazed by their fear of losing their privileges." This is, of course, a place we recognize from *The Player*. Nan's main squeeze is the studio's head of development, Burke Adler (Albert Brooks), whose level of fear has turned him into a dyspeptic mess, a kind of monster of insecurity and compulsive behaviors. She finally walks out on him in a restaurant where, for the umpteenth time, he's propelling himself from table to table, working the room like an automaton whose polish has begun to wear off. James Brooks, who demonstrates more satirical edge here than in anything else he's done, stages horrifying studio scenes involving a director (Ian McKellen) who isn't interested enough to stick around for acting auditions and discussions among the development staff that reduce talented actors to looks and sex appeal. The only "D person" with a shred of sensibility and individuality is Cathy Breslow (Joely Richardson), who knows Matt from an acting class and lands him the audition—and then a more important one, for the lead in a project she's managed to slam through. But she's as insecure in her way as Burke; she's forever caving in to the pressure of her colleagues, even though she has no respect for them.

The movie gets itself into a tangle in the last act, when Jeannie, hanging out at the studio during her dad's audition, is picked for a kids' show, and Matt has to navigate warring reactions—her sudden luck is thrilling, but it's probably the worst possible thing for her emotional development, especially now when he seems to be getting a handle on what it means to be a parent. For once he puts his daughter first; he learns not only that Cathy (who has become romantically involved with him) didn't support his screen test with the other "D people," but that she doesn't understand his priorities. So Cathy becomes the villain of the piece. (Nan tells her to her face that she isn't good enough for him.) It's a bad idea, and you wish the movie didn't simplify itself at the end. But it's tough to make the last act of a satirical high comedy work; Altman and Tolkin clutch at the end of *The Player*, too.

Of all Robert Altman's movies, *Gosford Park* (2001) is the most conventional high comedy, though it's blended with a murder mystery. That's not his invention, of course, or that of the screenwriter, Julian Fellowes (working from an idea by Altman and actor-producer Bob Balaban). British mystery writers of the thirties—when *Gosford Park* is set—loved to invoke the comedy-of-manners tradition, and in our own country *The Thin Man* adopts that mix, with a few strictly American vulgarities thrown in for flavor. Altman and Fellowes set out to make *Agatha Christie Meets "The Rules of the Game,"* with a shooting weekend in the country, a wide cast of characters that includes both aristocrats and domestics, and a variety of illicit couplings, including one that crosses class barriers—the host, Sir William McCordle (Michael Gambon), has been carrying on an affair with his daughter's maid, Elsie (Emily Watson). Another of the liaisons only seems to violate class rules but, like the romances of neoclassical comedies, is really a meeting of equals (or nearly equals) in disguise. Sir William's wife, Lady Sylvia (Kristin Scott Thomas), has it off with the valet (Ryan Philippe) of her American guest, a Hollywood producer named Weissman (Balaban). She doesn't know—nor do we—that Henry is really a movie actor doing research for a part in Weissman's next Charlie Chan picture. The joke is that when he reveals himself, nobody likes him; the other guests think he's been behaving boorishly and the servants feel betrayed. "You can't play on both teams at once," one of the maids explains to him.

In fact, the trouble with Fellowes's script is that it's so scrupulous about making a political point about the distinction between servants and masters in the England of the thirties that it fails to acknowledge how intricate and complex their interactions often were. There is one friendship across class lines—Elsie and her mistress, Isobel (Camilla Rutherford)—but the movie insists that all the other aristocrats treat their domestics like nonpersons, though anyone who's watched *Upstairs, Downstairs* would be surprised to hear it. In the most egregious scene, the fatuous Inspector Thompson (Stephen Fry), called in to investigate Sir William's murder, refuses to query the servants because he says they wouldn't be likely to know anything. We're meant to see the irony (especially when it turns out that a servant is the killer), but surely no one who made it all the way to inspector at Scotland Yard would make so serious an error.

When *Gosford Park* (the name of the McCordles' country estate) veers anywhere near social commentary, it becomes unconvincing melodrama; Fellowes's Oscar-winning script is the weakest element in the movie. Altman's work, by contrast, is impeccable and inspiriting. He swirls around the great house, picking up the most telling small details of the characters' lives and interactions; the conversations seem spontaneous, while the staging and camerawork are choreographed with effortless precision. And he's gathered the most gifted ensemble he's directed since *Nashville* (all but Balaban and Philippe are English), including Maggie Smith, Alan Bates, Helen Mirren, Richard E. Grant, Eileen Atkins, Tom Hollander, Derek Jacobi, Jeremy Northam, Clive Owen, Kelly Macdonald, and Sophie Thompson. It's a ticklish joke that Bates, Jacobi, Mirren, and Atkins—all members of British theatrical royalty—play servants. Mirren, as the housekeeper, Mrs. Wilson, gives the most subtle and astonishing performance, though her big scenes are written as melodrama. The movie's high-comic spirit is Maggie Smith, as the droll, gossipy dowager Lady Constance Trentham. She's playing an archetype—the bankrupt aristo who lives off the grudging charity of her nephew (Sir William)—but she does so much with lines like Lady Constance's complaint about the boredom of weekends in the country, "There's always so little to talk about after the first flush of recognition," or with her childish delight in a scrumptious breakfast in bed or a mean joke at another guest's expense that you don't think of her as a type at all. The other deft high-comic touch is the presence of one real-life character among the guests, the songwriter-actor Ivor Novello (Northam), who literally sings for his supper. He's forever at the piano, enchanting the others, especially the servants, with his plaintive melodies and brittle, slightly romantic-masochistic lyrics. (The exception is Lady Constance, who finds him tiresome and delivers a few priceless bons mots at his expense.) Novello's songs are second-tier Noël Coward, but since the same can be said for much of Coward's own output, that hardly seems like a flaw. They provide an ideal soundtrack for the movie.

Two writer-directors emerged in the nineties whose work, thus far, has been entirely in the realm of high comedy. Whit Stillman's debut film, the 1990 *Metropolitan*, depicts the courtship rites of upper-crust New York City WASPs—or, as one of them likes to call their crowd, UHBs (urban *hautes bourgeois*). There's an outsider, Tom (Edward Clements), whose manners are so good that the most exclusive group, encountering him at a party, takes him up; they don't realize that he lives in a middle-class neighborhood and his tux is rented. Tom struggles with his longing to belong to this set; he's the Macaulay Connor figure who starts out critical of the rich but quickly capitulates when he gets to know them. (In this movie, that means dropping his socialist pose and developing a taste for Jane Austen—to whom many critics, dutifully taking the hint, implausibly compared Stillman.) But Stillman isn't very skilled with his actors (and Clements barely seems to be an actor at all), so you don't feel the tension between Tom's style, which is acquired, and theirs, which is a birthright. And though the movie seems meant to be both affectionate and parodic, like a Mazursky picture, you can't place these young aristocrats or the era they belong to. Are there young people in 1990 who wear dinner clothes night after night? One character gets sick drunk; another takes mescaline; in one scene they play strip poker (though Stillman, who's no sensualist, cuts away before they reveal too much). Otherwise their conduct doesn't seem remotely like that of college students, and the banter Stillman has created for them, meant to be a stylized version of sparkling café chat, is so artificial that they always seem to be talking in quotation marks. That's clearly his intention—he's a very deliberate stylist. He's also a minimalist, and that doesn't work well with high comedy unless you're Eric Rohmer.

*Barcelona* (1994) is far more accomplished than *Metropolitan*, though perhaps even more baffling. The only holdovers among the cast from his earlier comedy are Chris Eigeman and Taylor Nichols, who gave the only good performances in it. Here they play cousins, white-bread Republicans in Spain at the twilight of the cold war, and the beautiful young women they romance look at them through perplexed but intrigued eyes. Stillman shapes the story of these young Yankees' adventures in Spain as a series of contained, small-cast dialogues; Rohmer must be one of his influences, along with Philip Barry.

But the way he uses his two protagonists, making them the butt of the joke while staying essentially on their side, recalls an entirely different tradition—the Yankee-clowns-abroad scenarios of the *Road* pictures Bob Hope and Bing Crosby made (mostly) in the forties. Stillman's version contains two Hopes and no Crosby. In those movies the exotic settings were a joke; Dorothy Lamour and the other performers who inhabited them were pure Hollywood. But you couldn't make films like those now, so Stillman scores points off the boys' lunkheadedness about cultural issues—their reflex defense of the United States, their complaint that Europeans don't know how to cook a hamburger, their shock at the anti-Americanism they encounter—while clearly sympathizing with their discomfort. The humor is evenhanded—maybe too evenhanded to work; there's no satiric sting, and the political subplot (involving the bombing of the USO building) makes you uncomfortable. Finally Stillman seems to be engaged in the same project as he was in *Metropolitan*: a chronicle of the Yankee WASP's last stand—the subject of most of A. R. Gurney's plays, twenty-something division. The issue has a limited appeal—an inherent colorlessness. (Stillman has directed a third film, *The Last Days of Disco* [1998], but throwing his style and his kind of characters in a seventies nightclub setting is an awful mistake.)

Lisa Cholodenko already had a sureness of tone, a sense of dramatic structure and a skill at coaching actors when she turned out her first movie, *High Art*, in 1998. It's a very strange film, though, combining a satirical, decidedly hip take on the Manhattan art (and art-mag) scene with a cautionary, relentlessly downbeat yet equally hip view of the SoHo junkie scene. Radha Mitchell plays Syd, an ambitious young assistant editor at a photography magazine called *Frame* who's treated like an intern by her deadpan bosses. (As played by Anh Duong and a very amusing, ponytailed David Thornton, they have so little pulse you expect to find out they're vampires.) But then she discovers that her upstairs neighbor, Lucy (Ally Sheedy, in a ravaged, high-stakes comeback performance), is a brilliant photographer, a one-time star who walked away from the New York art scene. Lucy still works, but at her leisure; the rest of the time she snorts heroin with her lover, a one-time Fassbinder actress named Greta (Patricia Clarkson, in a hilarious, beautifully calibrated Eurotrash impersonation), and their friends. When *Frame*'s editors hear Lucy's back in New York, they hire her to do a spread, and she insists on Syd as her editor. The rest of the story parallels Benjy Stone's travails with Alan Swann in *My Favorite Year*, except that the two women become lovers and the ending is predictably tragic. That's the addict-movie side kicking in. The intersection of the phony aristocracy of the Manhattan art world and the more courtly—and more detached—circle of junkies, who are like remnants from Andy Warhol's factory, is fascinating, though, and Cholodenko has a witty satirical eye. She doesn't shy away from her young protagonist's ambition and self-absorption—though Lucy's death is perhaps a cruel way of punishing Syd for them.

Unfortunately, that eye isn't sufficiently in evidence in her next picture, *Laurel Canyon* (2003), a confidently made comedy in which an uptight young man (Christian Bale) brings his fiancée (Kate Beckinsale) to live with his bohemian record-producer mom (Frances McDormand) in Los Angeles. Sam's adult life is an extended rebellion against his unconventional music-biz upbringing—Jane raised him by herself in a languid, druggy, sexually free atmosphere. Manic about order, he's launching a career in psychiatry, while Alex, his partner, is a biologist completing her dissertation. Jane drives him crazy. It wasn't his intention to share her Laurel Canyon house; she was supposed to have vacated it. But she's still there when he arrives, and her current lover, a young Brit named Ian (Alessandro Nivola), is ensconced in the studio next door with his band, completing a record. So while Sam is beginning his residency, and struggling to tamp down his desire for a gorgeous Israeli coworker (Natascha McElhone), Alex works away in her room. Inevitably, the strains of rock and roll, the sweet smell of marijuana, and Jane's charisma lure her away from her laptop. The setup—a repressed eastern blueblood primed for loosening up, a son trying to hold on to the normal lifestyle that he adopted in defiance of his free-spirit mother—is promising, if conventional, but Cholodenko's rhythms aren't right for this kind of comedy. In style and tone the movie might have been conceived by Sam: The scenes are shaped to make points. (It's the same impulse that made Cholodenko kill off Lucy in *High Art* with an overdose.) On the other hand, her heart is too much with freewheeling Jane, whom she softens so much that Sam comes across as the nutty one. A childhood spent with Jane must have been both heavenly and horrible. But Cholodenko won't acknowledge that people like her are generally narcissists who make dreadful parents. This is the kind of movie Mazursky became famous for, but in his version the temptations of Laurel Canyon would have been more sensuous, the tone more complex, the conflicts funnier. And it would have been more honest.

Filmmakers have used the high-comedy form for a range of effects and subjects. In *Jeffrey* (1995), written by the playwright Paul Rudnick and directed by Christopher Ashley, which covers the romantic and sexual tribulations of an attractive young homosexual actor (Steven Weber) in the age of AIDS, the gay subculture becomes the defining notion for the exclusive club, and also the movie's best running gag. Everyone Jeffrey comes in contact with—clothing salesmen, waiters, casting directors—is gay. Philip Kaufman's *Henry and June* (1990) takes a high-comic approach to the bohemian world of the Left Bank in early-thirties Paris. Anaïs Nin (Maria de Medeiros) and her banker husband, Hugo (Richard E. Grant), are aristocrats in a more traditional sense (they appear to have enough money for anything they desire), but the Kaufmans—the director's cowriter is his wife Rose—depict them as childlike, poor little rich kids hunting for experience. Anaïs, who scribbles erotic fiction while Hugo is asleep beside her, is the more adventurous of the two. When Hugo introduces her to the ex-pat writer Henry Miller (Fred Ward), Miller brings her into his world. It's a Parisian subculture she's never seen before—the cafés and clubs and brothels of the Left Bank. Henry hangs out with circus folk, and with the great photographer Brassaï (Artus de Penguern), who captures a demimonde Paris that's fresh and new. So, for a while, Anaïs hangs out with them too, starved as she is, she says, for people who are alive, restless for exotica. When, her typewriter clutched to her breast, she steps out of her husband's car in an unfamiliar, lower-class Paris neighborhood and into the flat Henry shares with his pal Osborne (Kevin Spacey), past the musicians and pickpockets in the street—Kaufman is quoting the famous opening of René Clair's 1930 *Under the Roofs of Paris* here (he even uses the same music)—she's joining a new club. And when she's through with Miller and his wife, June (Uma Thurman), the voracious bisexual vamp who does double service as Henry's muse and Anaïs's, she walks straight out of that flat to find the faithful Hugo waiting to ferry her back to her life.

Henry and June, with their thick Brooklyn accents, are perhaps the most oddball aristocrats ever to claim primacy in a comedy of manners. But their world, where the mixture of high and low culture reaches intoxicating intensity, is as insulated and self-defined as the bohemian elite Noël Coward characterized in *Design for Living* (which comes from the same era). It's a world of experimentation, in art and in life. Miller works away at *Tropic of Cancer*, Nin at *House of Incest*, and they argue over D. H. Lawrence. When they go to the movies it's to see Dreyer's *The Passion of Joan of Arc* or Sagan's *Mädchen in Uniform* or Buñuel and Dali's *Un chien andalou*, which the Paris art-house audience boos. "C'est obscène!" one patron cries, to which Anaïs stands up self-righteously and replies, "Fuck you, Jack!" Medeiros is wonderfully funny: Henry may have taught her to curse, but she discharges the expletive in an almost maidenly way, batting her eyes and then darting a glance back at him, like a mischievous schoolgirl. Everything in the movie—one of the most sensuous period pieces ever made by an American filmmaker—contributes to recreate the parameters of this aristocracy, which the Kaufmans adore, while they can see the humor in the interactions of a trio as self-conscious and self-involved as this one. The soundtrack includes Debussy's *Afternoon of a Faun* and "Parlez-moi d'amour" by the French chanteuse Lucienne Boyer and Bessie Smith's "Nobody Knows You When You're Down and Out." At the end, when Anaïs, safely stowed away in Hugo's car, drives past Henry on his bike, clowning around, we hear Bing Crosby croon "I Found a Million Dollar Baby (in a Five and Ten Cent Store)." This final musical choice is particularly witty. That's what Anaïs has been all along—a million-dollar baby slumming in a five-and-ten-cent neighborhood.

Robert Redford's *Quiz Show* (1994) tells the story of the game-fixing scandal on the TV show *21*, but Paul Attanasio's script plays with the tacit class boundaries between Jews and Gentiles in Eisenhower's America. When Herbie Stempel (John Turturro) is asked to throw a match in favor of Charlie Van Doren (Ralph Fiennes), he's sore because this WASP golden boy is walking away with the only crown Herbie's ever been allowed to win. The sponsor wants a winner on *21* who looks like he could get a *table* at 21, and Herbie, with his lower-middle-class background and his Bronx accent and aggressive personality, isn't it. His Jewishness is, of course, inseparable from those other qualities. Charlie, by contrast, is handsome, charming, with a gee-gosh boyishness; he never pushes too hard. And he's the son and heir to a fabulous WASP legacy: His parents, Mark (Paul Scofield) and Dorothy (Elizabeth Wilson), are a famous poet-critic-lecturer and a well-known novelist. *Quiz Show* is both a social-problem picture about the social effects of television (not a persuasive one) and a highly original comedy of manners about Gentile insiders and Jewish outsiders in the American class system of the fifties. The movie's pivot—and wild card—is Dick Goodwin (Rob Morrow), the dogged Jewish lawyer from the Boston suburbs who, biding time on the Legislative Oversight Subcommittee, sees that the presentment resulting from the grand jury probe of game-show corruption has been sealed. He smells a rat and starts to investigate. Goodwin graduated first in his class at Harvard Law; he's one of the lucky ones—he made it through Harvard's quota for Jews, probably because, unlike Stempel, he doesn't come across as Jewish. Herbie doesn't spot it; when Dick comes by to talk, Herbie offers him rugelach and thinks he has to explain what it is. "I'm familiar with rugelach," Dick answers with a trace of sarcasm, prompting an amazed Stempel to ask—as almost any Jew would have in 1957—"How'd a guy like you get into Harvard?" But when Charlie, whom Dick befriends, takes him for lunch at a ritzy club, Dick quips that the Reuben sandwich on the menu must be the only *other* Reuben in the room. This is a club that even Goodwin's Harvard credentials couldn't gain him entrée to unless he were the guest of a Van Doren.

Goodwin's personal struggle is that he falls in love with Charlie's WASP world. Meanwhile, in one of the film's many ironies, the producers of *21* (David Paymer and Hank Azaria), who see to it that every Jew who wins is ultimately defeated by a Gentile, and the Gentile always wins more money, are themselves Jews. *Quiz Show* is a terrific movie, but the casting of the central roles is flawed: To work on all cylinders, it would have to star three actors with the right style for high comedy. Judy Davis and Kevin Spacey, as the squabbling couple in Ted Demme's *The Ref* (1994) who are reconciled when a runaway thief holds them hostage, have that style in spades. Few of Spacey's roles have seemed as ideally suited to that killer verbal attack of his—the razor-blade irony backed up by chainsaw hostility. And Davis is witheringly brilliant trading insults with him. Davis made her name with both free-spirit roles (*My Brilliant Career* [1980], *High Tide* [1988]) and neurotic, repressed ones (*A Passage to India* [1984]); and in high comedy, which was her specialty in movies in the nineties, she gets to draw on that entire range. Her way of using idiosyncratic mannerisms—the pursed-lip smile, the folded-in-on-herself physicality, the comic-strip tipped-over-and-balanced-on-one-foot pose—to split open a character's anxieties and dilemmas is Katharine Hepburn–like, but her dark, benighted presence is nothing like Hepburn's. And what she can't do with a line! The critic Alan Dale writes about "that voice in which you can hear the grating of nutmeg" and "her archly jaded comic style."[2] You could argue that *The Ref*, with its inventive script by Richard LaGravenese and Marie Weiss, is a reconstructed romantic comedy, where the couple begins on the verge of divorce but comes back together again (as they do in certain classic screwball comedies, most famously *The Awful Truth*).[3] But, as Dale writes, "The mix of post-'70s frankness and screwball style make this a four-finger cocktail of a high comedy."[4]

Dale talks about the ways Judy Davis is like both Constance Bennett ("that combination of airiness and saturation. . . . And like Bennett, Davis's comic ability is inseparable from her glamour, which likewise feels fully attained rather than patrician, inborn") and Bette Davis in *All About Eve*. He's referring here to *The New Age* [1994], but you can also see the Bette Davis connection in Woody Allen's *Husbands and Wives* (1992), where, like her predecessor, she smokes with deadly conviction, using her cigarette like a weapon (usually aimed at herself). There are no straight readings in a Judy Davis performance; if there's such a thing as being compulsively elliptical, she is. Her rhythms are unpredictable. In *Husbands and Wives* she plays Sally, who divorces her husband (Sydney Pollack) and then returns to him, not very happily, when she can't find contentment with a sweet, uncomplicated swain (Liam Neeson), who settles for her best friend (Mia Farrow). *Husbands* and *Wives* is a miserable little movie, full of characters Allen seems barely able to contain his loathing for (specifically the female ones), but Davis goes breathtakingly far with her tamped-down, splayed-apart character.

In *The New Age*, written and directed by Michael Tolkin, she plays Katherine, married to Peter (Peter Weller) and living the high life in contemporary Los Angeles. Tolkin takes up where Paul Mazursky left off in his southern-California high comedies by taking the hip aristocrats into murky economic waters. In this movie, the bottom drops out of their lives, revealing an abyss that appears bottomless. One day Peter's talent-agency boss complains that he isn't as creative or as industrious as he used to be, so Peter walks out. Unfortunately, the same day Katherine erases all her business files because her clients owe her money that, in the post-boom economy of the nineties, they can't seem to pay. So both halves of the couples are at loose ends, and their restlessness extends to their sexual and spiritual lives, too. They give a big party where sex lingers in the air, as it does at the parties in *Shampoo*; she takes a younger lover (he's already got one); they consult their gurus; they open an elite clothing shop called Hipocracy, where a belt goes for $400 plus tax. When it folds, they consider suicide, but the last scenes find Katherine working as a saleswoman at someone else's shop and Peter training telemarketers to embrace economic greed in their lives and their careers.

The sexual experimentation in *The New Age* makes Bob and Carol's fumblings and Blume's reckless, unconsidered infidelity to Nina seem naive and rather sweet. Peter and Katherine agree to go on living together, but they entertain their lovers in separate rooms: While hers (Bruce Ramsay) mounts her, she can hear the sounds of sex from the living room, where his (Paula Marshall) is pinned against the piano. There's an ultramodern version of a Noël Coward scene at a spa, where all four of them, in their separate cubicles, discuss whether or not Peter and his mistress Alison should break up. And Peter gets invited to a party with "the usual art and politics and S&M crowd," where the first remark he overhears, as he wanders among the naked and semi-naked, the pierced and the chained, is "The problem with him is that he's still really just a swinger, and he pretends to be bisexual, but he comes to the parties, and all he does is try to make it with the women." Mazursky's shrinks have given way to the spiritual teachers—Sarah (Rachel Rosenthal), who teaches yoga to Katherine and invites her to a female drumming circle; Mary (Sandra Seacat), who spouts Zen wisdom while one of their friends, Laura (Maureen Mueller), suffering from cancer, ends her life with her husband and friends around for support (Mary calls it "self-deliverance"); and Jean (Patrick Bauchau), who has an elegantly remote quality, as if he didn't have any feeling beneath his words.

Though he spouts cryptic advice like "Live with the question," he might just as well be an aging gigolo as a guru.

What makes the tone of *The New Age* so unusual is that, though it's unmistakably satirical about the characters' solipsistic, privileged existences, and though it's very bleak, Tolkin doesn't make fun of the idea of their spiritual quest, caustic as he may be about the way they go about it. Tolkin stands in the same relation to spirituality as Flannery O'Connor; you shortchange them if you think they're being merely sardonic or glib. And it's audacious of him to bring death into the equation. There's nothing funny about Laura's death scene. It's hard to know how to react when Katherine recreates it later—when she and Peter seem to be at the end of their tether. She dresses in her most ostentatious cocktail-party dress (because "when you're calling on the Angel of Death, you have to call in style") and prepares a pitcher of margaritas ("So Mexican, so Day of the Dead")—only to leap up from their supposed deathbed to reveal that she's only fed Peter enough pills to knock him out for a few hours, and then it's his decision if he wants to go through with it; for her part, she wants to live. The scene seems to be ironic and celebratory at the same time. *The New Age*, with its ricocheting tone and its straight-faced satire, is the most radical high comedy any American filmmaker has ever come up with.

*"When you're calling on the Angel of Death, you have to call in style"*: Peter Weller and Judy Davis prepare for suicide in Michael Tolkin's The New Age *(1994). Credit: New Regency/The Kobal Collection/Bailey, K. C.*

The most remarkable high comedy of this two-and-a-half-decade sweep, however—the best one since *Shampoo* and *Nashville*—is Fred Schepisi's *Six Degrees of Separation* (1993), which John Guare adapted from his own play. It wasn't Guare's first foray into this genre. The acting edition for his wildly inventive 1977 comedy *Marco Polo Sings a Solo* counsels that it should be played like *The Philadelphia Story*, with a stage full of Katharine Hepburns and Cary Grants, and *Six Degrees* is another variant on Philip Barry. The main aristocrats are Ouisa (Stockard Channing) and Flan Kittredge (Donald Sutherland), Manhattan socialites (he's an art dealer) whose lives are disrupted when a young black man who calls himself Paul (Will Smith) bursts into their Central Park East apartment one evening, bleeding from a knife wound in his side that he says was inflicted by muggers. He claims to be a Harvard friend of their two older kids; more than that, he says he's the son of Sidney Poitier, who'll be in town tomorrow to start shooting his new movie, an adaptation of *Cats*. Paul disarms the Kittredges with his credentials, his alleged friendship with their children, his delightful company; he also charms their guest, a South African, Geoffrey (Ian McKellen), who they're hoping will invest in the Cézanne Flan needs to purchase for sale. Paul cooks them all dinner; he enchants them with a précis of his dissertation on *The Catcher in the Rye* (the muggers, he bemoans, stole his only copy). Geoffrey has such a wonderful time that he volunteers the money for the Cézanne and even hatches a scheme for an African American film festival in Johannesburg. (It's the kind of inspiration Tom Wolfe satirized in his essay "Radical Chic.") The Kittredges, utterly taken with this boy, insist on putting him up for the night and advancing him fifty bucks as "walking around money." But in the morning they interrupt him as he's being serviced by a male hustler he picked up in the park after they went to sleep, and they chase him out. Only afterward, when their friends Kitty and Larkin (Mary Beth Hurt and Bruce Davison) share a similar story, and their children disavow any knowledge of a Paul Poitier, do they realize they've been taken in by a stranger. A trip to the library confirms that Sidney Poitier has no son, only daughters.

In the interim before they hear from Paul again (it doesn't happen until quite late in the movie) they learn that he's an outsider tutored by one of their children's prep-school acquaintances, an M.I.T. student named Trent (Anthony Michael Hall) who picked him up on a street in the rain and invited him into his bed. Paul trades sexual favors for lessons in how to be an insider: how to speak, what to wear, whom to pretend to know. (Ouisa, amazed, calls Trent "the Henry Higgins of our time.") This information enables him to leap across class boundaries—to be accepted, for a night here, a night there, into the elite despite being gay, black, and homeless. Trent, though born to the lifestyle Paul covets, has his own outsider issues because of his sexuality; he fantasizes that if Paul becomes a member of the society he feels ostracized from, and he meets him in the parlors of the aristocrats he grew up with, then their relationship will receive the social sanction he feels it can't now. But Paul runs off, stealing—among other things—his address book. The Kittredges also find out that, after leaving them and their friends—and Dr. Fine (Richard Masur), the father of another of Trent's high-school connections—Paul lived for a while with a couple of aspiring actors he met in the park, Rick and Elizabeth (Eric Thal and Heather Graham), Utah émigrés eager for experience in the Big Apple. To them he reports, pointing up at the Kittredges' apartment building, that he's Flan's illegitimate son, shunted aside for his white wife and kids.

Paul theorizes at one point, when he's dazzling the Kittredges and Geoffrey with his cultivated cocktail-party chat, that collage is the art form of the twentieth century, and the structure of the movie—a collage of story fragments, mostly in flashback—reflects the nature of Paul himself, a hustler and a thief who has reinvented himself with parts of the people he's hustled. By the end, he's calling himself Paul Poitier-Kittredge. He wants to adopt Ouisa and Flan, move into their lives, become an art dealer just like Flan. He tells Ouisa, in the telephone conversation that will be the last connection she has with him, that they were the hosts he preferred because they let him use all the parts of himself. But what he used were parts of *the Kittredges* (and of others—the dissertation rap was culled from a commencement speech he read somewhere). A con man who believes his own con can be very convincing, very potent, and there are few things in the world more seductive than someone who wants to be you. "Everything we are in the world, this paltry thing—our life—he wanted it," Ouisa says with astonishment. "He stabbed himself to get into our lives." And he's found the perfect targets in Ouisa and Flan. The aristocrats in *The Philadelphia Story* have it all, as long as they remember not to be fooled by the wrong values. Their counterparts in *Six Degrees of Separation* live hollow, frantic lives. Flan is terrified of losing the Cézanne—and forfeiting their lifestyle. He and Ouisa are companions, business partners, but not lovers. (When Paul, explaining to Ouisa why he picked up the hustler that night, says that he was so happy he wanted to add sex to it, assuming she must do the same, she has to confess that she doesn't.) And while their real children are privileged monsters who delight in kicking their parents in the teeth, Paul tells them what they want to hear (he says their kids called them "kind"), and acts like the child they wish they had, a child who loves them and looks up to them and longs only to emulate them. "He did more for us in a few hours than our children ever did," Ouisa admits.

Paul is seductive in a number of ways. His purported relationship with Sidney Poitier is an irresistible invitation to celebrity by association (Ouisa doesn't have a good word to say for *Cats*, but she and Flan are tickled by the chance to be extras in this fictitious movie version of it). And Poitier's is a name that no good old-school liberal can resist. Yes, these people think of themselves as liberals, just as surely as Dave Whiteman in *Down and Out in Beverly Hills* does. When the put-upon hosts exchange their individual versions of Paul's scam, each points out with gasping admiration what a groundbreaker Poitier was; Dr. Fine says, with a straight face, that as a Jew he's always identified with the black actor's triumph. (When he learns from his son, however, that Paul is a fraud, his language alters: He calls the boy "that fucking black kid" and jumps to the conclusion that he's a crackhead.) To each person whose life he invades, Paul brings a weird mixture of fantasy and reality. To Trent, whose high-school yearbook and treasure trove of information about his classmates grease Paul's ventures into the aristocratic world Trent grew up in, he's a dream lover. Though he disappears after three months with all of Trent's electronic equipment, when Trent's asked if he plans to press charges, he answers dismissively, "Oh, please"; he figures he got his money's worth out of Paul. For Rick, he's the embodiment of Manhattan romance. Rick squanders his and Elizabeth's meager savings on an evening on the town with Paul, which culminates in a midnight carriage ride through Central Park and his first thrilling taste of gay sex. But Paul gives Rick more experience than he can handle: Guilt-ridden, the young actor leaps off the balcony of their apartment. And for the New York socialites whose doors he knocks on with fabricated tales about being mugged on the street below, he combines the articulate, expensively educated veneer they find comfortably familiar with an appreciative sweetness.

But Paul isn't the protagonist of *Six Degrees*. Profoundly mysterious, his own peculiar brand of shrewdness and delusion left largely unexplained, he's the catalyst (like Jerry in *Down and Out in Beverly Hills*). Ouisa is the protagonist. She's Guare's revamped version of a Philip Barry heroine who learns the necessity of wrestling with the accepted wisdom of her upbringing and holding on to whatever she can find in her life that's of genuine value. And like Tracy Lord (and Johnny Case), she comes, in due course, to the conclusion that she's chosen the wrong partner. We get the information about Paul in a series of stories—chapters in the big story all of the Kittredges' friends want to hear, as well as the stories of other characters that form some of these chapters (Ouisa hears the Trent-Paul episode from her daughter Tess, who heard it from Trent; Elizabeth tells the tale of her and Rick's involvement with Paul; and so forth). The recitations to members of the Kittredges' social set take

*"Everything we are in the world . . . he wanted it": Paul (Will Smith) reinvents himself to fit into the Manhattan aristocracy represented by Flan and Ouisa Kittredge (Donald Sutherland and Stockard Channing) in Fred Schepisi's film of John Guare's play* Six Degrees of Separation *(1993). Credit: MGM/Maiden/New Regency/The Kobal Collection/Aronowitz, Myles*

place at gallery openings, in Lincoln Center, at fancy weddings and baptisms, in high-priced restaurants—precisely the sorts of Manhattan backdrops you'd expect for these people's lives. (This is the main amendment Guare and Schepisi make to the stage play, where the fragments of the story are addressed to the audience.) But when Ouisa, pressed by their luncheon hostess (played by Kitty Carlisle Hart, a Manhattan aristo if there ever was one), tells the last chapter of the story, where she loses Paul forever, she suddenly realizes that these anecdotes trivialize the significance of her connection to him. One of the guests (Madhur Jaffrey, the famous Indian chef, who also turns up in *Vanya on 42nd Street* [1994]), hearing the ruefulness in her tone, asks, "Why does it mean so much to you?" and Flan, embarrassed by his wife's display of emotion, by the way the chic, flip, gossipy façade of social intercourse has unaccountably fallen, tries to restore it. But she won't let him: "We turn him into an anecdote to dine out on. As we are right now. But it was an experience. I will not turn him into an anecdote. How do we fit what happens to us into life without turning it into an anecdote with no teeth and a punch line we'll mouth over and over for years to come?" And she gets up and marches out of the party, making a decision to stop dining out on Paul—to opt for something real (the experience) rather than something artificial (the anecdote, style, social intercourse). The last conversation between her and Flan is the first one in the movie that has no audience (except us). And she looks at this man she's lived with for twenty-five years and realizes that his certainty about his place in the world and her tentativeness about hers, his control and her chaos—which echo the two sides of the double-painted Kandinsky that is their apartment's prize possession—are a terrible match. And if we watch the movie a second time, we realize that the filmmakers have been hinting that they are from the outset. One clue, perhaps my favorite: When Paul appears at their door, wounded, Flan observes that his *shirt* is bleeding. Ouisa corrects him: the *boy* is bleeding. It's apt that while she responds to the human situation, her husband remains distanced, observing the boy as if he were a painting.

The movie is rich in verbal and visual references to bursts of color. Flan makes an erudite allusion to the burst of color "that's asked to carry so much" in a Cézanne canvas; he dreams about the second-grade art teacher whose students' work suggests junior Matisses and Picassos. Visually Schepisi gives us the neon reflected in the pool of blood around Rick's body outside the roller disco beneath his and Elizabeth's apartment; the lights that play on the phone booth when Paul calls Ouisa from Greenwich Village; the flowers in the florist shop window that Ouisa passes after she's walked out on the luncheon and her marriage. These images suggest the real thing, experience, life, that Flan tries to aestheticize and that Ouisa realizes, with Paul's help, she wants to get at directly. She refers to herself as color without structure, and at the end she slips out of Flan's grasp, eluding his attempt to order her, to put her on a grid.

*Six Degrees of Separation* is partly about imagination. Paul's "dissertation" speech about *The Catcher in the Rye* culminates in these lines: "To face ourselves. That's the hard thing. The imagination. That's God's gift to make the act of self-examination bearable." In fact, Paul suffers from narcissism and delusion, two disorders that make true self-examination impossible. For Paul, imagination is inseparable from fiction. (That's why he can't be the protagonist.) But his presence allows others to release *their* imaginations: Trent, Rick, Ouisa. At the end of the movie, Ouisa does what Paul's madness prevents him from doing—she faces herself, buoyed up by her own imagination. And the movie is partly, of course, about connection. Guare gives Ouisa the speech that provides the title, in which she says that the six-degree closeness of human beings is both comforting and torturous: "I am bound—you are bound to everyone on this planet by a trail of six people. It's a profound thought. How Paul found us. . . . How every person is a new door, opening up into other worlds. Six degrees of separation between me and everyone else on this planet. But to find the right six people." The coincidences in the story (Larkin and Kitty happen to go to the roller disco the night Rick jumps; the body lands smack in front of them) underscore this theme of connection. The irony—and tragedy—is how hard it is to find the right six people. Ouisa and Flan find their children, who bring them nothing but pain, but she loses Paul; after he phones her and reestablishes contact, he's arrested before she and Flan can reach him. She's not family, she doesn't even know his real name, so she isn't permitted access to the information that might restore him to her.

Paul's coveting Ouisa's life gives it meaning, as well as, paradoxically, exposing its meaninglessness. His connection to her makes her realize how little connection there is in her life. His view of sex reminds her that her life is empty of erotics, empty of passion. His weird, unsolicited love for her—which is somehow delusional and real at the same time—brings out the love in *her*, giving her something to reach out to for the first time in so long. The burst of color he represents takes her away from Flan's aesthetics (color as theory) to something vibrant inside herself she's been out of touch with (color as feeling). *Six Degrees of Separation* returns us to the end of *The Philadelphia Story*, where Tracy confesses to Dexter, "Oh, I don't know anything anymore!" and he replies, "That sounds very hopeful." But in this extraordinary movie, which alters most of the conventions Barry adhered to, the notion of high comedy that he embodied has been complicated and deepened.

# Notes

1. Mel Weiser, *Nick Nolte: Caught in the Act* (Santa Monica: Momentum Press, 1999).

2. Alan Dale, *What We Do Best: American Movies Comedies of the 1990s* (published online, 2003).

3. Stanley Cavell calls these "comedies of remarriage." See Stanley Cavell, *Pursuits of Happiness: The Hollywood Comedy of Remarriage* (Cambridge: Harvard University Press, 1984).

4. Dale, *What We Do Best*.

# Filmography

*Alex in Wonderland.* Directed by Paul Mazursky. Screenplay by Paul Mazursky and Larry Tucker. With Donald Sutherland, Ellen Burstyn, Michael Lerner, Viola Spolin, André Philippe, Federico Fellini, Jeanne Moreau, and Paul Mazursky. 1970.

*Alice Adams.* Directed by George Stevens. Screenplay by Dorothy Yost, Mortimer Offner, and Jane Murfin. Based on the novel by Booth Tarkington. With Katharine Hepburn, Fred MacMurray, Ann Shoemaker, Fred Stone, Frank Albertson, Evelyn Venable, Grady Sutton, Charley Grapewin, Hedda Hopper, and Hattie McDaniel. 1935.

*Alice's Restaurant.* Directed by Arthur Penn. Screenplay by Venable Herndon and Arthur Penn. Inspired by the song by Arlo Guthrie. With Arlo Guthrie, James Broderick, Pat Quinn, Michael McClanathan, Joseph Boley, Tina Chen, Geoff Outlaw, Pete Seeger, Kathleen Dabney, William Obanhein, and Sylvia Davis. 1969.

*All About Eve.* Written and directed by Joseph L. Mankiewicz. With Bette Davis, Anne Baxter, George Sanders, Celeste Holm, Gary Merrill, Hugh Marlowe, Gregory Ratoff, Thelma Ritter, and Marilyn Monroe. 1950.

*Angel.* Directed by Ernst Lubitsch. Screenplay by Samson Raphaelson and Frederick Lonsdale (uncredited). Based on the play by Melchior Lengyel; English version by Guy Bolton and Russell Medcraft. With Marlene Dietrich, Herbert Marshall, Melvyn Douglas, Edward Everett Horton, Ernest Cossart, and Laura Hope Crews. 1937.

*The Animal Kingdom.* Directed by Edward H. Griffith. Screenplay by Horace Jackson, Edward H. Griffith (uncredited), and Adela Rogers St. John (uncredited). Based on the play by Philip Barry. With Ann Harding, Leslie Howard, Myrna Loy,

William Gargan, Neil Hamilton, Ilka Chase, Henry Stephenson, Leni Stengel, and Don Dillaway. 1932.

*Arsène Lupin.* Directed by Jack Conway. Screenplay by Lenore Coffee, Bayard Veiller, and Carey Wilson. Based on the play by Francis de Croisset and Maurice Le Blanc. With John Barrymore, Lionel Barrymore, Karen Morley, John Miljan, and Tully Marshall. 1932.

*Barcelona.* Written and directed by Whit Stillman. With Chris Eigeman, Taylor Nichols, Tushka Bergen, Mira Sorvino, Pep Munné, Helena Schmied, Nuria Badia, and Thomas Gibson. 1994.

*The Big Broadcast of 1938.* Directed by Mitchell Leisen. Screenplay by Russel Crouse, Walter DeLeon, Ken Englund, Howard Lindsay, and Francis Martin. Based on a story by Frederick Hazlitt Brennan. With W. C. Fields, Bob Hope, Shirley Ross, Martha Raye, Dorothy Lamour, Lynne Overman, Ben Blue, Leif Erickson, Patricia Wilder, Grace Bradley, Kristen Flagstad, Wilfred Pelletier, Tito Guízar, and Shep Fields and His Rippling Rhythm Orchestra. 1938.

*Bluebeard's Eighth Wife.* Directed by Ernst Lubitsch. Screenplay by Billy Wilder and Charles Brackett. Based on the play by Alfred Savoir; English version by Charlton Andrews. With Claudette Colbert, Gary Cooper, David Niven, Edward Everett Horton, Elizabeth Patterson, Herman Bing, Warren Hymer, and Franklin Pangborn. 1938.

*Blume in Love.* Written and directed by Paul Mazursky. With George Segal, Susan Anspach, Kris Kristofferson, Marsha Mason, Shelley Winters, Donald F. Muhich, Paul Mazursky, and Erin O'Reilly. 1973.

*Bob and Carol and Ted and Alice.* Directed by Paul Mazursky. Written by Paul Mazursky and Larry Tucker. With Robert Culp, Natalie Wood, Elliott Gould, Dyan Cannon, Donald F. Muhich, Horst Ebersberg, Lee Bergere, and Greg Mullavey. 1969.

*Bullets Over Broadway.* Directed by Woody Allen. Screenplay by Woody Allen and Douglas McGrath. With John Cusack, Dianne Wiest, Jennifer Tilly, Chazz Palminteri, Joe Vitarelli, Jim Broadbent, Jack Warden, Tracey Ullman, Mary Louise Parker, and Rob Reiner. 1994.

*Camille.* Directed by George Cukor. Screenplay by Zoe Akins, Frances Marion, and James Hilton. Based on the play *La dame aux camélias* by Alexandre Dumas *fils.* With Greta Garbo, Robert Taylor, Henry Daniell, Lionel Barrymore, Elizabeth Allan, Jessie Ralph, Lenore Ulric, Laura Hope Crews, and Rex O'Malley. 1936.

*Caught.* Directed by Max Ophüls. Screenplay by Arthur Laurents and John Berry (uncredited). Based (officially) on the novel *Wild Calendar* by Libbie Block. With Barbara Bel Geddes, Robert Ryan, James Mason, Ruth Brady, Curt Bois, Frank Ferguson, Natalie Schafer, and Art Smith. 1949.

*Citizen Kane.* Directed by Orson Welles. Written by Herman J. Mankiewicz, Orson Welles, and John Houseman (uncredited). With Orson Welles, Joseph Cotten, Dorothy Comingore, Ruth Warrick, Everett Sloane, Agnes Moorehead, Erskine

Sanford, Ray Collins, William Alland, Paul Stewart, George Coulouris, and Fortunio Bonanova. 1941.

*Cluny Brown.* Directed by Ernst Lubitsch. Screenplay by Samuel Hoffenstein and Elizabeth Reinhardt. Based on the novel by Margery Sharp. With Jennifer Jones, Charles Boyer, Richard Haydn, Una O'Connor, Reginald Owen, Peter Lawford, Helen Walker, Reginald Gardiner, C. Aubrey Smith, Margaret Bannerman, Sara Allgood, Ernest Cossart, and Florence Bates. 1946.

*Design for Living.* Directed by Ernst Lubitsch. Screenplay by Ben Hecht. Based on the play by Noël Coward. With Miriam Hopkins, Fredric March, Gary Cooper, Edward Everett Horton, and Franklin Pangborn. 1933.

*Desire.* Directed by Franz Borzage. Screenplay by Edwin Justus Mayer, Waldemar Young. Samuel Hoffenstein, Vincent Lawrence (uncredited), and Benn Levy (uncredited). Based on a play by Hans Szekely and R. A. Stemmle. With Gary Cooper, Marlene Dietrich, John Halliday, William Frawley, Ernest Cossart, Akim Tamiroff, Alan Mowbray, and Zeffie Tilbury. 1936.

*The Devil to Pay.* Directed by George Fitzmaurice and Irving Cummings (uncredited). Screenplay by Benjamin Glazer and Frederick Lonsdale. Based on a play by Frederick Lonsdale. With Ronald Colman, Frederic Kerr, Loretta Young, David Torrence, Florence Britton, and Myrna Loy. 1930.

*Dinner at Eight.* Directed by George Cukor. Screenplay by Frances Marion, Herman J. Mankiewicz, and Donald Ogden Stewart. Based on the play by George S. Kaufman and Edna Ferber. With John Barrymore, Lionel Barrymore, Billie Burke, Marie Dressler, Wallace Beery, Jean Harlow, Madge Evans, Edmund Lowe, Karen Morley, Lee Tracy, Jean Hersholt, Louise Closser Hale, Grant Mitchell, and May Robson. 1933.

*Dodsworth.* Directed by William Wyler. Screenplay by Sidney Howard. Based on the novel by Sinclair Lewis and the play by Sidney Howard. With Walter Huston, Ruth Chatterton, Mary Astor, David Niven, Gregory Gaye, Paul Lukas, Odette Myrtil, John Payne, Spring Byington, Harlan Briggs, and Maria Ouspenskaya. 1936.

*Down and Out in Beverly Hills.* Directed by Paul Mazursky. Screenplay by Paul Mazursky and Leon Capetanos. Based on the play *Boudu Saved from Drowning* by René Fauchois and the film by Jean Renoir. With Nick Nolte, Richard Dreyfuss, Bette Midler, Elizabeth Peña, Tracy Nelson, Evan Richards, Little Richard, Donald F. Muhich, Paul Mazursky, Valerie Curtin, Jack Bruskoff, Geraldine Dreyfuss, Barry Primus, Irene Tsu, and Michael Yama. 1986.

*Enemies, A Love Story.* Directed by Paul Mazursky. Screenplay by Roger L. Simon and Paul Mazursky. Based on the novel by Isaac Bashevis Singer. With Ron Silver, Anjelica Huston, Lena Olin, Margaret Sophie Stein, Judith Malina, Alan King, Paul Mazursky, Rita Karin, Phil Leeds, and Elya Baskin. 1989.

*Gosford Park.* Directed by Robert Altman. Screenplay by Julian Fellowes. Based on an idea by Robert Altman and Bob Balaban. With Maggie Smith, Michael Gambon,

Kristin Scott Thomas, Alan Bates, Helen Mirren, Emily Watson, Richard E. Grant, Eileen Atkins, Derek Jacobi, Ryan Philippe, Bob Balaban, Camilla Rutherford, Stephen Fry, Tom Hollander, Charles Dance, Jeremy Northam, Clive Owen, Kelly Macdonald, Geraldine Somerville, Natasha Wightman, Sophie Thompson, James Wilby, Claudie Blakley, Laurence Fox, Trent Ford, and Ron Webster. 2001.

*Grand Hotel.* Directed by Edmund Goulding. Screenplay by Frances Marion, Herman J. Mankiewicz, Donald Ogden Stewart, and Béla Balázs. Based on the novel and play by Vicki Baum; American version by William A. Drake. With Greta Garbo, John Barrymore, Wallace Beery, Lionel Barrymore, Joan Crawford, Lewis Stone, Jean Hersholt, Robert McWade, Rafaela Ottiano, Purnell Pratt, Ferdinand Gottschalk, and Tully Marshall. 1932.

*The Guardsman.* Directed by Sidney Franklin. Screenplay by Ernest Vajda and Claudine West. Based on the play by Fernc Molnár. With Alfred Lunt, Lynn Fontanne, Roland Young, ZaSu Pitts, Maude Eburne, and Herman Bing. 1931.

*Heaven Can Wait.* Directed by Ernst Lubitsch. Screenplay by Samson Raphaelson. Based on a play by Leslie Bush-Fekete. With Don Ameche, Gene Tierney, Laird Cregar, Spring Byington, Eugene Pallette, Marjorie Main, Allyn Joslyn, Charles Coburn, Louis Calhern, Signe Hasso, Tod Andrews, and Clarence Muse. 1943.

*The Heiress.* Directed by William Wyler. Screenplay by Ruth and Augustus Goetz. Based on their play and the novella *Washington Square* by Henry James. With Olivia De Havilland, Ralph Richardson, Montgomery Clift, Miriam Hopkins, Betty Linley, Vanessa Brown, Ray Collins, Mona Freeman, Selena Royle, and Paul Lees. 1949.

*Henry and June.* Directed by Philip Kaufman. Screenplay by Philip and Rose Kaufman. With Fred Ward, Maria de Medeiros, Uma Thurman, Richard E. Grant, Kevin Spacey, and Jean-Philippe Ecoffey. 1990.

*High Art.* Written and directed by Lisa Cholodenko. With Ally Sheedy, Radha Mitchell, Patricia Clarkson, Anh Duong, David Thornton, Gabriel Mann, Tammy Grimes, and Bill Sage. 1998.

*History Is Made at Night.* Directed by Frank Borzage. Screenplay by Gene Towne, Graham Baker, David Hertz, Vincent Lawrence, and Frank Borzage (uncredited). With Charles Boyer, Jean Arthur, Colin Clive, Leo Carrillo, and Ivan Lebedeff. 1937.

*Holiday.* Directed by Edward H. Griffith. Screenplay by Horace Jackson. Based on the play by Philip Barry. With Robert Ames, Ann Harding, Mary Astor, Hedda Hopper, Monroe Owsley, and William Holden. 1930.

*Holiday.* Directed by George Cukor. Screenplay by Donald Ogden Stewart and Sidney Buchman. Based on the play by Philip Barry. With Cary Grant, Katharine Hepburn, Doris Nolan, Lew Ayres, Henry Kolker, Edward Everett Horton, Jean Dixon, Henry Daniell, and Binnie Barnes. 1938.

*Husbands and Wives.* Written and directed by Woody Allen. With Woody Allen, Mia Farrow, Judy Davis, Sydney Pollack, Liam Neeson, Juliette Lewis, and Lysette Anthony. 1992.

*Idiot's Delight.* Directed by Clarence Brown. Screenplay by Robert E. Sherwood. Based on his play. With Clark Gable, Norma Shearer, Burgess Meredith, Edward Arnold, Charles Coburn, Joseph Schildkraut, Laura Hope Crews, and Skeets Gallagher. 1939.

*I'll Do Anything.* Written and directed by James L. Brooks. With Nick Nolte, Joely Richardson, Albert Brooks, Julie Kavner, Whittni Wright, Tracey Ullman, and Ian McKellen. 1994.

*Jeffrey.* Directed by Christopher Ashley. Screenplay by Paul Rudnick. Based on his play. With Steven Weber, Michael T. Weiss, Patrick Stewart, Sigourney Weaver, and Nathan Lane. 1995.

*Lady Windermere's Fan.* Directed by Ernst Lubitsch. Screenplay by Julien Josephson. Based on the play by Oscar Wilde. With Ronald Colman, May McAvoy, Irene Rich, and Bert Lytell. 1925.

*Laughter.* Directed by Harry d'Abbadie d'Arrast. Screenplay by Donald Ogden Stewart, Harry d'Abbadie d'Arrast, Douglas Doty, Herman J. Mankiewicz, and Donald Ogden Stewart. With Nancy Carroll, Fredric March, Frank Morgan, Glenn Anders, Diane Ellis, Leonard Carey, Ollie Burgoyne, and Eric Blore. 1930.

*Laura.* Directed by Otto Preminger. Screenplay by Jay Dratler, Samuel Hoffenstein, Betty Reinhardt, and Ring Lardner Jr. (uncredited). Based on the novel by Vera Caspary. With Dana Andrews, Gene Tierney, Clifton Webb, Judith Anderson, Vincent Price, and Dorothy Adams. 1944.

*Laurel Canyon.* Written and directed by Lisa Cholodenko. With Frances McDormand, Christian Bale, Kate Beckinsale, Alessandro Nivola, and Natascha McElhone. 2003.

*The Letter.* Directed by Jean de Limur. Screenplay by Monta Bell, Mort Blumenstock, Jean de Limur, and Garrett Fort. Based on the story and play by W. Somerset Maugham. With Jeanne Eagels, Reginald Owen, Lady Tsen-Mei, O. P. Heggie, Herbert Marshall, and Irene Browne. 1929.

*The Letter.* Directed by William Wyler. Screenplay by Howard Koch. Based on the story and play by W. Somerset Maugham. With Bette Davis, Herbert Marshall, James Stephenson, Gale Sondergaard, Frieda Inescort, Bruce Lester, Victor Sen Yung, Willie Fung, Cecil Kellaway, and Doris Lloyd. 1940.

*Letter from an Unknown Woman.* Directed by Max Ophüls. Screenplay by Howard Koch and Max Ophüls. Based on a story by Stefan Sweig. With Joan Fontaine, Louis Jourdan, Mady Christians, Marcel Journet, John Good, Art Smith, Carol Yorke, and Howard Freeman. 1948.

*A Letter to Three Wives.* Directed by Joseph L. Mankiewicz. Written by Joseph L. Mankiewicz and Vera Caspary. With Jeanne Crain, Jeffrey Lynn, Ann Sothern, Kirk Douglas, Linda Darnell, Paul Douglas, Florence Bates, Hobart Cavanaugh, Connie Gilchrist, Thelma Ritter, and the voice of Celeste Holm. 1949.

*Lolita.* Directed by Stanley Kubrick. Screenplay by Vladimir Nabokov and Stanley Kubrick (uncredited). Based on the novel by Vladimir Nabokov. With James Mason, Peter Sellers, Shelley Winters, and Sue Lyon. 1962.

*The Long Goodbye*. Directed by Robert Altman. Screenplay by Leigh Brackett. Based on the novel by Raymond Chandler. With Elliott Gould, Sterling Hayden, Nina Van Pallandt, Mark Rydell, Henry Gibson, Jim Bouton, Jo Ann Brody, David Arkin, Warren Berlinger, Steve Coit, and Arnold Schwarzenegger. 1973.

*The Magnificent Ambersons*. Directed by Orson Welles. Written by Orson Welles, Jack Moss (uncredited), and Joseph Cotten (uncredited). Based on the novel by Booth Tarkington. With Tim Holt, Joseph Cotten, Anne Baxter, Dolores Costello, Agnes Moorehead, Ray Collins, Richard Bennett, and Don Dillaway. 1942.

*The Man Who Came to Dinner*. Directed by William Keighley. Screenplay by Julius and Philip Epstein. Based on the play by George S. Kaufman and Moss Hart. With Monty Woolley, Bette Davis, Billie Burke, Ann Sheridan, Reginald Gardiner, Jimmy Durante, Mary Wickes, Elisabeth Fraser, Richard Travis, Grant Mitchell, George Barbier, Russell Arms, and Ruth Vivian. 1942.

*Manhattan*. Directed by Woody Allen. Written by Woody Allen and Marshall Brickman. With Woody Allen, Diane Keaton, Michael Murphy, Mariel Hemingway, and Meryl Streep. 1979.

*The Merry Widow*. Directed by Ernst Lubitsch. Screenplay by Samson Raphaelson, Ernest Vajda, Ernst Lubitsch (uncredited), and Marcel Achard (uncredited). Based on the operetta by Franz Léhar and English libretto by Victor Léon and Leo Stein. With Maurice Chevalier, Jeanette MacDonald, Edward Everett Horton, Una Merkel, and George Barbier. 1934.

*Metropolitan*. Written and directed by Whit Stillman. With Edward Clements, Chris Eigeman, Taylor Nichols, Carolyn Farina, Allison Parisi, Dylan Hundley, Isabel Gillies, Bryan Leder, Will Kempe, Elizabeth Thompson, Stephen Uys, Alice Connorton, and Linda Gillies. 1990.

*Midnight*. Directed by Mitchell Leisen. Screenplay by Billy Wilder and Charles Brackett. Based on a story by Edwin Justus Mayer and Franz Schulz. With Claudette Colbert, Don Ameche, John Barrymore, Mary Astor, Francis Lederer, Elaine Barrie, Hedda Hopper, Rex O'Malley, and Monty Woolley. 1939.

*Monsieur Verdoux*. Written and directed by Charles Chaplin. Based on an idea by Orson Welles. With Charles Chaplin, Martha Raye, Marilyn Nash, Mady Correll, Allison Roddan, Robert Lewis, Audrey Betz, Ada May, Isobel Elsom, Margaret Hoffman, Irving Bacon, Edwin Mills, and Virginia Brissac. 1947.

*Moscow on the Hudson*. Directed by Paul Mazursky. Screenplay by Paul Mazursky and Leon Capetanos. With Robin Williams, Maria Conchita Alonso, Cleavant Derricks, Alejandro Rey, Saveli Kramarov, Elya Baskin, Oleg Rudnik, Aleksandr Beniaminov, Tiger Haynes, and Connie Chung. 1984.

*Moulin Rouge*. Directed by Sidney Lanfield. Screenplay by Nunnally Johnson and Henry Lehmann. Based on the play by Lyon de Bri. With Constance Bennett, Franchot Tone, Tullio Carminati, Helen Westley, Andrew Tombes, Russ Brown, Russ Columbo, and the Boswell Sisters. 1934.

My *Favorite Year*. Directed by Richard Benjamin. Screenplay by Norman Steinberg and Dennis Palumbo. Based on a story by Dennis Palumbo. With Peter O'Toole, Joseph Bologna, Mark Linn-Baker, Jessica Harper, Bill Macy, Lainie Kazan, Anne De Salvo, Lou Jacobi, Basil Hoffman, Adolph Green, Tony DiBenedetto, George Wyner, Selma Diamond, and Cameron Mitchell. 1982.

My *Man Godfrey*. Directed by Gregory La Cava. Screenplay by Morrie Ryskind, Eric Hatch, and Gregory La Cava (uncredited). Based on the novel by Eric Hatch. With William Powell, Carole Lombard, Alice Brady, Gail Patrick, Eugene Pallette, Alan Mowbray, Jean Dixon, Mischa Auer, and Robert Light. 1936.

*Nashville*. Directed by Robert Altman. Screenplay by Joan Tewksbury. With Ronee Blakley, Henry Gibson, Michael Murphy, Allen Garfield, Ned Beatty, Lily Tomlin, Gwen Welles, Barbara Baxley, Barbara Harris, Karen Black, Geraldine Chaplin, Keith Carradine, Shelley Duvall, Keenan Wynn, Cristina Raines, David Hayward, Scott Glenn, Robert Doqui, Jeff Goldblum, Allan Nicholls, Timothy Brown, David Arkin, Bert Remsen, Dave Peel, Richard Baskin, Elliott Gould, and Julie Christie. 1975.

*The New Age*. Written and directed by Michael Tolkin. With Judy Davis, Peter Weller, Bruce Ramsay, Paula Marshall, Patrick Bauchau, Tanya Pohlkotte, Susan Traylor, Patricia Heaton, Rachel Rosenthal, Sandra Seacat, Maureen Mueller, John Diehl, Samuel L. Jackson, Audra Lindley, and Adam West. 1994.

*Next Stop, Greenwich Village*. Written and directed by Paul Mazursky. With Lenny Baker, Shelley Winters, Ellen Greene, Christopher Walken, Lois Smith, Antonio Fargas, Dori Brenner, Mike Kellin, Michael Egan, John Ford Noonan, Lou Jacobi, Rashel Novikoff, Helen Hanft, Jeff Goldblum, Rochelle Oliver, John C. Becher, and Joe Madden. 1976.

*Ninotchka*. Directed by Ernst Lubitsch. Screenplay by Billy Wilder, Charles Brackett, and Walter Reisch. Based on a story by Melchior Lengyel. With Greta Garbo, Melvyn Douglas, Ina Claire, Bela Lugosi, Sig Ruman, Felix Bressart, Alexander Granach, and Gregory Gaye. 1939.

*No Time for Comedy*. Directed by William Keighley. Screenplay by Julius and Philip Epstein. Based on the play by S. N. Behrman. With James Stewart, Rosalind Russell, Genevieve Tobin, Charlie Ruggles, Allyn Joslyn, Clarence Kolb, and Louise Beavers. 1940.

*The Philadelphia Story*. Directed by George Cukor. Screenplay by Donald Ogden Stewart and Waldo Salt (uncredited). Based on the play by Philip Barry. With Katharine Hepburn, Cary Grant, James Stewart, Ruth Hussey, John Howard, John Halliday, Mary Nash, Roland Young, Virginia Weidler, and Henry Daniell. 1940.

*Platinum Blonde*. Directed by Frank Capra. Screenplay by Robert Riskin, Jo Swerling, and Dorothy Howell. Based on a story by Harry E. Chandlee and Douglas W. Churchill. With Robert Williams, Jean Harlow, Loretta Young, Halliwell Hobbes, Reginald Owen, Edmund Breese, Don Dillaway, Walter Catlett, Claud Allister, and Louise Closser Hale. 1931.

*The Player.* Directed by Robert Altman. Screenplay by Michael Tolkin. Based on his novel. With Tim Robbins, Peter Gallagher, Greta Scacchi, Vincent D'Onofrio, Cynthia Stevenson, Richard E. Grant, Dean Stockwell, Fred Ward, Brion James, Whoopi Goldberg, Lyle Lovett, Dina Merrill, Angela Hall, and Leah Ayres. 1992.

*Pride and Prejudice.* Directed by Robert Z. Leonard. Screenplay by Aldous Huxley and Jane Murfin. Based on the novel by Jane Austen and the play by Helen Jerome. With Laurence Olivier, Greer Garson, Mary Boland, Edmund Gwenn, Melville Cooper, Edna May Oliver, Maureen O'Sullivan, Ann Rutherford, Frieda Inescort, Karen Morley, Heather Angel, Marsha Hunt, Bruce Lester, Edward Ashley, Marten Lamont, and E. E. Clive. 1940.

*Private Lives.* Directed by Sidney Franklin. Screenplay by Hanns Kraly and Richard Schayer. Based on the play by Noël Coward. With Robert Montgomery, Norma Shearer, Una Merkel, Reginald Denny, and Jean Hersholt. 1931.

*Quality Street.* Directed by George Stevens. Screenplay by Allan Scott, Mortimer Offner, and Jack Townley (uncredited). Based on the play by James Barrie. With Katharine Hepburn, Franchot Tone, Fay Bainter, Eric Blore, Cora Witherspoon, and Estelle Winwood. 1937.

*Quiz Show.* Directed by Robert Redford. Screenplay by Paul Attanasio. Based on the book by Richard N. Goodwin. With Ralph Fiennes, Rob Morrow, John Turturro, Paul Scofield, Elizabeth Wilson, David Paymer, Hank Azaria, Christopher Mc-Donald, Johann Carlo, Allan Rich, and Mira Sorvino. 1994.

*Rebecca.* Directed by Alfred Hitchcock. Screenplay by Robert E. Sherwood and Joan Harrison. Based on the novel by Daphne Du Maurier. With Joan Fontaine, Laurence Olivier, Judith Anderson, Florence Bates, Gladys Cooper, Nigel Bruce, George Sanders, Reginald Denny, C. Aubrey Smith, Melville Cooper, Leonard Carey, Leo G. Carroll, and Edward Fielding. 1940.

*Rebound.* Directed by Edward H. Griffith. Screenplay by Donald Ogden Stewart. Based on his play. With Ina Claire, Robert Ames, Myrna Loy, Hedda Hopper, Robert Williams, Hale Hamilton, Walter Walker, Louise Closser Hale, and Leigh Allen. 1931.

*The Ref.* Directed by Ted Demme. Screenplay by Richard LaGravenese and Marie Weiss. Based on a story by Marie Weiss. With Judy Davis, Kevin Spacey, Dennis Leary, Glynis Johns, Robert J. Steinmiller Jr., Raymond Barry, Richard Bright, Christine Baranski, Adam LeFevre, Phillip Nicoll, and Ellie Rabb. 1994.

*Reunion in Vienna.* Directed by Sidney Franklin. Screenplay by Ernest Vajda and Claudine West. Based on the play by Robert E. Sherwood. With John Barrymore, Diana Wynyard, Frank Morgan, Henry Travers, May Robson, Eduardo Ciannelli, Una Merkel, and Bodil Rosing. 1933.

*The Royal Family of Broadway.* Directed by George Cukor and Cyril Gardner. Screenplay by Herman J. Mankiewicz and Gertrude Purcell. Based on the play *The Royal Family* by George S. Kaufman and Edna Ferber. With Fredric March, Ina Claire, Henrietta Crosman, Mary Brian, Arnold Korff, Frank Conroy, and Charles Starrett. 1930.

*Shampoo*. Directed by Hal Ashby. Screenplay by Robert Towne and Warren Beatty. With Warren Beatty, Julie Christie, Goldie Hawn, Jack Warden, Lee Grant, Tony Bill, Carrie Fisher, Jay Robinson, and George Furth. 1975.

*The Shop Around the Corner*. Directed by Ernst Lubitsch. Screenplay by Samson Raphaelson and Ben Hecht (uncredited). Based on the play *Parfumerie* by Miklos Lászlo. With James Stewart, Margaret Sullavan, Frank Morgan, Joseph Schild-kraut, Sara Haden, Felix Bressart, William Tracy, and Inez Courtney. 1940.

*Six Degrees of Separation*. Directed by Fred Schepisi. Screenplay by John Guare. Based on his play. With Stockard Channing, Donald Sutherland, Will Smith, Mary Beth Hurt, Bruce Davison, Anthony Michael Hall, Eric Thal, Heather Graham, Ian McKellen, Richard Masur, Anthony Rapp, Osgood Perkins, Catherine Kellner, and Jeffrey Abrams. 1993.

*A Star Is Born*. Directed by William Wellman and Jack Conway (uncredited). Screenplay by Dorothy Parker, Alan Campbell, William Wellman, Ben Hecht (uncredited), Ring Lardner Jr. (uncredited), John Lee Mahin (uncredited), Budd Schulberg (uncredited), David O. Selznick (uncredited), and Adela Rogers St. John (uncredited). Based on a story by William Wellman and Robert Carson, and the film *What Price Hollywood?* (uncredited) by George Cukor. With Fredric March, Janet Gaynor, Lionel Stander, Adolphe Menjou, May Robson, Andy Devine, Owen Moore, Peggy Woody, Elizabeth Jenns, and Edgar Kennedy. 1937.

*A Star Is Born*. Directed by George Cukor. Screenplay by Moss Hart. Based on the earlier screenplay by Dorothy Parker, Alan Campbell, and William Wellman (and others). With Judy Garland, James Mason, Jack Carson, Charles Bickford, and Tommy Noonan. 1954.

*Strangers on a Train*. Directed by Alfred Hitchcock. Screenplay by Raymond Chandler, Czenzi Ormonde, Whitfield Cook, and Ben Hecht (uncredited). Based on the novel by Patricia Highsmith. With Robert Walker, Farley Granger, Ruth Roman, Leo G. Carroll, Laura Elliott, Marion Lorne, Patricia Hitchcock, Jonathan Hale, Howard St. John, John Brown, Robert Gist, and Norma Varden. 1951.

*The Stunt Man*. Directed by Richard Rush. Screenplay by Lawrence B. Marcus and Richard Rush. Based on the novel by Paul Brodeur. With Peter O'Toole, Steve Railsback, Barbara Hershey, Allen Garfield, Chuck Bail, Adam Roarke, Alex Rocco, Sharon Farrell, Philip Bruns, John Garwood, and Jim Hess. 1980.

*Sunset Boulevard*. Directed by Billy Wilder. Screenplay by Billy Wilder, Charles Brackett, and D. M. Marshman Jr. With Gloria Swanson, William Holden, Erich von Stroheim, Jack Webb, Nancy Olson, Fred Clark, Lloyd Gough, Cecil B. De-Mille, Buster Keaton, H. B. Warner, Anna Q. Nilsson, Ray Evans, and Jay Livingston. 1950.

*Sweet Smell of Success*. Directed by Alexander Mackendrick. Screenplay by Clifford Odets, Ernest Lehman, and Alexander Mackendrick (uncredited). With Burt Lancaster, Tony Curtis, Martin Milner, Susan Harrison, Emile Meyer, Barbara Nichols, Sam Levene, Jeff Donnell, Joe Frisco, Lawrence Dobkin, Lurene Tuttle, David White, Edith Atwater, and the Chico Hamilton Quintet. 1957.

*Sylvia Scarlett.* Directed by George Cukor. Screenplay by Gladys Unger, John Collier, and Mortimer Offner. Based on a novel by Compton MacKenzie. With Katharine Hepburn, Cary Grant, Edmund Gwenn, Dennie Moore, and Brian Aherne. 1936.

*The Talented Mr. Ripley.* Written and directed by Anthony Minghella. Based on the novel by Patricia Highsmith. With Matt Damon, Jude Law, Gwyneth Paltrow, Cate Blanchett, Philip Seymour Hoffman, Jack Davenport, James Rebhorn, Sergio Rubini, Philip Baker Hall, and Celia Weston. 1999.

*The Thin Man.* Directed by W. S. Van Dyke. Screenplay by Albert Hackett and Frances Goodrich. Based on the novel by Dashiell Hammett. With William Powell, Myrna Loy, Minna Gombell, Maureen O'Sullivan, Nat Pendleton, Porter Hall, Henry Wadsworth, William Henry, Harold Huber, Cesar Romero, Natalie Moorhead, Edward Brophy, Edward Ellis, Cyril Thornton, and Asta. 1934.

*Thirty Day Princess.* Directed by Marion Gering. Screenplay by Sam Hellman, Edwin Justus Mayer, Preston Sturges, and Frank Partos. Based on a story by Clarence Budington Kelland. With Sylvia Sidney, Cary Grant, Edward Arnold, Henry Stephenson, Edgar Norton, Ray Walker, Lucien Littlefield, Robert McWade, and George Baxter. 1934.

*Three Comrades.* Directed by Frank Borzage. Screenplay by F. Scott Fitzgerald and Edward A. Paramore. Based on the novel by Erich Maria Remarque. With Margaret Sullavan, Robert Taylor, Robert Young, Franchot Tone, Guy Kibbee, Lionel Atwill, Henry Hull, Charley Grapewin, and Monty Woolley. 1938.

*Tootsie.* Directed by Sydney Pollack. Screenplay by Larry Gelbart, Murray Schisgal, Elaine May (uncredited), and Barry Levinson (uncredited). Based on a story by Larry Gelbart and Don McGuire. With Dustin Hoffman, Jessica Lange, Charles Durning, Teri Garr, Bill Murray, Sydney Pollack, George Gaynes, Dabney Coleman, Geena Davis, and Doris Belack. 1982.

*Topaze.* Directed by Harry d'Abbadie d'Arrast. Screenplay by Ben Hecht, Benn W. Levy, and Charles MacArthur (uncredited). Based on the play by Marcel Pagnol. With John Barrymore, Myrna Loy, Reginald Mason, Jobyna Howland, Jackie Searle, Albert Conti, Frank Reicher, and Luis Alberni. 1933.

*Topper.* Directed by Norman Z. McLeod. Screenplay by Eric Hatch, Jack Jevne, and Eddie Moran. Based on the novel by Thorne Smith. With Cary Grant, Constance Bennett, Roland Young, Billie Burke, Alan Mowbray, Eugene Pallette, Arthur Lake, Hedda Hopper, Virginia Sale, Three Hits and a Miss, and Hoagy Carmichael. 1937.

*Tovarich.* Directed by Anatole Litvak. Screenplay by Casey Robinson. Based on the play by Jacques Deval; English version by Casey Robinson. With Claudette Colbert, Charles Boyer, Melville Cooper, Isabel Jeans, Basil Rathbone, Morris Carnovsky, Maurice Murphy, Anita Louise, Gregory Gaye, and Montagu Love. 1937.

*Trouble in Paradise.* Directed by Ernst Lubitsch. Screenplay by Samson Raphaelson and Grover Jones. Based on the play *The Honest Finder* by Aladar Laszlo. With Herbert Marshall, Miriam Hopkins, Kay Francis, Edward Everett Horton, Charlie Ruggles, Robert Greig, Luis Alberni, and Leonid Kinsky. 1932.

*Unfaithfully Yours.* Written and directed by Preston Sturges. With Rex Harrison, Linda Darnell, Barbara Lawrence, Rudy Vallee, and Kurt Kreuger. 1948.

*What Price Hollywood?* Directed by George Cukor. Screenplay by Gene Fowler, Roland Brown, Robert Presnell Sr., Jane Murfin, Ben Markson, and Allen Rivkin (uncredited). Based on a story by Adela Rogers St. John and Louis Stevens (uncredited). With Constance Bennett, Lowell Sherman, Neil Hamilton, Gregory Ratoff, and Louise Beavers. 1932.

*The Women.* Directed by George Cukor. Screenplay by Anita Loos, Jane Murfin, F. Scott Fitzgerald (uncredited), and Donald Ogden Stewart (uncredited). Based on the play by Clare Boothe Luce. With Norma Shearer, Joan Crawford, Paulette Goddard, Rosalind Russell, Mary Boland, Phyllis Povah, Joan Fontaine, Virginia Weidler, Lucile Watson, Marjorie Main, Virginia Grey, and Ruth Hussey. 1939.

~

# Bibliography

Agee, James. *Agee on Film, Volume One: Reviews and Comments by James Agee*. New York: Grosset & Dunlap, 1969.

Barry, Philip. *States of Grace: Eight Plays by Philip Barry*. New York: Harcourt Brace Jovanovich, 1975.

Behrman, S. N. *No Time for Comedy*. In *The Pocket Book of Modern American Plays*. New York: Pocket Books, 1942.

———. "Query: What Makes Comedy High?" *New York Times*, May 30, 1952.

Bergman, Ingmar. *Four Screenplays of Ingmar Bergman*. New York: Simon & Schuster, 1960.

Bolitho, William. "The Egg." *New York World*, February 7, 1929.

Carrington, Robert L. *The Magnificent Ambersons: A Reconstruction*. Berkeley and Los Angeles: University of California Press, 1993.

Cavell, Stanley. *Pursuits of Happiness: The Hollywood Comedy of Remarriage*. Boston: Harvard University Press, 1984.

Coward, Noël. *Play Parade*. New York: Doubleday, Doran, 1934.

Dale, Alan. *Comedy Is a Man in Trouble: Slapstick in American Movies*. Minneapolis, Minn.: University of Minnesota Press, 2000.

———. *What We Do Best: American Movie Comedies of the 1990s*. 2003, at www.weird professortype.com/introduction.html.

Fergusion, Otis. *The Film Criticism of Otis Ferguson*, edited by Robert Wilson. Philadelphia: Temple University Press, 1971.

Gassner, John, and Dudley Nicols, eds. *Great Film Plays*. New York: Crown Publishers, 1959.

Greene, Graham. *The Graham Greene Reader: Reviews, Essays, Interviews & Film Stories*. Edited by David Parkinson. New York: Applause Books, 1995.

Guare, John. *Marco Polo Sings a Solo*. New York: Dramatist's Play Service, 1998.
———. *Six Degrees of Separation*. New York: Random House, 1994.
Harvey, James. *Romantic Comedy in Hollywood, from Lubitsch to Sturges*. New York: Alfred A. Knopf, 1987.
Hastings, Jonathan. "Toward a Sense of Modern Comedy in Film and Dramatic Literature." Undergraduate thesis, College of the Holy Cross, 1998.
Haver, Ronald. *A Star Is Born: The Making of the 1954 Movie and Its 1983 Restoration*. New York: Applause Books, 1988.
Henderson, Brian. "*Semi-Tough* or Impossible? Romantic Comedy Today." *Film Quarterly* 31, no. 4 (1978).
Herman, Jan. *A Talent for Trouble: The Life of Hollywood's Most Acclaimed Director, William Wyler*. New York: G. P. Putnam's Sons, 1995.
Howard, Sidney. *Dodsworth*. New York: Harcourt, Brace, 1934.
Kael, Pauline. *The Citizen Kane Book*. New York: Limelight Editions, 1984.
———. *Deeper Into Movies*. New York: Little, Brown and Company, 1973.
———. *5001 Nights at the Movies*. 2nd ed. New York: Henry Holt, 1991.
———. Introduction to *Three Screen Comedies*, by Samson Raphaelson. Madison: University of Wisconsin Press, 1983.
———. *Reeling*. Boston: Little, Brown, 1976.
———. *When the Lights Go Down*. New York: Holt, Rinehart and Winston, 1980.
Kendall, Elizabeth. *The Runaway Bride: Hollywood Romantic Comedies of the 1930s*. New York: Cooper Square Publishers, 2002.
Lambert, Gavin. *On Cukor*. New York: G. P. Putnam's Sons, 1972.
Lane, Anthony. "Master of Ceremonies: The Films of Max Ophüls." *New Yorker*, July 8, 2002.
Levy, Emanuel. *George Cukor, Master of Elegance: Hollywood's Legendary Director and His Stars*. New York: William Morrow & Company, 1994.
Lewis, Sinclair. *Dodsworth*. In *Arrowsmith; Elmer Gantry; Dodsworth*. New York: Library of America, 2002.
Madsen, Axel. *Billy Wilder*. Bloomington: Indiana University Press, 1969.
———. *William Wyler*. New York: Crowell, 1973.
Maugham, W. Somerset. "The Letter." In *The Great Exotic Novels and Short Stories of W. Somerset Maugham*. New York: Avalon, 2001.
Peary, Gerald, and Roger Shatzkin, eds. *The Classic American Novel & the Movies*. New York: Frederick Ungar Publishing Company, 1977.
Raphaelson, Samson. *Three Screen Comedies*. Madison: University of Wisconsin Press, 1983.
Sawhill, Ray. "A Movie Called *Nashville*." *Salon*, June 27, 2000 , at dir.salon.com/ent/movies/feature/2000/06/27/nashville/index.html?sid=859833.
Sherwood, Robert E., and Joan Harrison. *Rebecca*. In *Great Film Plays*, edited by John Gassner and Dudley Nichols. New York: Crown, 1959.
Staggs, Sam. *All About "All About Eve."* Boston: St. Martin's Press, 2000.

Sturges, Preston. *Preston Sturges by Preston Sturges*. Adapted and edited by Sandy Sturges. New York: Simon & Schuster, 1990.

Tarkington, Booth. *Alice Adams*. New York: Bantam Books, 1997.

———. *The Magnificent Ambersons*. New York: Modern Library, 1998.

Taylor, John Russell. *Strangers in Paradise: The Hollywood Émigrés, 1933-1950*. New York: Holt, Rinehart & Winston, 1983.

Tolkin, Michael. *Three Screenplays*. New York: Grove Press, 1995.

Ursini, James. *Preston Sturges: An American Dreamer*. New York: Curtis Books, 1973.

Weales, Gerald. *Canned Goods as Caviar: American Film Comedies of the 1930s*. Chicago: University of Chicago Press, 1985.

Weiser, Mel. *Nick Nolte: Caught in the Act*. New York: Momentum Books, 1999.

# Index

~

# About the Author

Steve Vineberg is the author of *Method Actors: Three Generations of an American Acting Style*, which won the Joe A. Calloway Prize, and *No Surprises, Please: Movies in the Reagan Decade*. He writes regularly on movies and theater for the *Threepenny Review* and the *Boston Phoenix* and on movies for the *Christian Century* and the *Perfect Vision*. His work has also appeared in the *New York Times*, the *Chronicle of Higher Education*, *Pakn Treger*, and the *Oxford American*. He lives in Worcester, Massachusetts and has taught theater and film at College of the Holy Cross since 1985.